Jewish Activities in the United States

Volume II
of
The International Jew

Being a Reprint of a Second selection
from articles appearing in
The Dearborn Independent
from Oct. 9, 1920 to March 19, 1921

Reprinted 2004 by
Liberty Bell Publications
PO Box 890
York, SC 29745
www.libertybellpublications.com
803.684.4408

ISBN: 1-59364-012-9

FOREWARD
To the Bi-Centennial Edition

In the year1920 Henry Sr. published *The International Jew,* a comprehensive survey of Jewish Power in the United States and throughout the world. This four-volume work was originally serialized in the *Dearborn Independent,* the house organ of the Ford Motor Company.

These books have been best-sellers in many parts of the world, and have been translated into the languages of most civilized countries. Sadly, there are many countries today where possession of these books has been made punishable by confiscation or worse. In Germany, for example, a person who wants to borrow *The International Jew* from a library must first prove that he needs it for historical research. In other words, an ordinary tax-paying member of the public who supports the public library with his hard-earned money is unable to further his knowledge or satisfy his curiosity in this regard.

It is therefore in the interest of spreading truth that we republish these books in full so that new generations shall see for themselves how our problems of today are the same problems which have "mysteriously" occurred since the turn of the century. The fact that even the wealthy Henry Ford, Sr. could be forced to withdraw these books, starkly illuminates the power of the Jews, even in the 1920's. To reprint *The International Jew* now, when the Jews are so much more powerful, is some indication of the tremendous courage of the publisher.

Every American who loves his country should make it his duty to buy sufficient copies for donation to libraries, universities, business associations, etc. Most important, every American parent should have at least one set at home to pass on to his children.

In further support of the findings and conclusions of *The International Jew,* an excellent companion book, *The Dispossessed Majority,* by Wilmot Robertson, exposes the rapid increase of Jewish power since the first publication of Henry Ford's great work. No conscientious, thinking American should be without these amazing, fact-filled books.

Preface

A FORMER volume, containing the first twenty articles in the series of Jewish studies which began their appearance in THE DEARBORN INDEPENDENT of May 22, 1920, dealt largely with the theory of the Jewish World Program. The present volume gives a general view of some of the evidence which illustrates and substantiates that Program. As the first volume brought the subject forward a step, the present volume brings it forward another step. The Question is a very big one, the material is of mountainous proportions, so that it is very desirable that there be simplicity of method. The method therefore has been to lay the observable everyday facts alongside the Program, to see if they agree. It will be time enough to take up the authenticity of the Protocols when the parallel between them and the activities of the Jewish leaders is shown.

The articles thus far printed remain unanswered. They have been denounced and misrepresented, but not answered. A favorite evasion of Jewish editors is to say that the statements made about the Jews could be made about any other race, and that no race could refute the statements with facts. But these statements have not been made about any other race and could they be? If they were made about, say the Hungarians, Poles, Rumanians, Italians, English, Scotch, Irish, Russian or Syrian in our midst, could they not be met?

Not the mere fact that certain statements are made about the purposes of Jewish leaders, but the fact that people can *see* wherein the statements agree with actual conditions, is what gives strength to the statements. The same statements made about any other group would fall because the people could find nothing to sustain them. Say-so and hearsay have no weight at all. Neither has abuse or prejudice. If the statements made in these articles are false, they are of a nature which can be refuted with facts. If there is no parallel between the written Program of the Protocols and the actual program as followed under Jewish leadership, surely that can be shown. If it has not been shown, it is because the parallel exists, and Jewish leaders know it exists.

The following chapters take up numerous matters, chiefly the interference of the Jew with educational and religious interests of the majority of the people; the moral menace in the Jew-controlled theater and movie; the fight of the New York Stock Exchange against Jewish domination; a discussion of the question whether the Jews are a "religious denomination" or a race, only Jewish authorities being quoted; and a very slight beginning on the endless subject of Jewish influence during the Great War. Bernard M. Baruch, although secondary in the real Jewish counsels, proclaimed himself to a Congressional committee as "the most powerful man in the war," and the records show that he was.

This volume does not complete the case. It is issued to meet the demand of new readers who call for the articles from the beginning. The editions of The Dearborn Independent being long ago exhausted, the publication of these two volumes was undertaken to enable readers to begin with the first article. The omission of several single articles from this compilation is in the interest of compactness, and may be restored in another volume. The omitted articles are "The Jews' Complaint Against 'Americanism,' " Oct. 23; "Gentile Fall Involved in Hope of Jewish Rule," Dec. 25

April, 1921

Contents

"The distinctive character of the Jew does not arise solely from his religion. It is true that his race and religion are indissolubly connected, ... but whatever be the cause of this function of the race idea with the religion, it is very certain that the religion alone does not constitute the people. A believer in the Jewish faith does not by reason of that fact become a Jew. On the other hand, however, a Jew by birth remains a Jew, even though he abjures his religion."
— Leo. N. Levi,
President of the B'nai B'rith 1900-1904

XXI.

How Jews in the U. S.
Conceal Their Strength

HOW many Jews are there in the United States? No Gentile knows. The figures are the exclusive property of the Jewish authorities. The government of the United States can provide statistics on almost every matter pertaining to the population of the country, but whenever it has attempted in a systematic way to get information about the Jews who are constantly entering the country, and the number now resident here, the Jewish lobby at Washington steps in and stops it.

For more than 20 years the fight for the right of the United States Government to make a complete census of the people has been going on, and for the same period the Jewish lobby at the Capitol has been strong enough to win.

The alarming increase in Jewish immigration at the present time has brought the question to public attention again. For the first time in the history of the United States a national conviction is forming upon this subject. From Europe came the first news which startled this country. The reports told of vast mobilizations of Jewish people at stated rendezvous in Europe. Great barracks were built for them. Large bodies of trained men went from the United States, under orders of Jewish secret societies here, to expedite "passport work," as it is termed among these bodies. Immigration into the United States became a business—a strictly Jewish business.

Why is that statement made?—"a strictly Jewish business." For this reason: there are countries in Europe from which today no Gentile can be admitted to the United States. From Germany, from Russia, from Poland, it is with the utmost

7

difficulty that even one person can be won permission to enter this country. But Jews from Poland, Germany, and Russia by the thousands come in most freely, in utter disregard of the laws, in open contempt of the health regulations —a strictly Jewish business of getting another million Jews into the United States. It is like moving an army, which having done duty in Europe for the subjugation of that continent, is now being transferred to America.

When the conditions overseas were made known in this country and it became apparent that Jewish societies in the United States were the principal aids in this stampede to America, the newspapers for the first time in American history began to comment on a Jewish Question in tones of alarm. This in itself is an indication that the facts are becoming too challenging to be longer ignored.

Even the ordinary immigration officials, who for years have watched the human stream as it flowed over Ellis Island, have this year been startled into attention and action by the sharp change that has come in the character of the stream. And what has startled them?

First, it is composed almost entirely of Jews. Real Ukrainians, real Russians, real Germans cannot come in. But Jews can come from anywhere, and are coming from almost everywhere. Why this special privilege? —is being asked.

Second, they do not come as refugees, as people fleeing from hunger and persecution: they come as if they own the country. They arrive as special guests. As on the other side the passport business is "arranged," so on this side the entrance business is "arranged." The laws are set aside. Health regulations are ignored. Why should they not behave as if they own the United States? They see officials of Jewish secret societies override officials of the United States Immigration Bureau. Their first glimpse of life here shows a Jewish control as potent and complete as it is in Russia. No wonder then that they literally beat down the walls and gates with all the éclat of a victorious invasion. Is not this America—"The Jews' Country," as it is called in the smaller nations of Europe?

Third, there is a perfect organization which over-comes the numerous objections which arise against admission of known revolutionary Jews. European Jews are potential revolutionists. They are the revolutionists of Italy, Germany, Russia and Poland today. They are the Red and I. W. W. leaders of the United States today. When one man whose record is known presents himself at Ellis Island—and of course he is one in a thousand whose records are not known – he is held up. Immediately there start across the country telegrams to Congressmen, editors, state and municipal officials telling them in peremptory tones to "get busy" in behalf of Mr. So-and-So who is detained at Ellis Island. And the same day there start back to Washington telegrams from Congressmen, editors and others of influence, insisting on the spotless character of Mr. So-and-So and demanding his immediate admittance into the United States. Sometimes also the Russian embassy—so called—is used in this work.

It is an invasion—nothing but an invasion; and it is helped by influences within the United States. It is thinly cloaked with sentiment—"these people are fleeing from persecution." It is cleverly assisted by photographs showing groups of forlorn looking women and children—never by photographs showing the groups of husky young revolutionists who are just as ready to despoil the United States as they were to despoil Russia.

That, however, is the present situation. What this and a subsequent article propose to do for the reader is to put him in possession of some of the facts concerning the government's fight on this question during the last quarter century.

The question is not peculiar to America, and it may throw a sidelight on the American phase to note some of the facts developed at the hearings of the British Royal commission on Alien Immigration which sat in London in 1902, a feature of whose proceedings was the testimony of Theodor Herzl, the great propagandist of Zionism.

In his initial statement to the Commission, Herzl made these statements, among others:

"The fact that there is now for the first time since Cromwell a perceptible number of our people in England is the true cause

9

of this Commission being called together. * * * That a serious pressure exists in England, the fact of your Commission sitting is full proof."

Then the examination proceeded until the following was brought out: (the answers are Herzl's)

Q. Looking at the question of alien immigration from the standpoint of the United States for a moment, you have referred to the fact that America excludes?

A. Yes.

Q. The exclusion is a partial exclusion?

A. Exclusion, as I know, is worked in this way: The immigrant must show a certain amount of money at the moment of his landing.

Q. You are aware that the stream of immigration into the United States is twice as much as the immigration into the United Kingdom?

A. I know that. New York has now the greatest Jewish population of all the towns in the world.

Q. And the actual exclusion is the actual exclusion of a small proportion?

A. Yes; but they go, however, to America. I think it is so easy to evade such a prohibition. For instance, *if they joined a small company, it would lend the necessary amount to each immigrant, and the immigrant shows it and comes in, and sends back by post the amount he has borrowed.* There are no efficacious measures to prevent that.

Q. I took it that your reference to the United States was an approval of the action of that country as an act of self-preservation.

A. No.

A little later on in the examination, the question of immigration to the United States was again brought in. The answers are still Dr. Herzl's—remember that the date is still 1902.

Q. Are you aware whether it is the fact or not that the leading Jews in America have informed their correspondents here that they cannot receive and distribute any more Jewish immigrants?

A. I have heard of difficulties of emigration, and that *they are overcrowded with Jews.* As to that information I cannot say.

Q. In your opinion would not the stream of emigration to America have been much greater if no such law had existed?

A. I think this law did not alter it much. The prohibition could not change it.

Q. On what grounds do you believe that?

A. *It is a question of coasts and harbors. They come in.* How will you prevent a man from coming in?

Q. Do you mean they are smuggled in?

A. No, I do not believe that. But they always find means to come in.

Now, discussion of immigration in the United States has never been free. We have talked a great deal about it in general terms, but not in terms of specific races except the Chinese and Japanese. However, Herzl seems to have known that wherever the Jews congregate in noticeable number they become a trouble (his words are: " * * * America, where so soon as they form a perceptible number they become a trouble and a burden to the land") and he also knew that efforts would be made to meet that condition. But more than that, he dropped what must be construed as a warning, that such efforts would be resisted. He said:

"There exists a French proverb, *'cet animal est tres impatient; il se defend quand on l'attaque.'* If the Jews are attacked, they will defend themselves, and you will get something like internal troubles."

The time apparently did come in the United States when some far-seeing official began to wonder what the Jewish invasion portended. Already it was too strong to be openly attacked. The

Jewish lobby at Washington was powerful even at that time. So, apparently, this official concluded that the best way to set about so momentous a task was to collect the information.

But in order to get the information, Congress had to give its permission; and to get the permission of Congress, hearings had to be ordered. Hearings were ordered, and the records of them, though very scarce, still exist. The reader will be given important extracts from them presently, and he will see for himself how certain American statesmen reacted to the whole matter.

A remark is in order just here, namely, that the Jewish lobby eventually became more skillful in such matters. It now takes very good care that no officials shall be appointed who shall make suggestions which shall precipitate congressional hearings on the Jewish matter. The time is coming, of course, when the whole Jewish Question may be threshed out by the government of the United States, but it will not be because an official precipitated it; it will be because the people will demand it.

Officials are now much too wary to meddle with this Question. They know too well the consequences. During the war many a secret trail of danger led into Jewish quarters, and the secret service man who loyally made his reports was often surprised to find himself lifted completely off that trail. Why? All Jewish trails in this country were powerfully protected by hidden influences during the war.

Well, the time came in the United States, when it was obviously desirable to know what elements were comprising our population; whether we were an Anglo-Saxon nation, Semitic, Latin, or what. The situation was this, and was so stated by government officials at the time:—In the '80's, and previously, it could be safely assumed that an immigrant from Ireland was Irish, an immigrant from Norway or Sweden was Scandinavian, an immigrant from Russia was Russian, and immigrant from Germany was German, and so on.

But times changed. Previous to 1880, the entry on a man's record—"born in Russia"—indicated that he was a Russian. But, says a statement made by a government official with reference to the 10 years following 1880—"So many Hebrews have come from that country to the United States, that 'born in Russia" has come in popular opinion to mean a 'Russian Jew.' " And then the same official goes on to show that during a 10-year period when 666,561 Jews came from Russia, there came also from Russia large numbers of Poles, Finns, Germans and Lithuanians.

Now, to make a census enumeration of these peoples under the heading "Russian" was plainly misleading, and not only misleading but valueless for census purposes. The racial identity would be lost, and our knowledge of the racial make-up of the nation very incomplete. Therefore, the census authorities asked Congress for permission to classify people by "race" as well as by "country of birth." It seemed perfectly reasonable. Of what possible use is it to classify 3,000,000 Jews as "Russians" when there are very few real Russians in the country, and when the Russian and the Jew are so deeply different one from another?

Senator Simon Guggenheim arose in the committee to object. He used the common formula in such cases. He said:

"Personally I object to it, not because I am a Hebrew, but because it is not in place."

That is the common Jewish formula of objection. The B'nai B'rith says the same thing when it forces Shakespeare's "Merchant of Venice" out of the public schools. That society's "anti-defamation circular" always includes the thought:—"We do not base our request on the embarrassment which may be caused to the Jewish students in class, nor is our attitude in this regard based on thin-skinned sensitiveness. Our objection is made because of the effect upon the non-Jewish children who subconsciously will associate in their minds the Jew as Shakespeare portrayed him with the Jew of today." So Senator Guggenheim, therefore, was playing the game according to the rules made and established in such cases.

At this hearing, Senator LaFollette was chairman. Senator Guggenheim's contention was that "Jew" was the name of a member of a religious denomination, and not of a race.

Chairman LaFollette—"I can see broad ethnological reasons why some time it would be important to know from what blood and race the man came."

Senator Guggenheim—"Why not ask his religion?"

Senators McCumber and Bailey came to the support of Senator Guggenheim's contention, that "Jew" is a religious and not a racial term.

Chairman LaFollette—"I do not just get your objection to this, Senator Guggenheim. What objection can one have to having the race to which he belongs correctly entered?"

Senator Guggenheim—"Because it is not correct when stated in that way. The Jews are not a race. * * * "

Later on in the hearing, Senator Cummins entered the discussion in response to a pro-Jewish remark made by Senator Bailey:

Senator Bailey—"If I were a Hebrew and I had been born here and they wanted me to say I was anything but an American, I would have a difference with the enumerator. I perhaps would refuse to answer their questions."

Senator Cummins—"I would not have any hesitancy in stating from what blood I was."

Senator Bailey—"No; but in the case that I refer to, it would be a matter of religion."

Senator Guggenheim—"That is the point; it is a question of religion."

That was in April, 1909. In December, 1909, Simon Wolf was the chief witness for the pro-Jewish contention. Simon Wolf is a very interesting character. From before the days of President Lincoln, he has been lobbyist for the Jews at the National Capitol, and has been in contact with every President from Lincoln to Wilson. At the hearing where Mr. Wolf testified, Senator Dillingham acted as chairman, and the whole proceeding was enlivened and clarified by the vigorous part which Senator Lodge took in it. Certain extracts, which entirely reproduce the spirit and argument of the hearing, follow:

Mr. Wolf—"The point we make is this: A Jew coming from Russia is a Russian; from Rumania, a Rumanian; from France, a Frenchman; from England, an Englishman; and from Germany, a German; that Hebrew or Jewish is simply a religion."

Senator Lodge—"Do I understand you to deny that the Jews are a race?"

Mr. Wolf—"How?"

Senator Lodge—"Do you deny that the word "Jew" is used to express a race?"

Mr. Wolf—"As the representative of the Union of American Hebrew Congregations—which I have been for nearly 30 years—I took up the matter and propounded a series of interrogations to some of the leading Jews of the United States, among others * * * Dr. Cyrus Adler, who was librarian of the Smithsonian * * * and every one of them states that the Jews are not a race."

Senator Lodge—"That, I think, is an important point. I have always supposed they were. I find in the preface of The Jewish Encyclopedia, which is signed by Cyrus Adler, among others, this statement:

'An even more delicate problem that presented itself at the very outset was the attitude to be observed by the encyclopedia in regard to those Jews who, while born within the Jewish community, have, for one reason or another, abandoned it. As the present work *deals with the Jews as a race,* it was found impossible to exclude those who were of that *race,* whatever their *religious affiliations* might have been.'

"In the same encyclopedia is a statement by Joseph Jacobs, B.A., formerly president of the Jewish Historical Society of England:

'Anthropologically considered, *the Jews are a race* of markedly uniform type, due either to unity of race or to similarity of environment.'

"Do you mean to deny—I want to understand your position—that the word 'Jew' is a racial term?"

Mr. Wolf—"I have made my statement, and my opinions are in this pamphlet."

Senator Lodge—"Let me get at it. How would you classify Benjamin Disraeli? Was he a Jew?"

Mr. Wolf—"He was born a Jew."

Senator Lodge—"He was baptized as a Christian. He then ceased to be a Jew?"

Mr. Wolf—"Yes; religiously he ceased to be a Jew.

Senator Lodge—"Ah! Religiously. He was very proud of the fact that he was a Jew, and always spoke of himself in that way. Did the fact that he changed his religion alter his race?"

Mr. Wolf—"It did not change the fact that he was born a Jew; not at all; and I know the Jewish people throughout the world have claimed him, Heine, and Borne, and others who were born of their blood, as being Jews, when they speak of persons who have accomplished something wonderful in the world. But they ceased to be Jews from the standpoint of religion—"

Senator Lodge—"Undoubtedly. What I want to get at is whether the word 'Jew' or 'Hebrew' is not a correct racial term?"

Mr. Wolf—"If you will pardon me, you will find a letter from Dr. Cyrus Adler right at the close of the pamphlet, which perhaps you might read for the benefit of the committee."

Senator Lodge—"It never occurred to me until I heard you were coming here that the classification as made by the immigration authorities had anything to do with religion. I supposed it was a race classification. It is important, very important, to get the race classification as nearly as we can."

Mr. Wolf—"You are aware that the Census Bureau some time ago attempted to classify in the same manner and it was prohibited from doing so."

Senator Lodge—"The word 'race' was stricken out of the census bill. *I think it was a great mistake.* It makes the returns almost valueless."

16

Mr. Wolf—"I can simply repeat what I have said—that I am voicing the opinions of those whom I represent—the Union of American Hebrew Congregations, and the Order of B'nai B'rith. They are opposed to the classification as made in the last few years and as contemplated, so far as I am informed, in the report of the commission."

The hearings continued, Julian W. Mack later appearing for the Jewish contention.

From the extracts given in this article, four matters become very clear:

First, the Jew is opposed to any restrictive legislation against his entrance into a country.

Second, the Jew is opposed to any racial classification of himself after he has entered a country.

Third, the Jewish argument to the Gentile authorities is that the Jew represents religion and not race.

Fourth, that at least one indication has appeared in which the Jew has one view to present to the Gentiles, and another which he cherishes among his own people, on this question of Race.

Another point might be made, as this: When the authorities disregard as untenable the argument of religion, not race, the Jewish spokesmen fall back on the fact that their organizations don't want certain things and won't have certain things—argument or no argument, commission or no commission.

The Jewish lobbyists had their way. There is no enumeration of Jews in the United States. There are 46 other classifications, but none for the Jew. The Northern Italians are distinguished in the records from the Southern Italians; the Moravians are distinguished from the Bohemians; the Scotch from the English; the Spanish-American from the Spanish-European; the West Indians from the Mexicans—but the Jew is not distinguished at all.

None of the other races made objection. On this point the report of the commission reads;

"As far as ascertained by the commission, the practice of classifying the foreign-born by race or people,

17

rather than by country of birth, is acceptable to the people of the United States *with one exception.* "

The officials, who were endeavoring to have the Census Report show with scientific accuracy the actual racial components of the population of the United States, were compelled to see their recommendation eliminated.

What is the result? If you ask the government of the United States how many Frenchmen there are in the country, it can give you the figures. If you ask for the number of Poles, it is there. If you ask for the number of Africans, it is known. Or down a long list you may make your inquiries, and you will find that the government knows.

But ask the government of the United States how many Jews are in the country—and it cannot tell; there are no records. If you want information upon that point, you will have to go to the officials or representatives of the Jewish Government in the United States.

Of course, if "Jew " is a religious term, like Baptist, Catholic, Christian Scientist or Quaker, then there is merit in the argument that religious questions are not proper for the government to ask unless the religion comes in conflict with, or is a menace to, the ideals of the Republic. But if "Jew" is a racial term, or a national term, then the government is properly interested in making record of all the inhabitants of this land who bear it.

Like all questions pertaining to the Jews, this can be settled by their own words. What the Jews teach the Jews on this matter should be the determining point. In the next article we shall see what Jews themselves have to say about "race or religion?"

Issue of October 9, 1920

18

XXII.

Jewish Testimony on "Are Jews a Nation?"

"I will give you my definition of a nation, and you can add the adjective 'Jewish.' A Nation is, in my mind, an historical group of men of a recognizable cohesion held together by a common enemy. Then, if you add to that the word 'Jewish' you have what I understand to be the Jewish nation.

—Theodor Herzl

"Let us all recognize that we Jews are a distinct nationality of which every Jew, whatever his country, his station, or shade of belief, is necessarily a member."

—Louis D. Brandeis
Justice of the United States Supreme Court

T HIS article is designed to put the reader in possession of information regarding the Jew's own thought of himself, as regards race, religion and citizenship. In the last article we saw the thought which Jewish representatives wish to plant in Gentile minds concerning this matter. The Senate committee which was to be convinced was made up of Gentiles. The witnesses who were to do the convincing were Jews.

Senator Simon Guggenheim said: "There is no such thing as a Jewish race, because it is the Jewish religion."

Simon Wolf said: "The point we make is this * * * that Hebrew or Jewish is simply a religion."

Julian W. Mack said: "Of what possible value is it to anybody to classify them as Jews simply because they adhere to the Jewish religion?"

The object of this testimony was to have the Jews classified under various national names, such as Polish, English, German, Russian, or whatever it might be.

Now, when the inquirer turns to the authoritative Jewish spokesmen who speak not to Gentiles but to Jews about this matter, he finds an entirely different kind of testimony. Some of this testimony will now be presented.

The reader will bear in mind that, as the series is not written for entertainment but for instruction into the facts of a very vital Question, the present article will be of value only to those who desire to know for themselves what are the basic elements of the matter.

It should also be observed during the reading of the following testimony that sometimes the term "race" is used, sometimes the term "nation." In every case, it is recognized that the Jew is a member of a separate people, quite aside from the consideration of his religion.

First, let us consider the testimony which forbids us to consider the term "Jew" as merely the name of a member of a religious body only.

Louis D. Brandeis, Justice of the Supreme Court of the United States and world leader of the Zionist movement, says:

"Councils of Rabbis and others have undertaken at times to prescribe by definition that only those shall be deemed Jews who professedly adhere to the orthodox or reformed faith. But in the connection in which we are considering the term, it is not in the power of any single body of Jews—or indeed of all Jews collectively—to establish the effective definition. The meaning of the word 'Jewish' in the term 'Jewish Problem' must be accepted as co-extensive with the disabilities which it is our problem to remove * * * Those disabilities extend substantially to all of Jewish blood. The disabilities do not end with a

renunciation of faith, however sincere * * * Despite the medita-
tions of pundits or the decrees of councils, our own instincts and
acts, and those of others, have defined for us the term 'Jew' "
("Zionism and the American Jews.")

The Rev. Mr. Morris Joseph, West London Synagogue of
British Jews: "Israel is assuredly a great nation * * * The very
word 'Israel' proves it. No mere sect or religious community could
appropriately bear such a name. Israel is recognized as a nation
by those who see it; no one can possibly mistake it for a mere sect.
To deny Jewish nationality you must deny the existence of the
Jew." ("Israel a Nation.")

Arthur D. Lewis, West London Zionist Association: "When
some Jews say they consider the Jews a religious sect, like the
Roman Catholics or Protestants, they are usually not correctly
analyzing and describing their own feelings and attitude. * * *
If a Jew is baptized, or, what is not necessarily the same thing,
sincerely converted to Christianity, few people think of him as
no longer being a Jew. His blood, temperament and spiritual
peculiarities are unaltered." ("The Jews a Nation.")

Bertram B. Benas, barrister-at-law: "The Jewish entity is
essentially the entity of a People. 'Israelites,' 'Jews,' 'Hebrews'—
all the terms used to denote the Jewish people bear a specifically historical meaning, and none of these terms has been
convincingly superseded by one of purely sectarian nature. The
external world has never completely subscribed to the view that
the Jewish people constitute merely an ecclesiastical denomination. * * * " ("Zionism—The National Jewish Movement.")

Leon Simon, a brilliant and impressive Jewish scholar and
writer, makes an important study of the question of "Religion
and Nationality" in his volume, "Studies in Jewish Nationalism." He makes out a case for the proposition that the Religion
of the Jews is Nationalism, and that Nationalism is an integral
part of their Religion.

"It is often said, indeed, that Judaism has no dogmas. That
statement is not true as it stands." He then states some of the
dogmas, and continues—"And the Messianic Age means for the
Jew not merely the establishment of peace on earth and good will

to men, but the universal recognition of the Jew and his God. It is another assertion of the eternity of the nation. Dogmas such as these are not simply the articles of faith of a church, to which anybody may gain admittance by accepting them; they are the beliefs of a nation about its own past and its own future." (p.14.)

"For Judaism has no message of salvation for the individual soul, as Christianity has; all its ideas are bound up with the existence of the Jewish nation." (p. 20.)

"The idea that Jews are a religious sect, precisely parallel to Catholics and Protestants, is nonsense." (p. 34.)

Graetz, the great historian of the Jews, whose monumental work is one of the standard authorities, says that the history of the Jews, even since they lost the Jewish State, "still possesses a national character; it is by no means merely a creed or church history. * * * Our history is far from being a mere chronicle of literary events or church history."

Moses Hess, one of the historic figures through whom the whole Jewish Program has flowed down from its ancient sources to its modern agents, wrote a book entitled "Rome and Jerusalem" in which he stated the whole matter with clearness and force.

"Jewish religion," he says, "is, above all, Jewish patriotism." (p.61.)

"Were the Jews only followers of a certain religious denomination, like the others, then it were really inconceivable that Europe, and especially Germany, where the Jews have participated in every cultural activity, 'should spare the followers of the Israelitish confession neither pains, nor tears, nor bitterness.' The solution of the problem, however, consists in the fact that the Jews are something more than mere 'followers of a religion,' namely, they are a race brotherhood, a nation. * * * " (p.71.)

Hess, like other authoritative Jewish spokesmen, denies that forsaking the faith constitutes a Jew a non-Jew." * * * Judaism has never excluded anyone. The apostates severed themselves from the bond of Jewry. 'And not even them has Judaism forsaken,' added a learned rabbi in whose presence I expressed the above-quoted opinion."

"In reality, Judaism as a nationality has a natural basis which cannot be set aside by mere conversion to another faith, as is the case in other religions. A Jew belongs to his race and consequently also to Judaism, in spite of the fact that he or his ancestors have become apostates." (pp. 97-98.)

"Every Jew is, whether he wishes it or not, solidly united with the entire nation." (p. 163.)

Simply to indicate that we have not been quoting outworn opinions, but the actual beliefs of the most active and influential part of Jewry, we close this section of the testimony with excerpts from a work published in 1920 by the Zionist Organization of America, from the pen of Jessie E. Sampter:

"The name of their national religion, Judaism, is derived from their national designation. An un-religious Jew is still a Jew, and he can with difficulty escape his allegiance only by repudiating the name of Jew." (Guide to Zionism," p.5.)

It will be seen that none of these writers—and their number might be multiplied among both ancients and moderns—can deny that the Jew is exclusively a member of a religion without at the same time asserting that he is, whether he will or not, the member of a nation. Some go so far as to insist that his allegiance is racial in addition to being national. The term "race" is used by important Jewish scholars without reserve, while some, who hold the German-originated view that the Jews are an offshoot of the Semitic race and do not comprise that race, are satisfied with the term "nation." Biblically, in both the Old Testament and the New, the term "nation" or "people" is employed. But the consensus of Jewish opinion is this: the Jews are a separate people, marked off from other races by very distinctive characteristics, both physical and spiritual, and they have both a national history and a national aspiration.

It will be noticed how the testimony on the point of "race" combines the thought of race and nationality, just as the previous section combined the thought of nationality with religion.

Supreme Justice Brandeis, previously quoted, appears to give a racial basis to the fact of nationality.

He says: "It is no answer to this evidence of nationality to declare that the Jews are not an absolutely pure race. There has, of course, been some intermixture of foreign blood in the three thousand years which constitute our historic period. But, owing to persecution and prejudice, the intermarriages with non-Jews which have occurred have resulted merely in taking away many from the Jewish community. Intermarriage has brought few additions. Therefore the percentage of foreign blood in the Jews of today is very low. Probably no important European race is as pure. But common race is only one of the elements which determine nationality."

Arthur D. Lewis, a Jewish writer, in his "The Jews a Nation," also bases nationality on the racial element:

"The Jews were originally a nation, and have retained more than most nations one of the elements of nationality—namely, the race element; this may be proved, of course, by the common sense test of their distinguishability. You can more easily see that a Jew is a Jew than that an Englishman is English."

Moses Hess is also quite clear on this point. He writes of the impossibility of Jews denying "their racial descent, and says: "Jewish noses cannot be reformed, and the black, wavy hair of the Jews will not turn through conversion into blond, nor can its curves be straightened out by constant combing. The Jewish race is one of the primary races of mankind that has retained its integrity, in spite of the continual change of its climatic environment, and the Jewish type has conserved its purity through the centuries."

Jessie E. Sampter, in the "Guide to Zionism," recounting the history of the work done for Zionism in the United States, says: "And this burden was nobly borne, due partly to the commanding leadership of such men as Justice Louis D. Brandeis, Judge Julian W. Mack, and Rabbi Stephen S. Wise, partly to the devoted and huge labors of the old-time faithful Zionists on the Committee, such as Jacob de Haas, Louis Lipsky, and Henrietta Szold, and partly to *the aroused race consciousness of the mass of American Jews.*"

Four times in the brief preface to the fifth edition of "Coningsby," Disraeli uses the term "race" in referring to the Jews, and Disraeli was proud of being racially a Jew, though religiously he was a Christian.

In The Jewish Encyclopedia, "the Jewish race" is spoken of. In the preface, which is signed by Dr. Cyrus Adler as chief editor, these words occur: "An even more delicate problem that presented itself at the very outset was the attitude to be observed by the Encyclopedia in regard to those Jews who, while born within the Jewish community, have, for one reason or another, abandoned it. As the present work deals with the Jews as a race, it was found impossible to exclude those who were of that race, whatever their religious affiliations might have been."

But as we are not interested in ethnology, the inquiry need not be continued further along this line. The point toward which all this trends is that the Jew is conscious of himself as being more than the member of a religious body. That is, Jewry nowhere subscribes in the persons of its greatest teachers and its most authoritative representatives, to the theory that a Jew is only "a brother of the faith." Often he is not of the faith at all, but he is still a Jew. The fact is insisted upon here, not to discredit him, but to expose the double minds of those political leaders who, instead of straightforwardly meeting the Jewish Question, endeavor to turn all inquiry aside by an impressive confusion of the Gentile mind.

It may be argued by the small body of so-called "Reformed Jews" that the authorities quoted here are mostly Zionists. The reply is this: there may be, and quite possibly are, two Jewish programs in the world—one which it is intended the Gentiles should see, and one which is exclusively for the Jews. In determining which is the real Program, it is a safe course to adopt the one that is made to succeed. It is the Program sponsored by the so-called Zionists which is succeeding. It was made to succeed through the Allied Governments, through the Peace Conference, and now through the League of Nations. That, then, must be the true Jewish program, because it is hardly possible that the Gentile governments could have been led as they are being led, were they not convinced that they are obeying the behests of the real Princes of the Jews. It is all well enough to engage the plain Gentile people with one set of interesting things; the real thing is the one what has been put over. And that is the program whose sponsors also stand for the racial and national separateness of the Jews.

The idea that the Jews comprise a nation is the most common idea of all—among the Jews. Not only a nation with a past, but a nation with a future. More than that—not only a nation, but a Super-Nation.

We can go still further on the authority of Jewish statements: we can say that the future form of the Jewish Nation will be a kingdom.

And as to the present problems of the Jewish Nation, there is plenty of Jewish testimony to the fact that the influence of American life is harmful to Jewish life; that is, they are in antagonism like two opposite ideas. This point, however, must await development in the succeeding article.

Israel Friedlaender traces the racial and national exclusiveness of the Jews from the earliest times, giving as illustrations two Biblical incidents—the Samaritans, "who were half-Jews by race and who were eager to become full Jews by religion," and their repulse by the Jews "who were eager to safeguard the racial integrity of the Jews"; also, the demand for genealogical records and for the dissolution of mixed marriages, as recorded in the Book of Ezra. Dr. Friedlaender says that in post-Biblical times "this racial exclusiveness of the Jews became even more accentuated." Entry into Judaism "never was, as in other religious communities, purely a question of faith. Proselytes were seldom solicited, and even when ultimately admitted into the Jewish fold they were so on the express condition that they surrender their racial individuality."

"For the purposes of the present inquiry," says Dr. Friedlaender, "it is enough for us to know that the Jews have always *felt* themselves as a separate race, sharply marked off from the rest of mankind. Anyone who denies the racial conception of Judaism on the part of the Jews in the past is either ignorant of the facts of Jewish history *or intentionally misrepresents them.*"

Elkan N. Adler says: "No serious politician today doubts that our people have a *political future.*"

This future of political definiteness and power was in the mind of Moses Hess when he wrote in 1862— mark the date!— in the preface of his "Rome and Jerusalem," these words:

"No nation can be indifferent to the fact that in *the coming European struggle* for liberty, it *may have another people* as its friend or foe."

Hess had just been complaining of the inequalities visited upon the Jews. He was saying that what the individual Jew could not get because he was a Jew, the Jewish Nation would be able to get because it would be a Nation. Evidently he expected that nationhood might arrive before the "coming European struggle," and he was warning the Gentile nations to be careful, because in that coming struggle there might be another nation in the list, namely, the Jewish Nation, which could be either friend or foe to any nation it chose.

Dr. J. Abelson, of Portsea College, in discussing the status of "small nations" as a result of the Great War, says: "The Jew is one of these 'smaller nations,' " and claims for the Jew what is claimed for the Pole, the Rumanian and the Serbian, and on the same ground —that of nationality.

Justice Brandeis voices the same thought. He says:

"While every other people is striving for development by asserting its nationality, and a great war is making clear the value of small nations * * * Let us make clear to the world that we too are a nationality clamoring for equal rights. * * * "

Again says Justice Brandeis: "Let us all recognize that we Jews are a distinct nationality, of which every Jew, whatever his country, his station, or shade of belief, is necessarily a member."

And he concludes his article, from which these quotations are made, with these words:

"Organize, organize, organize, until every Jew must stand up and be counted—counted with us, or prove himself, wittingly or unwittingly, of the few who are against their own people."

Sir Samuel Montague, the British Jew who has been appointed governor of Palestine under the British mandate, habitually speaks of the Jewish Kingdom, usually employing the expression "the restoration of the Jewish Kingdom." It may be of significance that the native population already refer to Sir Samuel as "The King of the Jews."

Achad ha-Am, who must be regarded as the one who has most conclusively stated the Jewish Idea as it has always existed, and whose influence is not as obscure as his lack of fame among the Gentiles might indicate, is strong for the separate identity of the Jews as a super-nation. Leon Simon succinctly states the great teacher's views when he says:

"While Hebraic thought is familiar with the conception of a Superman (distinguished, of course, from Nietzsche's conception by having a very different standard of excellence), yet its most familiar and characteristic application of that conception is not to the individual *but to the nation*—to *Israel as the Super-Nation* or 'chosen people." In fact, the Jewish nation is presupposed in all characteristically Jewish thinking, just as it is presupposed in the teaching of the Prophets."

"In those countries," says Moses Hess, "which form a dividing line between the Occident and the Orient, namely, Russia, Poland, Prussia and Austria, there live millions of our brethren who earnestly believe in the restoration of *the Jewish Kingdom* and pray for it fervently in their daily services."

This article, therefore, at the risk of appearing tedious, has sought to summon from many sides and from many periods the testimony which should be taken whenever the subject of Jewish nationalism comes under discussion. Regardless of what may be said to Gentile authorities for the purpose of hindering or modifying their action, there can be no·question as to what the Jew thinks of himself: He thinks of himself as belonging to a People, united to that People by ties of blood which no amount of creedal change can weaken, heir of that People's past, agent of that People's political future. He belongs to a race; he belongs to a nation; he seeks a kingdom to come on this earth, a kingdom which shall be over all kingdoms, with Jerusalem the ruling city of the world. That desire of the Jewish Nation may be fulfilled; it is the contention of these articles that it will not come by way of the Program of the Protocols nor by any of the other devious ways through which powerful Jews have chosen to work.

The charge of religious prejudice has always touched the people of civilized countries in a tender spot. Sensing this, the Jewish spokesmen chosen to deal with non-Jews have emphasized the point of religious prejudice. It is therefore a relief to tender and uninstructed minds to learn that Jewish spokesmen themselves have said that the troubles of the Jew have never arisen out of his religion, the Jew is not questioned on account of his religion, but on account of other things which his religion ought to modify. Gentiles know the truth that the Jew is not persecuted on account of his religion. All honest investigators know it. The attempt to shield the Jews under cover of their religion is, therefore, in face of the facts and of their own statements, an unworthy one.

If there were no other evidence, the very evidence which many Jewish writers cite, namely, the instant siding of the Jews one with another upon any and every occasion, would constitute evidence of racial and national solidarity. Whenever these articles have touched the International Jewish Financier, hundreds of Jews in the lower walks of life have protested. Touch a Rothschild, and the revolutionary Jew from the ghetto utters his protest, and accepts the remark as a personal affront to himself. Touch a regular old-line Jewish politician who is using a government office exclusively for the benefit of his fellow Jews as against the best interests of the nation, and the Socialist and anti-government Jew comes out in his defense. Most of these Jews, it may be said, have lost a vital touch with the teachings and ceremonials of their religion, but they indicate what their real religion is by their national solidarity.

This in itself would be interesting, but it becomes important in view of another fact, with which the next article will deal, namely, the relation between this Jewish nationalism and the nationalism of the peoples among whom the Jews dwell.

Issue of October 16, 1920

(Special Dispatch to the Evening Telegram.)

A CHANGE IN THE THANKSGIVING PROCLAMATION.

HARRISBURG, Nov. 10th— *An important change has been made in the Thanksgiving proclamation. In the last paragraph the words "Christian Commonwealth" have been altered to read: "A Commonwealth of freemen." This change has been made because of animadversions made by prominent Israelites. Gov. Hoyt says he used the word "Christian " in the sense of "civilized" and not particularly in a religious sense.*

—Vol. 20, American Jewish Historical Society "Documents regarding the Thanksgiving Proclamation of Gov. Hoyt, of Pennsylvania (1880)"

XXIII.

Jew Versus Non-Jew in New York Finance

THE Jewish problem in the United States is essentially a city problem. It is characteristic of the Jew to gather in numbers, not where land is open nor where raw materials are found, but where the greatest number of people abide. This is a noteworthy fact when considered alongside the Jews' claim that the Gentiles have ostracized them; the Jews congregate in their greatest numbers in those places and among those people where they complain they are least wanted. The explanation most frequently given is this: the genius of the Jew is to live off people; not off land, nor off the production of commodities from raw material, but off people. Let other people till the soil; the Jew, if he can, will live off the tiller. Let other people toil at trades and manufacture; the Jew will exploit the fruits of their work. That is his peculiar genius. If this genius be described as parasitic, the term would seem to be justified by a certain fitness.

In no other city of the United States can the Jewish Problem be studied with greater profit than in the city of New York. There are more Jews in New York than in all Palestine. The communal register of the Jewish Kehillah (or Kahal) of New York sets the population at about 1,527,778. "The next largest Jewish community in the world, that of the city of Warsaw, is estimated to have been between 300,000 and 330,000 Jews, about one-fifth as many as we estimate for New York." (Communal Register, 1917-1918.) "If we accept the estimate of the number of Jews in the world as about 14,000,000, one Jew out of every ten resides in New York."

31

As a population, the Jews exert more power in New York than they have ever exerted during the 'Christian Era in any place, with the exception of the present Russia. The Jewish Revolution in Russia was manned from New York. The present Jewish government of Russia was transported almost as a unit from the lower East Side of New York. The New York Ghetto has long since overflowed the lower East Side. Brownsville, Brooklyn, is a Jewish town, with its own language, theatres and press. The upper East Side of New York is practically in large sections a Jewish ghetto. The prosperous West Side and the middle class section of the city north of Central Park are practically Jewish.

With the exception of one great department store and a few lesser ones, all the large department stores in New York are Jewish. Men and women's ready-to-wear apparel, laundries, furriers, the general run of shopkeeping is practically monopolized by Jews. The legal profession is predominantly Jewish. It is estimated that of the 27,000 news stands that control the distribution of New York's reading matter, 25,000 are in the hands of Jews. There are 360 synagogues on the East Side of New York alone.

The New York Kehillah is a very powerful organization, whose membership strength is not accurately known. It may be described as the Jewish government of that city. It was organized in 1908 as the result of a statement by General Bingham, then police commissioner of New York, that the Jewish population, which then amounted to 600,000, contributed 50 percent of the criminals of the city. The Kehillah is the bar before which the authorities must answer for statements or acts touching the Jewish community. Its power is very great and its methods far reaching.

Politically, while the rest of the country is entertained with the fiction that Tammany Hall rules the politics of New York, the fact is rarely published that the Jews rule Tammany.

But it is not the possession of power that constitutes an indictment of any people; it is their use or misuse of it. And if the fact of power is established, no misuse of it being found, the fact has a commendatory side. If the Jews who flock to New York become American, and if they do not work ceaselessly to twist Americanism into something else; if they strengthen the principles and traditions of America, and do not cease to vitiate the one and abolish the other, the judgment upon them must be one of friendship.

However, to establish the fact of Jewish power, one need not remain in the ghetto, nor in the mercantile districts. There are higher fields awaiting survey.

In Wall Street, the Jewish element is both numerous and powerful, as might be expected of a race which from early days has played an important part in the financial operations of the world.

This is not to say, however, that Jewish influence in American financial affairs is paramount. At one time it threatened to be, but American financiers have always been silently aware of the International Jewish Financier, and have endeavored quietly to block his game. Time and again the contest has seemed to turn in favor of the Jew, but when the widespread secret wrestlings of the two powers have been suspended for a moment, it has been found that American finance has maintained its superiority, if only in a slight degree. The Rothschilds were the first to be beaten on American soil; the story of their hidden hand in American finance, politics and diplomacy is a voluminous one; but even their finesse did not avail against the sterling worth of American Business—not "American business" as it has come to be known now that thousands of Jews are scattered about the world, representing themselves to be "American business men" although they can scarcely speak English!—but American Business as represented by the combination of American ability and American conscience. If the reputation of American business has suffered, it is because something other than American methods have been used under the American name.

In the New York financial district, Jewish finance makes itself felt through its private banking institutions. As distinct from the great trust companies and banks of deposit, the private banker utilizes his own capital and that of his partners and associates.

Jewish finance differs radically from non-Jewish finance in the fact that Jewish bankers are essentially money-lenders. They may underwrite great flotations of bond and stock issues for railroad and industrial companies, governments and municipalities, but these securities are immediately sold to the public. There is a quick money turnover. The public carries the bonds; the Jewish financier gets his money. The Jewish banker himself rarely has a permanent interest in the corporations he finances. Non-Jewish bankers usually feel obligated to retain a connection with the enterprises they have financed, in order to assure the investors a proper administration of funds; they feel obligated to contribute to the success of the investments which they handle for other people.

The Jewish banker keeps his capital liquid. The cash is always in his coffers. This is essential to his position as one who deals in money. And when the inevitable day of financial stress arrives, he profits greatly by the higher value then placed on liquid capital.

Far and away the leading Jewish banking house in Wall Street is that of Kuhn, Loeb & Company. The head of this great firm was the late Jacob Schiff, whose associates were his son Mortimer, Otto H. Kahn, Paul M. Warburg, and others, who have taken prominent parts both in public life and giant financial operations. Other private Jewish banking houses may be named as follows: Speyer & Company; J. and W. Seligman & Company; Hallgarten & Company; Knauth, Nachod & Kuhne; Goldman, Sachs & Company, as well as others of relatively less prominence. These firms enjoy a high reputation for financial integrity. They are cautious bankers, skillful in their operations, and sometimes brilliant in their financial strategy.

There is much control of industry, from the financial side, represented by Jewish power in Wall Street, and they have gained a monopoly of many metal markets. Large, prosperous Jewish brokerage houses are on every hand. The further one goes down the line of speculative operations, the more of the

Jewish race one finds to be active in the work of company promotions and the marketing of oil and mining stocks.

Yet one amazing fact stands out from the mass: there is not, at this writing, a Jewish bank president on Wall Street; that is, a president of a bank of public deposit. Of all the great banks of public deposit and corporation finance, the enormous trust companies whose individual resources often run up to $400,000,000 and whose combined resources approximate many billions, not one of them has Jewish management or Jewish officers.

Why is this so? Why have the powerful banking families of Wall Street surrounded themselves so carefully with non-Jewish associates? Why has this great dividing line been drawn between members of the Jewish and non-Jewish races in the financial district that manages the financial resources of the nation?

Why? The answer to the question is in the custody of the stronger and sounder financial heads of Wall Street.

Only here and there one will discover a Jewish director in the boards of some of the lesser banking institutions.

The situation may be due merely to a shrewd analysis of the public mind. Rightly or wrongly the public prefers not to confide its money to an institution under Jewish control. It is true that in certain uptown sections of New York there are a few banks of a local character which are completely under Jewish management. But even the Jews prefer to deposit their money in banks which are free of Jewish control.

The situation may also be the effect of the unfortunate experience which the public has had with Jewish management of banks in the past. Several large failures have served to impress upon the public mind a certain peculiarity which attached to the Jewish element in those failures. The public has not forgotten, among others, the failure of Joseph G. Robin, whose real name was Robonovitch. He was an Odessa Jew. In an incredibly short space of time he built up four large banking institutions in which public money was deposited. He wrecked them all. His failure was most sensational and caused untold suffering. Robonovitch's career illustrated very vividly the extent of the gifts and energies of the Jew from Russia, his wonderful faculty for building up large concerns through chicanery, and his cowardice and duplicity in the hour of defeat. This banking career ended in a felon's cell.

However, one fact of importance, a fact that should be reassuring to the general public, is that the men to whom is entrusted the crucial task of putting to work and keeping at work the financial resources of the United States have hedged themselves about with a non-Jewish wall of great strength and long standing.

The effort of Jewish interests to gain control of the Stock Exchange is also an interesting story, and although the record shows a steady Jewish gain toward the end they desire, it is slow; but there are indications that the relentless persistence for which the Jew is noted, will prevail in the end—that is, if stock gambling continues to prove an alluring source of wealth.

When the Jews gain control of the Stock Exchange they will, for the first time, possess the power to wrest public banking control from the non-Jewish group.

There is a silent resistance to Jews on the Stock Exchange also, in virtue of a unwritten law, just as there is in the banking world of Wall Street, and the story of the counter resistance calls for an historian.

It is related by Sereno S. Pratt that in 1792 there was a little office at No. 22 Wall Street for the public sale of stocks. A number of men, engaged in the business of buying and selling, were accustomed to meet near a large buttonwood tree which stood near 68 Wall Street. In 1817, the New York Stock Exchange, about as present constituted, was organized.

The Stock Exchange is a private institution. It is practically a commission club in private hands. It is not incorporated.

Its membership is strictly limited to 1,100 men.

There are only two ways by which an outsider can become owner of a seat on the Exchange—by obtaining it from the executor of a deceased member, or by purchasing from a retiring or bankrupt member.

These memberships or seats cost at present more than $100,000. About ten years ago a seat could be bought for $77,000.

The Stock Exchange is ruled by a Governing Committee of 40 members. For many years no Jew was elected to this Committee. Of recent years, an occasional Jewish broker has succeeded in being admitted to this upper group, but not often. This position, however, has not been the main objective of Jewish traders. When they secure a sufficient number of seats on the Exchange, they will take care of the matter of control in their own well-known way.

The two barriers which at present operate to prevent a large inroad of Jews are these: first, a silent resistance on the part of the other members against the admission of Jews, a resistance which is said to date from the earliest formation of this famous trading institution. And, second, the restrictions which are placed by the constitution of the Stock Exchange itself on all applications for membership.

The Governing Committee of 40 has a Committee on Admissions which comprises 15 members and which considers all applications for membership. As the membership is fixed at 1,100 and as no new seats are ever sold, a new member can gain entrance only through the transfer of an existing seat. But even such a transfer is under the strict control of the Committee on Admissions, to whose scrutiny the name of the applicant must be submitted, and whose two-thirds approval is necessary to his being seated.

But one outstanding characteristic of the Jewish race is its persistence. What it cannot attain this generation, it will attain next. Defeat it today, it does not remain defeated; its conquerors die, but Jewry goes on, never forgiving, never forgetting, never deviating from its ancient aim of world control in one form or another. So, though it would seem impossible that Jewish membership in the Stock Exchange could increase under these conditions, the plain fact is that it has increased. Slowly but surely the Jews are gaining numerical power on the floor of the Exchange. And they are doing it with a subtlety that is amazing.

How do they do it? In the first place, no Jewish member ever transfers his seat to a non-Jew. In times of market dullness, when the prices of seats drop, and the demand is not so keen as usual, Jewish bidders offer, invariably, the highest sums to the seller. Then, in the case of the bankruptcy of a non-Jewish member, the receiver is almost compelled by the demand of creditors to accept the highest bid for the transfer of his membership; and, of course, a Jew is always at hand to make the bid as high as necessary. These are the two principal methods by which Jewish membership in the Exchange is being increased.

Another method, however, is more insidious than all the others combined. It is based on the rather common practice of adopting non-Jewish names or professing some phase of the Christian faith. The "changed name," or, as Jews know it, "the cover name," is a very potent part of the policy of concealment. In an advertisement, on business stationery, at the head of a magazine or newspaper article, such names as Smith, Adams, Robin, serve as a "blind." The stage is flooded with Jewish actors and actresses, but their names are very distinguished Anglo-Saxon. Jewish papers often print jokes based on this habit of changing names. For long-distance dealing, or any business that is carried on "unsight and unseen," the name-veil is very useful. On this account, many Gentiles would be surprised to learn the extent to which they are involved with Jews, whose names give no indication of Jewishness. And this very system, an old American name, coupled with membership in some Christian sect (preferably one of the newer sects), has accounted for some memberships in the Stock Exchange which probably would not otherwise exist.

It is interesting to tabulate the growth of Jewish membership as shown by the old directories of the Exchange.

In the year 1872, with a total of 1,009 members, there were 60 Jews.

In 1873, with a total of 1,006 members, the Jewish membership decreased to 49.

In 1890, with membership limited to 1,100, there were 87 Jews.

In 1893, with the same limit of membership, there were 106 Jews.

At the present time, still with the same rigid limitation of membership, there are 276 Jewish members.

It is said that the Jewish membership is really somewhat larger than the last figures indicate, owing to the fact that some of the Jewish members bear non-Jewish names and have adopted some phase of the Christian faith and have cut themselves off, outwardly at least, from the Jewish community.

The figures show, therefore, that Jewish membership increased from 5 7/8 per cent of the total in 1872 to 25 per cent in 1919.

In its reference to the Stock Exchange under the head of "Finance," the Jewish Encyclopedia states that Jewish membership is "only 128," "a little more than 10 per cent." The date of these Jewish statistics is not given. The article quoted has, however, an argumentative as well as informative purpose. The statement concerning the 10 per cent membership on the Exchange is made to call attention to the fact that "Jews form at least 20 per cent of the whole population of New York, and much more than that percentage of the business section." The Jewish population of New York City has since increased to 25 per cent of the whole, and the membership on the Stock Exchange has increased to the same point.

But it has taken 47 years for the Jews to gain that 25 per cent membership. Their control of the Exchange, at the given rate of progress, is only a question of time.

In spite of these details, it is probably a fact that the Jewish speculators in the New York financial district greatly outnumber the non-Jewish speculators. Speculation and gambling are known historically as special propensities of the Jewish race. While many Jews patronize non-Jewish firms, the great mass of them follow in the speculative path of the leaders of their race. In Europe, where their financial control is more firmly fixed and of longer standing than here, it is rarely that the Jews are caught in speculative failure. They are sometimes found in speculative scandals, but seldom in any scandal involving losses to themselves. As a rule they dabble in "Jewish" securities, and in

Wall Street one hears many stories concerning the victories or defeats of "the Jewish following."

Some of the biggest Jewish sensations which ever occurred in the United States, sensations which disclosed by their lurid light the interlocking of Jewish finance, politics and racial objectives, have been brought to light by occurrences in Wall Street. It is probably the nature of these disclosures which accounts for the strong and silent anti-Jewish resistance which characterizes straight American finance.

Meanwhile, to leave the exalted sphere of Wall Street, banking and brokerage activities, let us descend to the street level of the Curb Market in Broad Street. Here the Jewish brokers flourish in their oil, mining and stock promotion offices. They are so numerous as to give a Semitic cast to the vicinity, as if it were a quarter in a foreign city. It is true that these concerns are frequently operated under non-Jewish names, but that is merely part of the Jew's consciousness that, in financial matters; whether rightly or wrongly, he is under suspicion. Gentile names carry with them no such handicap.

Going still further down the line, in shadier lanes, in semi-hidden offices, may be seen numerous members of the Jewish race who are identified with no established market which deals in securities. These are the true parasites of the Wall Street environment, they are the camp followers without status. Their work is that of fraudulent stock promotion, and they enter upon it with a zeal and an energy which nothing can dismay. Their purpose is to make money without labor, to get money without giving value, and in this they are immensely successful. It is amazing the number of these men who make immense fortunes; it is equally amazing the continuous crop of unwary, poorly informed, and unsuspecting Gentiles who send their money from all parts of the United States for the worthless bits of paper in which these Jewish parasites deal. It is a most heartless business; it has not even brilliance in its deviltry. It is the old-time shell game in other terms. The operations of these men are mostly conducted by mail or telephone. They deal in "sucker lists," and they circulate "market letters" by which, under the pretense of giving disinterested advice to investors, they seek to boom their own shady game. These "market letters" are, of course, innocuous to those who are informed and who can read their fraudulent import between the lines, but they are dangerous to the honest but uninformed minds of tens of thousands of thrifty people.

Pursued by detective agencies, watched constantly by the government secret service, exposed by the newspapers, placed on trial in the courts, convicted and sentenced to terms in prison, this type of Jewish swindler is undeterred. Where other men would regard exposure as a lifelong shame, this type regards it simply as a trifling interruption, as a sailor would regard an accidental tumble overboard.

There are lower depths still, where bald theft and violence prevail. The persons most found there are the henchmen of the lower type of speculators. The stories of criminality in Wall Street, a numerous and startling list, involving sometimes the high, but mostly the low, and all marked with a peculiar racial and groupal cast, have at times challenged the attention of the whole world, but as is usually the case with the general publication of such stories, the fundamental explanatory facts are omitted.

But it will be seen, as the story of actual conditions in Wall Street and its financial environs is unrolled, that there are always the two elements—Jewish and non-Jewish. It is perhaps the only non-Jewish coalition in America, this silent resistance which American finance is making to Semitic control. It is, in a sense, unnatural to the American mind, but has been forced as a defensive against the strong offensive operations of the Semitic coalition. If there is ever in the United States a strong non-Jewish combination, it will be the direct result of the ancient Jewish coalition against non-Jews. The condition in the United States at this moment, with regard to the financial question, is this: The Jewish coalition goes lower, but it does not yet go higher, but has thus far been estopped. It is believed that when the people are made aware of what is transpiring, it will be forever estopped.

As readers of former articles will remember, the attack upon Capital represented by the disorderly forces who operate under the forged banner of "Progress," is an attack against Gentile capital only. The only financial managers attacked in the United States are Gentile managers. In England also, the same attack is made. Readers of the newspapers know what strenuous efforts are being made in that country to wreck railroad and coal mine administration by a constant series of strikes. But what readers of newspapers are not told is that the railroad and coal mines are still in Gentile hands, and that the Bolshevist-led strike is a Jewish financial weapon to wreck these forms of Gentile business, that they may easily fall into Jewish hands.

Issue of November 13, 1920

"Economic crises were created by us for the Gentiles only by the withdrawal of money from circulation. . . . The present issue of money does not coincide with the need per capita, and consequently it cannot satisfy all the needs of the working classes . . . . You know that gold currency was detrimental to the governments that accepted it, for it could not satisfy the requirements for money, since we took as much gold as possible out of circulation."
—Protocol 20.

XXIV.

The High and Low of Jewish Money Power

J EWISH high finance first touched the United States through the Rothschilds. Indeed it may be said that the United States founded the Rothschild fortune. And, as so often occurs in the tale of Jewish riches, the fortune was founded in war. The first twenty million dollars the Rothschilds ever had to speculate with was money paid for Hessian troops to fight against the American colonies.

Since that first indirect connection with American affairs, the Rothschilds have often invaded the money affairs of the country, though always by agents. None of the Rothschild sons thought it necessary to establish himself in the United States. Anselm remained in Frankfort, Solomon chose Vienna, Nathan Mayer went to London, Charles established himself in Naples, and James represented the family in Paris. These were the five war-lords of Europe for more than a generation, and their dynasty was continued by their successors.

The first Jewish agent of the Rothschilds in the United States was August Belmont, who came to the United States in 1837, and was made chairman of the Democratic National Committee at the outbreak of the Civil War. The Belmonts professed Christianity and there is today a Belmont memorial, called the Oriental Chapel, in the new Cathedral of St. John the Divine on Morningside Heights.

Rothschild power, as it was once known, has been so broadened by the entry of other banking families into governmental finance, that it must now be known not by the name of

43

one family of Jews, but by the name of the race. Thus it is spoken of as International Jewish Finance, and its principal figures are described as International Jewish Financiers. Much of the veil of secrecy which contributed so greatly to the Rothschild power has been stripped away; war finance has been labeled for all time as "blood money"; and the mysterious magic surrounding large transactions between governments and individuals, by which individual controllers of large wealth were made the real rulers of the people, has been largely stripped away and the plain facts disclosed.

The Rothschild method still holds good, however, in that Jewish institutions are affiliated with their racial institutions in all foreign countries. There are Jewish banking firms in New York whose connections with firms in Frankfort, Hamburg and Dresden, as well as in London and Paris, can be traced by the mere matter of the signs over the doors. They are one.

As a leading student of financial affairs puts it, the world of high finance is largely a Jewish world because of the Jewish financier's "absence from national or patriotic illusions."

To the International Jewish Financier the ups and downs of war and peace between nations are but the changes of the world's financial market; and, as frequently the movement of stocks is manipulated for purposes of market strategy, so sometimes international relations are effected for mere financial gain.

It is known that the recent Great War was postponed several times at the behest of international financiers. If it broke out too soon, it would not involve the states which the international financiers wished to involve. Therefore, the masters of gold, that is, the international masters, were compelled several times to check the martial enthusiasm which their own propaganda had aroused. It is probably quite true, as the Jewish press alleges, that there has been discovered a Rothschild letter dated 1911 and urging the Kaiser against war. The year 1911 was too early. There was no such insistence in 1914.

Not only do these foreign financial affiliations cast a different light on purely national matters affecting the peace and prestige of the peoples, but they tend toward an extra- or super-

44

nationality. When these foreign affiliations enable Jewish bankers to excel in the more highly specialized forms of finance, such as foreign exchange, they also enable them to exercise almost complete control over international money movements.

There is no question whatever of International Jewish Finance being deeply concerned in the matters of war and revolution. This is never denied as to the past; but it is just as true of the present. The league against Napoleon, for example, was Jewish. Its headquarters were in Holland. When Napoleon invaded Holland, the headquarters were moved to Frankfort-on-the-Main. It is remarkable how many of the International Jewish Financiers have come out of Frankfort—the Rothschilds, the Schiffs, the Speyers, to name but a few. The racial affiliations running all through the world of international finance are readily recognized.

These associations produce in Jewish banking circles a constant tendency toward control or monopoly of certain lines of industry which are identified with the fields of finance. The rule is, once control is gained, all non-Jewish interests must be driven out. "Jewish financial interests have rarely been connected with industrials," says the Jewish Encyclopedia, "Except as regards some of the precious stones and metals, the Rothschilds, controlling mercury, Barnato Brothers and Werner, Beit & Company diamonds, and the firms of Lewisohn Brothers and Guggenheim Sons controlling copper, and to some extent silver." To this, of course, may be added whiskey, wireless, theaters, the European press and part of the American, and a number of other fields. The list will be made complete in this series of articles before they are finished.

The Jewish Encyclopedia continues:

"It is, however, mainly in the direction of foreign loans that there has been any definite predominance of Jewish financiers, this being due, as before stated, to the international relations of the larger Jewish firms."

In order that the senseless denials of certain portions of the Jewish press may be checked, it may be said that Jewish authorities do not deny such statements as are made about

45

Jewish international financial control, although they declare it is not as strong as it once was. "Of more recent years," says The Jewish Encyclopedia, "non-Jewish financiers have learned the same cosmopolitan method, and, on the whole, the control is now rather less than more in Jewish hands than formerly."

This is true, at least so far as the United States is concerned. Previous to the war, the status of many of the Jewish financial concerns in Wall Street was stronger than it is now. The war brought about a condition which threw a new light on the internationalism of Jewish finance. During the years of American neutrality there was opportunity to observe the extent of the foreign affiliations of certain men, and also the extent to which ordinary national loyalty was subordinated to the business of international finance. The war really forced a coalition of Gentile capital on one side of the struggle, as against certain blocks of Jewish capital which were willing to play both sides. The old Rothschild maxim, "Do not put all your eggs in one basket," becomes perfectly plain when transposed into national and international terms. Jewish finance treats political parties the same—bets on them both, and so never loses. In the same way, Jewish finance never loses a war. Being on both sides, it cannot miss the winning side, and its terms of peace are sufficient to cover all advances to the side that lost. This was the significance of the great swarming of Jews at the Peace Conference.

Many of the Jewish houses on Wall Street were originally the American branches of long established houses in Germany and Austria. These international firms were accustomed to support one another with capital, and maintained other intimate associations. Some of them are linked by intermarriage. But the bond above all is the Jewish racial bond. Most of these houses received a severe setback during the war, because their over-sea associations were not of the right kind. But this setback is expected to be only temporary, and the Jewish financiers will again be ready to give battle for the entire financial control of the United States.

46

Whether they will be successful, the future will decide. But a strange fatality seems to follow all forms of Jewish supremacy. Just as the capstone is ready to be placed upon the edifice of Jewish triumphs, something occurs and the structure shrinks. It occurs so often in Jewish history that the Jews themselves have been exercised to find an explanation. In many cases "anti-Semitism" offers the readiest excuse, but not always. Just at the present time, when the light which was shed by the fires of war has revealed so many matters formerly hidden in shadow, the awakening of world attention is called "anti-Semitism," and the explanation is given that "after every war the Jew becomes the scapegoat"—a curious admission which would lead a less self-centered people to inquire, Why?

But so handy and so untrustworthy an explanation as "anti-Semitism" does not account for the failure of Jewish financial interests to become absolutely dominant in a country like the United States. Anti-Semitism among the people does not surge high enough to injure those securely entrenched behind great financial influence. The silent resistance of the Wall Street financial group or of the New York Stock Exchange, for example, is not anti-Semitism. It is not a hindrance to the Jews in doing business; it is opposition to an apparent program for total control which is sought not for the general good, but for a racial benefit.

It was only a few years ago that the banking house of Kuhn, Loeb & Company was commonly regarded as being destined in the near future to win complete financial supremacy in Wall Street as an underwriting and money-lending institution. There were many reasons for this belief, among them the fact that Kuhn, Loeb & Company were the financial backers of Harriman in his terrific railroad duel with James J. Hill. But the prophecy regarding this financial institution was never realized. Untoward events intervened, in no way affecting the financial integrity of the firm, but bringing it into the light of undesirable publicity not of a financial character.

In the firm of Kuhn, Loeb & Company, Jewish finance in the United States reached its high-water mark. The head of this firm was the late Jacob Schiff, who was born in Frankfort-on-the-Main and whose father was one of the Rothschld's brokers. One of Jacob Schiff's associates, Otto Kahn, was born in Mannheim, and was early associated with the Speyers, who also originated in Frankfort-on-the-Main. Another associate, Felix Warburg, married into Jacob Schiff's family. Jewish finance has spread, but it has not risen higher than in this firm.

A flank movement, however, has been attempted which may bring Jewish ambitions nearer the goal of their desire. Checked in Wall Street, Jewish financiers have sought out other American centers, and even foreign centers whose future influence on American affairs promises to be considerable. The first flank movement is toward Central and South America. It may be said that the financial assistance, practical and advisory, offered to Mexico during the most unsatisfactory period of her relations with the United States, was given by Jewish financial groups. The attempt to gain influence with Japan seems to have come off rather badly. It is known, of course, that Jacob Schiff gave material assistance to Japan in the war with Russia. This was explainable on the ground of good business and also of a desire to revenge Russia's treatment of the Jews. Mr. Schiff used the opportunity also to instill the principles, which have since grown up into Bolshevism, into the minds of Russian prisoners in Japanese war camps. But more than that, the idea appears to have been to add the newly rising Japanese power to the string of Jewish financial conquests. Jewish finance already has a foothold in Japan, but it appears that Mr. Schiff's hopes in this respect were not fully realized. The Japanese are credited with knowing much more about "the Jewish peril" than even the United States does, and they were exceedingly wary. They kept the business deal strictly a business deal, and Mr. Schiff was said to have been displeased with Japan generally. This is well worth knowing at this time, especially in view of the propaganda which seeks constantly to cause misunderstandings to arise between the United States and the Empire of Japan.

But South America appears to be the latest objective. It must be remembered that the Jews exercise world control in two departments: in movements of men, and in movements of money. No government, no church, no school of thought could order the movement of 250,000, half a million, or even a million people, from one part of the world to another, shifting them as a general shifts his army, but the Jews can do that. They are doing it now. It is only a matter of ships. From Poland, where Jewish special privileges have been written into the law of the land by the all-powerful Peace Conference, and where it would seem that the Jews have every reason to remain, there is a great movement westward. It is not a stampede, as the American Commissioner of Immigration says, although it may look so from this side. It is an orderly movement, as can be seen when the American Jewish directors on the other side are observed. And part of it is being directed to South America. It is said that after a period of training in the United States, some of the immigrants who are now landing here will be shipped south again.

The other mastery which the Jews exert in a world degree is that over the movement of gold. Without giving expression to what the purpose may be, there is this to be said: a large movement of Jewish men and Jewish gold proceeds toward South America these days. And there is said to be a large movement of other materials, which when interpreted by the Protocols can mean but one thing.

The next attempt for control of the Americas may come from the South, where the Jews are already stronger than their numbers would indicate, and where their revolutionary proclivities have already come into play as between the various states.

These rebuffs and these strategic flank movements do not, however, complete the record. We are now speaking of American finance only. The Jews have not been restrained elsewhere as they have been in Wall Street. They exercise a very ominous control in a number of other fields, each of which will be taken up in detail in due time. For the present, out attention is being directed to New York and its financial district.

We have just shown the high-water mark of Jewish control as it has been reached up to date in the Street. There is another aspect of Jewish influence on the financial affairs of America which is not so flattering to that race. If Jewish financial activity does not go higher, it goes lower and finds its way into darker channels than does any other form of financial activity in the country.

It would make a sordid tale, the operations of the Robins, the Lamars, the Arnsteins and the others who have contributed to the long roll of criminality produced within the shadow of Wall Street and the only point that could be served by its retelling is that such criminality is predominantly Jewish. This is not to say that it has the approval of the Jewish community, but it is very significant that while whole volumes of abuse have been heaped upon THE DEARBORN INDEPENDENT'S very modest effort to state the status of the Jewish Question in America, the leaders of Jewry have been silent about the criminal financial operations of those who could be made to feel the displeasure of their race. The Jewish passion for the defense of the race, regardless of the degree of guilt, is well known to every prosecuting attorney, although it must be said that during the investigation made some years ago which revealed the business of commercialized vice to be under Jewish control, certain public-spirited Jews commendably aided the work. This aid, however, did not prevent the severest opposition to certain publications which gave notice of the facts which the investigators were finding.

The country was lately astounded by the revelation that stocks and Liberty bonds to the value of $12,000,000 had been lost through a systematic series of thefts in Wall Street.

Beginning with the spring of 1918, messengers sent out by New York Stock Exchange firms to make deliveries of stocks and bonds to other houses, in the course of ordinary business, began to disappear as if the earth had swallowed them up. For a time these disappearances were without explanation.

Wall Street is really a small district. Most of its business is done within the space of a city block. Messengers on their trips sometimes went only to another floor in the same building, or to an office across the street. Yet in those short trips they would disappear with all their securities, seldom to be heard of again. Up to the summer of 1918 the absconding messenger boy was a rarity. The type was regarded with good-humored indulgence on the Street. They were generally happy-go-lucky youngsters, and the steadier heads among them graduated into clerks in the commission houses.

The labor shortage struck Wall Street, along with other sections of the country, and messenger boys were difficult to find. During this period there was also a great expansion in business. Nearly everyone in the country possessed bonds of some kind, and these changed hands in unparalleled quantities. On the floor of the Stock Exchange, daily transactions in bonds up to $20,000,000, and in stocks up to one or two million shares, were common. Following the sales, the stocks and bonds were transferred from seller to buyer by messenger boy. It was not unusual for irresponsible lads to be running from office to office in Wall Street with $250,000 each under the arms.

Then, with the shortage of boys, another type of messenger began to appear, and with this type the trouble began. Disappearances and losses became more frequent and costly. The indemnities paid by the insurance companies reached such staggering figures that the custom of issuing blanket insurance was withdrawn. Various expedients were adopted to solve the mystery; boys were required to travel in pairs, guards were posted throughout Wall Street, the best detectives in the land were assigned to the matter, but without avail.

There was a strong disinclination in Wall Street toward publishing the figures of the losses, for fear the publication might be destructive of public confidence in the Street's financial condition. But the news was known in the underworld and drew to New York criminals from all parts of the country. For a time all efforts were fruitless; the losses continued and the mystery deepened.

Then, suddenly, in the early part of 1920, certain arrests were made and confessions obtained, which disclosed one of the most amazing criminal conspiracies in the history of the United States.

There was proved the existence of a vast Jewish conspiracy to loot Wall Street. It was found that a band of astute Jewish criminals, many of them wealthy men, some of them ex-convicts, had created an organization by which Wall Street financial houses were to be plundered.

Bands of young Jews, mostly of Russian origin and living on the East Side, had been shaped into being. These lads, instructed by clever Jewish principals, applied to Wall Street messenger agencies for employment in brokerage houses. It was part of the plan for them to assume good, honest-sounding Anglo-Saxon names. The "cover name"—how often we meet it!

These lads turned over their stolen stocks and bonds to the heads of their organizations, who in turn passed the securities on to the Jewish principals, who were for the most part members of the criminal band of "confidence men" in the White Light district—the "bank-roll men," whose immunity from punishment has always been one of the standing puzzles of Gentiles residing in New York.

These Jewish criminals were aided by Jewish lawyers in their transactions. The stolen stocks and bonds were taken to Cleveland, Boston, Washington, Philadelphia and parts of Canada, where they were pledged as collateral for loans in an apparently legitimate course of business.

One of the messenger boys refused to deliver his stolen securities for the small sum he was offered for them, and ran away to enjoy alone his ill-gotten wealth. His hiding place was discovered and members of a band of Harlem assassins were sent for him, with instructions to find where the securities were. If they were on the boy's person, he was to be killed at once. This band entertained the boy with drinks and women for several days until they learned that the securities were sewed inside the lining of his coat. They took him for a "joy-ride" into the country, and his dead body was afterward found, typically slain, with about two dozen dagger wounds in his body.

In one instance a non-Jew was inveigled into the nefarious scheme, and the method was also typical. The Jewish principals wished for another clearing-house through which to dispose of their securities, and were "tipped off" that a young non-Jewish broker was on the verge of bankruptcy. He was "helped out" and given what appeared to him to be a very profitable piece of business. Once in the power of his "friends," and deeply entangled in their game, he tried to get out of it. He was threatened with death. The Jewish principal said to him: "I don't want any double-crossing here, or I'll kill you in a minute. If I can't do it—if I am locked up— there are plenty of my gang who will do it."

Upon the arrest and confession of this non-Jew, many of the Jewish principals fled New York, traveling, as usual, under their assumed Christian names. But their identity had at last become known, and although many of their messenger-boy dupes have been made to suffer the penalty for their crimes, the leaders are at this writing yet free, and the most powerful influences seem to be invoked to protect them from the ordinary operations of the law. A few have been captured, but although their accusers are the most powerful banking, brokerage and surety companies on Wall Street, a power greater still seems to defend them from the treatment usually accorded known criminals.

One of the ringleaders has defied the courts with impunity and still walks the streets. Jewish theatrical managers in New York have headlined his actress wife, a Jewess, presumably because of the added prestige it gave her to be the wife of the world-defying bond thief.

That is the element which strikes something like consternation to the heart of the ordinary lover of law and order—the insolence with which these wealthy Jewish criminals regard all the agencies of the law. They are defended by clever lawyers, and the attitude of the Jewish press and Jewish population toward them is compact of sympathy and admiration. Why not?—since most of the individual victims of the thievery are Gentiles, and the general victim is Gentile capitalism itself!

There is complete silence on the Jewish side regarding this reign of crime. And yet inevitably the Jews themselves must suffer most from it. The New York Kehillah has completely ignored this outbreak and its exposure. The spokesmen of Jewry, so voluble against non-Jews, have no word to say to those whom they would probably call their "co-religionists." Yet it is well enough understood that so closely combined are all the influences in New York Jewry that a determined effort on the part of the leaders could clean up many untoward conditions now existing. But there seems to be a distinct aversion to anything that will indicate a division of one class of Jews against another. It is a racial instinct, evidently, to protect the threatened one no matter how richly he may deserve punishment.

It is this fact which puts the finishing Jewish touch on the whole matter. It may, of course, be an accident that all the criminals and their tools, with an occasional exception, are Jews. That of itself might not be a reason, in the extreme sense, for labeling the condition with a racial name. But the silence, the approbation in some quarters, the very active sympathy in others, all combining as a racial protectorate around the wrong-doers, is the more regrettable manifestation of the two.

Issue of November 20, 1920

XXV.

"Disraeli of America"—A Jew of Super-Power

A LTHOUGH the war had the effect of decreasing Jewish power in Wall Street by temporarily hindering, but perhaps not altogether breaking off, the communication between Jewish financial houses in the United States and their associates overseas, it also had the effect of greatly increasing Jewish wealth in this country. It is stated upon the authority of a well-informed Jewish source that in New York City alone fully 73 per cent of the "war millionaires" are Jews.

The mistake should not be made of assuming that because of the temporary setback in Wall Street, the war meant a total setback for the Jewish program. It did not. Jewry emerged from the war more strongly entrenched in power, even in the United States, than it was before. And in the world at large the ascendancy of the Jew, even where he was in control before, is very marked.

A Jew is now President of the League of Nations.

A Zionist is President of the Council of the League of Nations.

A Jew is President of France.

A Jew was President of the committee to investigate the responsibility for the war, and one incident of his service was the disappearance of vital documents.

In France, Germany and England of the Jews, as well as the filtration of their dangerous ideas of social disorder, have greatly increased.

It is a most remarkable fact that in those countries which can justly be called anti-Semitic, the rule of the Jew is stronger than anywhere else. The more they are opposed, the more they show their power. Germany is today an anti-Semitic nation. Yet, in spite of all that the German people have done to rid themselves of the visible show of Jewish power, it has entrenched itself more firmly than before, above and beyond the reach of the German popular will. France becomes increasingly anti-Semitic, and as the anti-Jewish wave rises, a Jewish President appears. Russia itself is anti-Semitic to the core, and the Jew is Russia's new tyrant. And at a moment when, as all Jewish spokesmen inform us, there is a world wave of anti-Semitics—which is their name for a new awakening of the nations to what has been going on—what should occur but that at the head of the League of Nations, in a position which but for the absence of the United States would constitute the Chief Magistracy of the World, a Jew appears. Nobody seem to know why. Nobody can explain it. Neither previous fitness nor public demand pointed him out—yet there he is!

In our own country we have just had a four-year term of Jewish rule, almost as absolute as that which exists in Russia. This appears to be a very strong statement, but it is somewhat milder than the facts warrant. And the facts themselves are not of hearsay origin, nor the product of a biased point of view; they are the fruits of an inquiry by the lawful officials of the United States who were set aside in favor of a ready-made Jewish Government, and they are forever spread upon the official records of the United States.

The Jews have proved for all time that the control of Wall Street is not necessary to the control of the American people, and the person by whom they proved this was a Wall Street Jew.

This man has been called "the pro-consul of Judah in America."

It is said that once, referring to himself, he exclaimed: "Behold the Disraeli of the United States!"

To a select committee of the Congress of the United States he said:

*"I probably had more power than perhaps any other
man did in the war; doubtless that is true."*
And in saying so he did not overstate the case. He *did* have
more power. It was not all legal power, this much he admitted.
It reached into every home and store and factory and bank and
railway and mine. It touched armies and governments. It
touched the recruiting boards. It made and unmade men without a word. It was power without responsibility and without
limit. It was such a power as compelled the Gentile population
to lay bare every secret before this man and his Jewish
associates, giving them a knowledge and an advantage that
billions of gold could not buy.

Doubtless not one in every 50,000 of the readers of this paper
ever heard of this man before 1917, and doubtless the same
number have clear knowledge of him now. He glided out of a
certain obscurity unlighted by public service of fame, into the
high rulership of the nation at war. The constituted government had little to do with him save vote the money and do his
bidding. He said that men could have appealed over his head to
the President of the United States but, knowing the situation,
men never did.

Who is this figure, colossal in his way, and most instructive
of the readiness of Judah to take the rule whenever he desires?

His name is Bernard M. Baruch. He was born in South
Carolina 50 years ago, the son of Dr. Simon Baruch, who was a
medical man of some consequence. "I went to college with the
idea of becoming a doctor, but I did not become a doctor," he told
the Congressional Committee. He was graduated at the College
of the City of New York when he was just under 19 years of age.
This college is one of the favorite educational institutions with
the Jews, its president being Dr. S. E. Mezes, a brother-in-law of
Colonel E. M. House, the colonel whose influence and disfavor at
the White House has for a long time been a favorite subject of
wondering speculation on the part of the American people,
though it scarcely need be so any longer.

Apparently young Baruch knew exactly what he wanted to
do, and set out to do it. He says he spent "many years" after his

graduation in certain studies, "particularly economics" as related to railroads and industrial propositions. "I tried to make Poor's Manual and the financial supplement of the Financial Chronicle my bible for a number of years."

He could not have spent very "many years" in these pursuits, for after going down to Wall Street as a clerk and a runner, and when he was "about 26 or 27" he became a member of the firm of A. A. Housman & Company. "In about 1900 or 1902" he left the firm, but he had meanwhile gained a seat on the Stock Exchange.

He then went into business for himself, a statement which must be taken literally in view of his testimony that he "did not do any business for anybody but myself. I made a study of the corporations engaged in the production and manufacture of different things, and a study of the men engaged in them."

In answer to questions intended to disclose the exact nature of his operations before he suddenly appeared as the man who "had *more power than perhaps any other man in the war,*" he stood off from any intimations that he perhaps engaged in mere buying and selling of stock. "My business then became the organization of various enterprises," he said, "and in connection with that, I, of course, did buy and sell stocks * * * If I organized any concern, I naturally took a large interest in it, or I would not organize it if I did not believe in it, and I stayed with the development of that concern; and then if I cared later on to sell it, I would sell it."

Pressed by the examiners for a still more detailed account of his activities in business, he said:

"Well, I was instrumental in the purchase of the Liggett & Myers Tobacco Company; in the purchase of Selby Smelter, Tacoma Smelter, and various copper, tungsten, rubber—I was instrumental in building up one of the great industries in rubber in Mexico, which was the establishment of the source of supply of rubber, and developed a large concern there for the production of raw material, which is still going on * * *

"I became interested in the new process of concentration of low-grade ores in the Mesaba Range, but the interest I had particularly in steel was in the study of the present-day organization, in order to get myself posted so that I could intelligently buy or sell their securities * * * "

It is an important point, one not made very clear in the testimony, what interests Mr. Baruch held at the beginning of the war. His previous activities in various fields, principally perhaps the field of metals, had been important and numerous. In any case, as a young man, he is found to be master of large sums of money, and there is no indication that he inherited it. He is very wealthy. What change the war made in his wealth, if it made any change at all, is a matter on which nothing may be said now. Certainly many of his friends and closest associates reaped great quantities of money from their activities during the war.

Now, as to the point of his business connections just prior to the war, this testimony appears:

Mr. Graham—"You continued in the operation of these various businesses, in the formation of companies and the flotation of their stocks, and in your business in the Stock Exchange and elsewhere *up until the time of the beginning of the war?"*

Mr. Baruch—"I was gradually getting myself away from business, because I had made up my mind to retire, and I had been getting less active with that end in view, and I was not very much in sympathy with the organization of companies. I am not criticising other men who engage in business that resulted in profits even before we had gotten into war. *I had made up my mind to leave* and do some other things that I hope to be able to do now; *but that process was interrupted by my appointment as member of the advisory commission* without any suggestion or without any knowledge or idea it was coming."

Does he mean that the process of getting out of business was interrupted by his appointment on the advisory commission, which appointment led straight to his complete rulership of the United States at war?

Mr. Jefferis—"Had any of the members of the advisory commission been engaged in the production of raw materials or in manufactured products, or not?"

Mr. Baruch—"I had."

Mr. Jefferis—"In what way?"

Mr. Baruch—"I had made a rather deep study of the production and the distribution and manufacture of many of these raw materials. I had to make an intensive study of these things in order to do the things I was engaged in."

Mr. Jefferis—"You were not running any raw material production?"

Mr. Baruch—"*I was interested in concerns* —I was interested in the study and production of a great many of these things, because I developed and organized concerns which did it."

Does he mean that he was interested in concerns at the time of his appointment? This would be an interesting point to clear up.

Another matter which would be not only of interest, but of great usefulness in explaining the gathering of a Jewish government around the President during the war, is the question of Bernard M. Baruch's acquaintance with Woodrow Wilson. When did it begin? What circumstances or what persons brought them together? There are stories, of course, and one of them may be true, but the story ought not to be told unless accompanied by the fullest confirmation. Why should it occur that a Jew should be the one man ready and selected for a position of greatest power during the war?

Mr. Baruch, in his testimony, sheds no light on this question. He had opportunity to do so, had he wished.

Mr. Graham—"I assume that you were personally acquainted with the President prior to the outbreak of the war?"

Mr. Baruch—"Yes, sir."

Mr. Graham—"Up to the time that you were appointed as a member of the advisory commission, had you ever had any personal conferences with the President about these matters?"

Mr. Baruch—"Yes, sir."

Mr. Graham—"Had he called you in consultation or had he talked to you about these matters and about the matter of your appointment before you were appointed?"

Mr. Baruch—"Never suggested anything about the appointment, because I would have told him that I would prefer not to be appointed."

Mr. Graham—"Do you now recall, Mr. Baruch, how long before you were actually appointed as a member of that advisory commission you had your last conference with the President?"

Mr. Baruch—"No * * * "

That is not all of Mr. Baruch's answer, but it is his reply to the question. Having said "No," Mr. Baruch became very communicative on another matter. His complete reply is—

"No; but I can tell you something that may be of interest, and that is probably what you want to know. I had been very much disturbed by the unprepared condition of this country, so much so that I was one of the first men to support General Wood in the Plattsburg encampment, and I think he will admit I gave him the first money and told him whatever he did I would guarantee to stand behind that movement, which happily only took a few thousand dollars so far as I was concerned, having caught the public approval and it went ahead, and in that relation naturally one had to think about the mobilization of the industries of the country, because people do not fight alone with their hands; they have got to fight with things."

It is thus shown that Mr. Baruch was a forehanded gentleman. It was only the year 1915. The European war had then not become more than an amazing spectacle to the mass of the American people. But still Mr. Baruch was convinced we were going to have war, and he spent money on his guess. The government which was then "keeping us out of war" was also consulting with Mr. Baruch who was already ahead of the government in creating the atmosphere of war in this country. If the reader, by a mental effort, can reconstruct the year of 1915, and then put into his picture of that year the element of which he was not then possessed, namely, the activity of Mr. Bernard M. Baruch and other Jews, he will see that he did not know much about what was going on, even if he did read the newspapers with attention!

To proceed with the examination, following the place where Mr. Baruch made his interesting disclosure of his part in the Plattsburg experiment:

Mr. Graham—"That was about 1915, was it not?"

Mr. Baruch—"Yes, 1915; and I had been thinking about it very seriously, and I thought we would be drawn into the war. I went off on a long trip, and it was while on this trip that I felt there ought to be some mobilization of the industries, and I was thinking about the scheme that practically was put into effect and was working when I was chairman of the board. When I came back from that trip I asked for an interview with the President. It was the first time I had seen the President since his election, so far as I can remember now."

Mr. Graham—"You mean his first election?"

Mr. Baruch—"His first election, yes."

So it is probable that Mr. Baruch, if any stress may be placed on the manner of his words, had known the President before. Ordinary men, who meet the President seldom, usually have a very clear recollection of those meetings. The fact probably is that Mr. Baruch saw the President so frequently that he found it difficult to distinguish the meetings in his memory. He describes the visit referred to:

"I explained to him as earnestly as I could that I was very deeply concerned about the necessity of the mobilization of the industries of the country. The President listened very attentively and graciously, as he always does * * * and the next thing I heard—some months afterward * * * my attention was brought to this Council of National Defense. Secretary Baker brought it to my attention. This was the first time I had met the Secretary of War. He asked me what I thought of it."

Mr. Graham—"That was before the bill was passed; before it became a law?"

Mr. Baruch—"I think it was. I am not certain about that. *I said I would like to have something different.*"

This is rather important. A council is a *council.* Mr. Baruch wanted *something different.* Eventually he did get something different. He got the President so to change matters as to make Mr. Baruch the most powerful man in the war. The Council of National Defense eventually became the merest side show. It was not a Council of Americans that ran the war, it was an autocracy headed by a Jew, with Jews at every strategic point down the line. What Mr. Baruch did was very masterly, but it was not in the American manner. He did what he set out to do, but it is seriously to be questioned whether any man ought to have done what he did, and probably no one but a member of his race would have wanted to do it.

Mr. Graham—"Did the President express any opinion about the advisability of adopting the scheme you proposed?"

Mr. Baruch —"I think *I did most of the talking.* I do not remember what the President said on that subject, but I think it can be best seen as expressed in the bill."

Mr. Graham—"Did you impress him with your belief that we were going to get into the war?"

Mr. Baruch—"I probably did. I would like to tell you exactly, but I do not want to guess at it."

Mr. Graham—"That was your opinion at the time?"

Mr. Baruch—"Yes; *I thought we were going to get into the war. I thought a war was coming long before it did.*"

The examination then reverted to Mr. Baruch's conference with the Secretary of War, in which the former had said he "would like to have something different."

Mr. Graham—"Mr. Baker said he thought that was the best that could be gotten at that time?"

Mr. Baruch—"I got that impression. Whether he said so or not, I do not know, but I got that impression that that was the best that could be gotten at that time."

If the event had not turned out exactly as Mr. Baruch planned it, a great deal of his testimony might be discounted on the principle of the natural boastfulness of the Jew after a scheme has succeeded; but there is no discounting anything that he says. The President did exactly what Baruch wanted in a thousand matters, and what Baruch apparently wanted most of all was a ruling hand upon productive America. And that he got. He got it in a larger measure than even Lenin ever got Russia; for here in the United States the people saw nothing but the patriotic element; they did not see the Jewish Government looming above them. Yet it was there.

The Council of National Defense, as originally constituted—"the best that could be gotten at that time," though Mr. Baruch "would like something different"—was headed by six secretaries of the Cabinet, the secretaries of War, Navy, Interior, Agriculture, Commerce and Labor. Beneath this official group was an advisory commission, of seven men, three of whom were Jews; one of these Jews was Mr. Baruch. Beneath this advisory commission were scores and hundreds of men, and many committees. One of the groups subordinate to the two groups just mentioned was the War Industries Board, of which Mr. Baruch was originally merely a member, Daniel Willard being the chairman.

Now, it was this War Industries Board which became the "whole thing" later on, and it was Mr. Baruch who became the "whole thing" in that board. The place where he was put became the corner stone; he became the chief pillar of the war administration. The records show it; he himself admits it.

What influence reached into this Council of hundreds of Americans and chose a single Jew to be their undoubted lord and master for the duration of the war? Was it Baruch's brains that elevated him? Or was it the suggestion of Jewish finance already well forward in its work of mobilization?

There is no desire to minimize the Baruch brain. Brains and money are the Jews' two greatest weapons. No Jew is picked for a key place who has not brains. Baruch has brains. He is a ceaseless wonder among men who know him. He can do six things at once and control the most colossal operations without fuss or fever. He has both brains and money.

But there is something for Jewry to learn: brains and money are not enough. There is another element which even brains cannot cope with, and which renders money cheap. The chess-playing expert may mystify and compel admiration; but the chess-player does not rule the world.

So, Baruch did things. But Trotsky also has done things. The point is this: Are people to be carried away by an appeal deliberately made to their imagination, or are they to scrutinize what has been done, and weigh its consequences?

The Jews could do greater things in the United States than even Baruch has done, if the opportunity offered, acts of superb ease and mastery—but what would it signify? The ideal of a dictator of the United States has never been absent from the group in which Baruch is found—witness the work, "Philip Dru, Administrator," commonly attributed to Colonel E. M. House, and never denied by him.

As a matter of fact, Baruch could probably do a better job than Trotsky did. Certainly, the recent experience which he had in governing the country during the war was a very valuable education in the art of autocracy. Not that it is by any means Mr. Baruch's possession alone; it is also the possession of scores of Jewish leaders who flitted about from department to department, from field to field, receiving a post-graduate course in the art of autocracy, not to mention other things.

Before Mr. Bernard M. Baruch got through, he was the head and center of a system of control such as the United States Government itself never possessed and never will possess until it changes its character as a free government.

Mr. Jefferis—"In other words, *you determined what anybody could have?"*

Mr. Baruch—"Exactly; there is no question about that. I assumed that responsibility, sir, and *that final determination rested within me."*

Mr. Jefferis—"What?"

Mr. Baruch—"That final determination, as the President said, rested within me; *the determination of whether the Army or Navy should have it rested with me; the determination of whether the Railroad Administration could have it, or the Allies, or whether General Allenby should have locomotives, or whether they should be used in Russia, or used in France."*

Mr. Jefferis—"You had considerable power?"

Mr. Baruch—"Indeed I did , sir. * * * "

Mr. Jefferis—"And all those different lines, really, ultimately, centered in you, so far as power was concerned?"

Mr. Baruch—"Yes, sir, it did. I probably had more
power than perhaps any other man did in the war;
doubtless that is true."

What preceded Mr. Baruch's attainment of this power, how
far his power reached and how it was used will be our next inquiry.

Issue of November 27. 1920

> *"The King of Israel must not be
> influenced by his passions, especially by
> sensuality. No particular element of his
> nature must have the upper hand and
> rule over his mind. Sensuality, more
> than anything else, upsets mental
> ability and clearness of vision by
> deflecting thought to the worst and
> most bestial side of human nature.*
>
> *"The Pillar of the Universe in the
> person of the World Ruler, sprung from
> the seed of David, must sacrifice all
> personal desires for the benefit of his
> people."*
>
> *—Protocol 24*

XXVI.

The Scope of Jewish Dictatorship in the U. S.

T HE common criticism made against President Wilson that "he played a lone hand" and would not avail himself of advice, can be made only by those who are in ignorance of the Jewish government which continually advised the President on all matters.

While the President is supposed to have been extremely jealous of his authority, this view of him can be maintained only by remaining blind to the immense authority he conferred on the members of the Jewish War Government. It is true he did not take Congress into his confidence; it is true that he made little of the members of his Cabinet; it is also true that he ignored the constitutional place of the United States Senate in the advisory work of making treaties; but it is not true that he acted without advice; it is not true that he depended on his own mind in the conduct of the war and the negotiations at Versailles.

Just when Bernard M. Baruch, the Jewish high governor of the United States in war affairs, came to know Mr. Wilson is yet to be told; but just when he got into and out of the war are matters about which he himself has told us. He got into the war at Plattsburg, two years before there was a war; and he got out of the war when the business at Paris was ended.

"I came back on the *"George Washington,"* he testified, which means that he remained at Paris until the last detail was arranged.

It is said that Mr. Baruch was normally a Republican until Woodrow Wilson began to loom up as a Presidential possibility. The Jews made much of Woodrow Wilson, far too much for his own good. They formed a solid ring around him. There was a time when he communicated to the country through no one but a Jew. The best political writers in the country were sidetracked for two years because the President chose the Jewish journalist, David Lawrence, as his unofficial mouthpiece. Lawrence had the run of the White House offices, with frequent access to the President, and for a time he was the high cockalorum of national newspaperdom, but neither that privilege nor the assiduous boosting of the Jewish ring availed to make him a favorite with the American public.

American Jewry was Democratic until it had secured the last favor that Woodrow Wilson could give, and then it left the Democratic party as with the indecent haste of rats leaving a sinking ship. Baruch stayed, rather ostentatiously spending his money for motion picture appeals in favor of the League of Nations, but it is entirely probable that he has a genuine interest in the new administration.

For one thing, there may be investigations. It remains to be seen whether the investigations which the Republican majority in the House began to make with regard to war expenditures will be continued. There are those who profess to believe that they will not be continued, the explanation being that such investigation as was made before election was solely for the purpose of securing campaign data, or creating a political atmosphere unfavorable to the Democrats.

It is sincerely to be hoped that the Republicans will not rest under the imputation, but that they will rigorously pursue the investigations that have been begun. There are two reasons why this should be done; first, that the country may know, with a view to future contingencies, what was "put over" on the government during the war; second, that the full sweep of Jewish influence in this country may be exposed. The second reason is not expected to appear very weighty to practical politicians, and that is no matter, for if the first reason is deemed sufficient, and if the investigations are honestly made, then inevitably the Jewish power will be further exposed. It is linked up at every stage of the business.

This may have had something to do with the sudden desertion of the Democratic party by the Jews. They may have swung over in order to have something to say about the pursuit of further investigations. Already the counsel is being heard, "Let bygones be bygones," "The people are tired of investigations, and don't want any more"; already attempts are being made to introduce fresher issues to deflect the public mind from war affairs, and the attempts are doubtless Jewish in their origin.

That portion of the public who are awake to the Jewish Question will do well to observe with care the attitude of the new administration toward completing the investigations. The Jews did not flock to the Republicans for nothing. The country is entitled to know what was done with the fabulous amounts of money spent during the war. The people are entitled to know who were their masters, and who were responsible for certain strange situations which were created.

Members of the House, Senators, and other officials should, at the very least, pay particular attention to the directions from which influences against further inquiry come.

Now, as to Mr. Bernard M. Baruch, who for some as yet undefined reason was made head and front of the United States at war, we have his own word on several occasions that he was the most important man in the war.

"I probably had more power than perhaps any other man did in the war; doubtless that is true," he told Representative Jefferis.

And again: "We had the power of priority, which was the greatest power in the war * * * Exactly; there is no question about that. I assumed that responsibility, sir, and that final determination rested within me."

And when Representative Jefferis said "What?" to that startling statement, Mr. Baruch repeated it:

"That final determination, as the President said, rested within me."

Representative Graham said to him: "In other words, I am right about this, Mr. Baruch, that yours was the guiding mind*** "

And Mr. Baruch replied: "That is partly correct—I think you are entirely correct * * * "

Now, in what did Baruch's power consist? Briefly, in this—in the dictatorship of the United States. He once expressed the opinion that the United States could have been managed that way in time of peace, but he explained that it was easier in war time, was made easy because of the patriotic mood of the people.

It is not sufficient, however, to say that Mr. Baruch's rule constituted a dictatorship of the United States; it remains to be shown just how rigid and far-reaching that dictatorship was. The reader may recognize at what point the Jewish rule touched his affairs also.

Mr. Baruch, who had the "final determination" of everything, says that his power extended to the needs of the Army and Navy, the Shipping Board, the Railroad Administration, touched also the Food and Fuel Administrations, and besides all that had a vital control of the Allies' purchases not only in the United States, but also in other countries with reference to certain materials.

There were $30,000,000,000 (Thirty Billions of dollars) spent by the United States Government during the war, all of it raised by taxation and bonds. Of this sum, $10,000,000,000 (Ten Billions) was loaned to the Allies and spent here—all of the purchases being viséed under Mr. Baruch's authority.

As told by himself, his power consisted in the following authorities:

1. *Authority over the use of capital in the private business of Americans.*

This authority was nominally under the Capital Issues Committee, the controlling factor of which was another Jew, Eugene Meyer, Jr. Here is another inexplicable circumstance. Was he the only banker in the United States capable of exercising a dominant influence? Why did it happen that a Jew should be found in this important position, too? Is it only accident? Was there no design involved?

Well, it was necessary during the war for anyone wishing to use capital in business enterprise, to lay all his cards on the table. He was required to reveal his plans, his ground for expecting success—in brief, tell the Jewish rulers and their

Jewish representatives all that he would tell in confidence to his banker in negotiating a loan. The organization which a few Jews perfected was the most complete business inquisition ever set up in any country. And that the knowledge thus gained should always be sacredly guarded, or always honestly used, would be expecting too much of human nature.

Mr. Baruch gave some instances of this, though they were not the instances that are calculated to throw the most light on the inner workings of the organization. He said:

"The Capital Issues Committee (*where Mr. Meyer reigned*), in the Treasury Department, had a man who sat with the War Industries Board (*where Mr. Baruch reigned*), and who always came to the War Industries Board to find out whether the individual or the corporation who wanted this money was going to use it for the purpose to win the war. To cite a case that happened at Philadelphia, that city wanted to make extensive public improvements; New York City wanted to spend $8,000,000 for schools, which would take an enormous amount of steel, labor, materials and transportation. We said, 'No, that won't help win the war. You can postpone that until later on. We cannot spare the steel on all these various things.'"

Very well. Does Mr. Baruch know of an enormous theater which a Jewish theatrical owner was permitted to build in an eastern city during the war?

Did he ever hear of non-Jews being refused permission to go ahead in a legitimate business which would have helped produce war materials, and that afterward—afterward—on almost identically the same plans, and in the same locality, a Jewish concern was given permission to do that very thing?

This was a terrible power, and far too great to be vested in one man; certainly it was such a power as should never have been vested in a coterie of Jews. The puzzle of it becomes greater the deeper it is probed. How did it occur? How *could* it occur--that always, at the most critical and delicate points in these matters, there sat a Jew enthroned with autocratic power?

Well could Mr. Baruch say—"I had more power than any man in the war." He could even have said: "We Jews had more power than you Americans did in the war" —and it would have been true.

2. Authority over all materials.

This, of course, included everything. Mr. Baruch was an expert in many of the lines of material involved, and had held interests in many of them. What the investigators endeavored to learn was in how many lines he was interested during the war.

In lines where Mr. Baruch was not expert he, of course, had experts in charge. There was Mr. Julius Rosenwald, another Jew, who was in charge of "supplies (including clothing)" and who had a Mr. Eisenman to represent him. Mr. Eisenman was on the stand for a considerable period with regard to uniforms, the change made in their quality, the price paid to the manufacturers (mostly Jewish) and other interesting questions.

The great Guggenheim copper interests, who sold most of the copper used during the war, were represented by a former employe; but undoubtedly Mr. Baruch himself, who was much interested in copper during his business career, was the principal expert in that line.

It is impossible to escape the names of Jews all down the line in these most important departments. But, for the present, attention is called to the scope of Mr. Baruch's control in the country at large. It is best stated in his own words: "No building costing more than $2,500 could be erected in the United States without the approval of the War Industries Board. Nobody could get a barrel of cement without its approval. You could not get a piece of zinc for your kitchen table without the approval of the War Industries Board."

3. Authority over industries.

He determined where coal might be shipped, where steel might be sold, where industries might be operated and where not. With the control over capital needed in business, went also control of the materials needed in industry. This control over industry was exercised through the device called priorities, which Mr. Baruch rightly described as "the greatest power in the war." He was the most powerful man in the war, because he exercised this power.

Mr. Baruch said there were 351 or 357 lines of industry under his control in the United States, including "practically every raw material in the world."

"I had the final authority," he said. Whether it was sugars or silk, coal or cannon, Mr. Baruch ruled its movements.

Mr. Jefferis—"For instance, this priority that you had would decide whether civilians should have any commodities for building?"

Mr. Baruch—"Yes; if we had not had that priority committee the civilians would have had nothing."

Mr. Jefferis—"Did they get anything?"

Mr. Baruch—"They got all there was."

Mr. Jefferis—"Did you sit with these priority boards at any time, or not?"

Mr. Baruch—"Sometimes; not very frequently. I was ex-officio of every one of the committees, and made it my business to go around as far as I could and keep in touch with everything."

Mr. Jefferis—"And all these different lines, really, ultimately, centered in you, so far as power was concerned?"

Mr. Baruch—"Yes, sir, it did. I probably had more power than perhaps any other man did in the war; doubtless that is true."

That, however, was not the full extent of Mr. Baruch's control over industry. The heart of industry is Power. Mr. Baruch controlled the Power of the United States. The dream of the Power Trust, an evil dream for this country, was realized for the first time under the organization which this single individual formed. He says:

"Not only did we endeavor to control the raw materials, but as well the manufacturing facilities of the country. We established priority uses also for power * * * "

4. *Authority over the classes of men to be called to military service.*

Baruch pointed out, virtually pointed out to the Provost Marshal of the United States, the classes of men to be taken into the army. "We had to decide virtually the necessity of such things," he said. "We decided that the less-essential industries would have to be curbed, and it was from them that man power would have to be taken for the army." In this way he ruled chauffeurs, traveling salesmen, and similar classes into military service. It was, of course, necessary that some such ruling should be made, but why one man, why always this one man?

5. *Authority over the personnel of labor in this country.*

"We decided upon a dilution of men with women labor, which was a thing that had always been fought by the labor unions."

6. And now behold as complete an illustration of one part of the Protocols as ever could be found in any Gentile government. Readers of previous articles will remember the passage:

"We will force up wages which, however, will be of no
benefit to the workers, for we will at the same time cause
a rise in the prices of necessities."

Mr. Baruch at one time was inclined to sidestep the matter of fixing wages; he did not like the expression. But that the reader himself may decide, we quote the testimony in full:

Mr. Jefferis—"Did the War Industries Board fix the price of labor?"

Mr. Baruch—"If you can call it that way, but I would not say so; no, sir."

Mr. Jefferis—"I am trying to get at what you did."

Mr. Baruch—"No, sir; we did not fix the price of wages."

Mr. Jefferis—"What did you do?"

Mr. Baruch—"Just what I told you."

Mr. Jefferis—"Probably I am a little dense, but I did not catch it if you told me."

Mr. Baruch—"When the price-fixing committee fixed the price of steel, we will say, they said, 'This price is agreed upon, and you shall keep wages where they are'—and those were the wages that were prevailing at the price we fixed. At the time prices were fixed at first they were very much higher than the prices that we fixed."

Mr. Jefferis—"When you got the price of any of these low materials you would fix the price of labor that was to be employed in producing them?"

Mr. Baruch—"To the extent that it should remain at the maximum of what it was when we fixed the price."

Considering the weight of Mr. Baruch's authority, and the stipulations he made, this was to all intents and purposes a fixing of the rate of wages.

Now, as to the fixing of prices, Mr. Baruch is much more positive. In answer to a question by Mr. Garrett, Mr. Baruch said:

"We fixed the prices in co-operation with the industries, but *when we fixed a price we fixed it for the total production,* not alone for the army and the navy, but for the Allies and *the civilian population."*

The minutes of one of the meetings of Mr. Baruch's board show this:

"Commissioner Baruch directed that the minutes show that the commission had consumed the entire afternoon in a discussion of *price-fixing, particularly with reference to the control of the food supply, grain, cotton, wool,* and raw materials generally."

Mr. Graham—"Tell me something else: How much personal attention did you give to the matter of price-fixing?"

Mr. Baruch—"In the beginning, considerable * * *"

At another time Mr. Baruch said—*"There was no law at all in the land to fix prices."*

Mr. Jefferis—"We grant that, *but you did it."*

Mr. Baruch—*"Yes, we did it,* and we did a great many things in the stress of the times."

Here was one man, having supreme dictatorial power, at both ends of the common people's affairs.

He admits that of the 351 or 357 lines of essential industry which he controlled, he fixed the prices at which the commodities should be sold to the government and to civilians. In fixing the prices, however, he made wage stipulations. The matter of wages came first—it entered into Mr. Baruch's computation of the cost, on which, to a vast extent, he based the price. Then, having decided what the producer was to receive in wages, he decided next what the producer should pay for living. The producer himself may answer the question as to how it all turned out! Wages were "high," but not quite so high as "living"; and the answer to both is in the testimony of Barney Baruch.

That is not the whole story by any means. It is inserted here merely to find its place in the list of authorities conferred on Mr. Baruch.

How completely Baruch felt himself to be the "power" is shown by a passage which occurred when he was trying to explain the very large profits made by some concerns with which he did business.

Mr. Jefferis—"Then the system which you did adopt did not give the Lukens Steel & Iron Company the amount of profit that the low-producing companies had?"

Mr. Baruch—"No, but we took 80 per cent away from the others."

Mr. Jefferis—"The law did that, didn't it?"

Mr. Baruch—"Yes; the law did that."

Mr. Graham—"What did you mean by the use of the word 'we'?"

Mr. Baruch—"The government did that. Excuse me, but I meant we, the Congress."

Mr. Graham—"You meant that the Congress passed a law covering that?"

Mr. Baruch—"Yes, sir."

Mr. Graham—"Did you have anything to do with that?"

Mr. Baruch—"Not a thing."

Mr. Graham—"Then I would not use the word 'we' if I were you."

Whether Mr. Baruch slipped up there, he best knows. Just as he had power to give the workers wages, and take it away again by price-fixing, so he had power to allow the raw material corporations to make fabulous profits—and it would not be at all unthinkable that he also had something to do with taking part of it away again. He said once, "We took away 80 per cent"; then he confessed it was a slip. Of the tongue, or of his prudence?

Certainly, the profits he allowed were so large that even where the 80 per cent was paid back— where it *was* paid back (there were all kinds of evasions and frauds)—the profits were still enormous.

And 73 per cent of the "war millionaires" of New York, in spite of the 80 per cent, are Jews.

Issue of December 4, 1920

XXVII.

Jewish Copper Kings Reap
Rich War-Profits

W ITH this article we shall dismiss Mr. Bernard M. Baruch for the present. His activities are not by any means to be construed as the main effort of Judah in the United States, nor is he himself to be regarded as an important factor in the Jewish World Program. Indeed, it is to be doubted that he has been entrusted with many of the secrets of the Elders. But he has been found to be a useful man, willing to play the Jewish game with Jews, and consciously bound as all Jews are by an obligation to see that Jewish interests get the better of the balance wherever possible.

Mr. Baruch, of course, is much pleased with the role he was permitted to play in the government of the United States during the war; but he probably has sense enough to know that he was chosen for other than mere personal reasons.

Indeed, one of the keys to the controlling part which a few Jews were permitted to play in American affairs during the war is to be found just here in the question, Why was Mr. Baruch chosen? What had he been, what had he done, that he should have been chosen as head and front of government power in the war? His antecedents do not account for it. Neither his personal nor commercial attainments account for it. What does?

There was no elected member of the United States Government who was closer, or even as close, to the President during the war as was this Jew out of Wall Street. No one whom the people sent to represent them at Washington ever came within leagues of the privileges accorded to Mr. Baruch. Plainly this is an unusual situation, not explainable by the emergency at all, certainly not explainable by anything that is as yet a matter of public knowledge.

As one man out of many, all together serving the country, Mr. Baruch, of course, would be perfectly explainable. But as *the* man, *the* man whose single committee was run up through the fabric of the Council of National Defense until it formed the focus of the war government, he is not explainable.

It was not only during the war, but also after the armistice, that these tokens of signal choice were showered upon Mr. Baruch. He went to the Peace Conference. Resigning as chairman of the War Industries Board on December 31, 1918—

"I went down to my place in South Carolina, and there received a wireless message from the President to come to Paris. I then went to Paris. I think I sailed about the first or second of January. I know one vessel broke down and I had to transfer from one to the other. But I had no further activities in connection with the government; that is, the War Industries Board."

Mr. Graham—"How long were you in Paris?"

Mr. Baruch—"I sailed, returning June 28 or 29. I came back on the George Washington." (This means that he was a part of the President's entourage.)

Mr. Graham—"What were you doing there, Mr. Baruch?"

Mr. Baruch—"I was economic advisor connected with the peace mission."

Mr. Graham—"You stayed until the Peace Treaty was concluded?"

Mr. Baruch—"Yes, sir."

Mr. Graham—"Did you frequently advise with the President while there?"

Mr. Baruch—"Whenever he asked my advice I gave it. *I had something to do with the reparation clauses. I was the American Commissioner in charge of what they called the 'Economic Section.' I was a member of the Supreme Economic Council in charge of raw materials.*"

Mr. Graham—"Did you sit in the council with the gentlemen who were negotiating the treaty?"

Mr. Baruch—*"Yes, sir; sometimes."*

Mr. Graham—*"All except the meetings that were participated in by the Five?"* (Meaning the Big Five premiers.)

Mr. Baruch—*"And frequently those also."*

This, then, is a sidelight on what has been called the "Kosher Conference," a name given to the Peace Conference by Frenchmen who were astounded to see thousands of Jews from all parts of the world appear in Paris as the chosen counsellors of the rulers of the nations. Jews were so conspicuous in the American mission as to excite comment everywhere. A Persian representative left on record this protest: *When the United States delegation * * * accepted a brief for the Jews* and imposed a Jewish semi-state on Rumania and Poland, *they were firm as the granite rock,* and no amount of opposition, no future deterrents, made any impression on their will. Accordingly, they had their own way. *But in the case of Persia they lost the fight,* although logic, humanity, justice, and the Ordinances solemnly accepted by the Great Powers were all on their side."

The comment is rather humiliating. But it is true. The Jewish World Program was the only program that passed through the Peace Conference without hindrance or revision.

So numerous and ubiquitous were the International Jews at Paris, so firmly established in the inner councils, that the keen observer, Dr. E. J. Dillon, whose book, "The Inside Story of the Peace Conference" (*Harper's)* is the best that has appeared, was constrained to say this:

"It may seem amazing to some readers, but it is none the less a fact, that a considerable number of *delegates believed that the real influences behind the Anglo-Saxon peoples were Semitic."* (p. 496.)

And again:

"They confronted the President's proposal on the subject of religious inequality, and in particular, the odd motive alleged for it, with the measures for the protection of minorities which he subsequently imposed on the lesser states, and which had for their keynote to satisfy the Jewish elements in Eastern Europe. And they concluded that *the sequence of expedients framed and enforced in this direction were inspired by the Jews, assembled in Paris for the purpose of realizing their carefully thought-out program, which they succeeded in having substantially executed.* However right or wrong these delegates may have been, it would be a dangerous mistake to ignore their views, seeing that they have since become one of the permanent elements of the situation. The formula into which this policy was thrown by the members of the Conference, whose countries it affected, and who regarded it as fatal to the peace of Eastern Europe, was this: *'Henceforth the world will be governed by the Anglo-Saxon peoples, who, in turn, are swayed by their Jewish elements.'* " (p.497. The italics are ours.)

There are other matters pertaining to Mr. Baruch which must await the development of this study, but it is worth while just now to possess ourselves of the information at hand regarding his peculiar handling of the copper situation during the war.

Mr. Baruch is known as a copper man. Copper is Jewish. That metal, throughout the world, is under Jewish domination. The Guggenheims and the Lewisohns, two Jewish families, are the copper kings of the planet—not that they confine themselves to copper; for example, their output of silver throughout the world is one-fourth more than is produced in the entire United States.

By his own testimony, Mr. Baruch was interested in copper concerns. What his holdings were during the war he did not disclose. But what his actions were has been very clearly set forth bit by bit in various inquiries.

Before the United States entered the war, Mr. Baruch rounded up the copper kings.

"I went to New York and saw there Mr. John D. Ryan and Mr. Daniel Guggenheim," he said in his testimony. This was in February or March, 1917, he wasn't sure which, but he said it was "before we went into the war."

Now, who were these gentlemen? Mr. Ryan was apparently in charge of the reorganized Lewisohn properties, while Mr. Guggenheim was chief of the seven Guggenheims who form "a business family and a family business." They divided business during the war. The United Metals Selling Company, which sold the United States Government its copper during the war, was the Lewisohn business reorganized, of which Tobias Wolfson was vice president; and the American Smelting and Refining Company was, apparently, the Guggenheim interests.

There was no competition between these two during the war!

How did it come about that these two worked together? Their case is clear on paper: their answer is that Mr. Baruch asked them to! And Mr. Baruch is clear, too; was he not a government official? And did they not show patriotism in doing as the government official bade them?

It came to this: the "Government" made a rule that it would do business only through the American Metals Selling Company as the representative of the copper producers of the United States. This meant, of course, that if the few competitors of this Jewish copper combine were to do business with the government, they too had to make arrangements with the American Metals Selling Company.

Mr. Graham—"But how did it happen that you were representing the other companies who were your competitors?"

Mr. Wolfson—"Well, at the request of the War Industries Board, we offered a copper producers' committee."

Mr. Graham—"Who requested that?"

Mr. Wolfson—"Mr. Eugene Meyer, Jr., representing Mr. B. M. Baruch."

Mr. Graham—"Now let us find out who Mr. Eugene Meyer, Jr., was. Do you know him?"

It develops that Mr. Eugene Meyer, Jr., is another Wall Street man who "had large investments in copper," though whether he retained them during the war, Mr. Wolfson did not know.

Mr. Graham—"Then Eugene Meyer, Jr., went into the War Industries Board and took up with the copper producers the question of furnishing copper, did he?"

Mr. Wolfson—"Yes, sir."

As a result of that request a meeting was held at 120 Broadway, at which were present, among a few others, S. S. Rosenstamm, L. Vogelstein, Julius Loeb, T. Wolfson, G. W. Drucker and Eugene Meyers, Jr.

Mr. Graham—"Any army officers there?"

Mr. Wolfson—"No."

The witness here quoted, Tobias Wolfson, was one of the most active instruments in the actual passage of business, but the Washington representative was a Mr. Mosehauer. The interesting thing about Mr. Mosehauer is that he represented both the American Metals Selling Company and the American Smelting and Refining Company—the Lewisohns and the Guggenheims—and by order of Baruch, with the approval of the government, the business was done with these two corporations.

How did they divide? It was very simple. Mr. Wolfson euphoniously describes it as a division of labor: the Lewisohn group took the trade with the United States; the Guggenheim group took over the foreign business with the Allies.

Now, the next interesting point is the special committee through which Baruch's board dealt with the copper producers. This committee, representing the government, consisted of three persons: Pope Yeatman, chief; E. C. Thurston, assistant; Andrew Walz, assistant.

Pope Yeatman was a mining engineer employed by the Guggenheims at $100,000 a year.

E. C. Thurston was Pope Yeatman's assistant in that private employment.

Andrew Walz was consulting mining engineer for the Guggenheims.

Everything was all set. The Jewish metal monopoly was assured of control on both sides of the Atlantic.

It was perhaps thought desirable, in view of the bad political odor which had accompanied the copper power in several states, mostly in connection with the "copper Senators," like Clarke, of Nevada (readers of this series will remember, in connection with the name of Guggenheim, that it was Senator Simon

Guggenheim who fought against the census officials), that something be done to gild the arrangement.

It was apparently necessary to do something to disarm the protest that might arise against this thorough Judaizing of the war metals, therefore a very fine show of patriotism was made. This is worthy of notice in view of the "show institutions" mentioned in the Protocols. The American Public is becoming accustomed to these "show institutions"—proposals which promise everything and then fade away into nothingness. It is one of the most effective methods of destroying the morale of a people.

When Mr. Baruch saw the heads of the two copper families, he says he found them willing to think of nothing but giving copper to the government—money was of no consideration whatever.

Mr. Baruch—"They said that so far as the United States Government itself was concerned they would give Uncle Sam all the copper he wanted for his preparedness campaign * * * at any price that was decided upon. In order to arrive at some price we took *the average price for 10 years which was about 16 2-3 cents;* and that is how the price happened to be arrived at. At the time that they said this, *copper was selling somewhere around 32 and 35 cents a pound."*

There, then, was a magnanimous thing! The government was to be given copper at half the market price. But did the government get it at this price? Wait —the story is a good one.

This unheard-of sacrifice of profits for patriotism was extensively advertised. The secretary of the Council of National Defense wrote a stirring story for one of the best magazines, in which he said:

"Mr. Baruch first announced his presence in the tremendous task of mobilizing American industry by procuring 45,000,000 pounds of copper for the army and navy at about half the current market price, saving the government in the neighborhood of $10,000,000."

Mr. Baruch himself, in his testimony, expanded with the generosity of it all. In an apparent mood of "help yourself to all you want" he said:

"On inquiry we found that * * * the army and navy * * * wanted only 45,000,000 pounds, which used to be a lot of copper before we got to dealing in astronomical figures; and they were given all the opportunity to consider what they wanted. They could just as well have had 450,000,000 pounds as 45,000,000 pounds, because there was an open offer."

Now for the effect which this produced on the country at large:

"The effect of that offer of the copper producers was electrical," said Mr. Baruch. *It showed that there was in this country a desire to set aside selfishness*, so far as our government was concerned in its need * * * 'Make us any price you want.' So that was practically the attitude that the producers took."

But the government did not get copper at that much-advertised patriotic price.

Mr. Graham—"They did not pay 16 2-3 cents for the 45,000,000 pounds?"

Mr. Baruch—"Oh, no; not these other large quantities of materials."

He said that the copper was furnished to the government without receiving money for it; price-fixing was yet in the future. "Then we came to the point, 'Well, what about the civilian population?' So we made a rule that became a policy, that whatever price was fixed it should be for everybody; that what was fair for the army and navy was fair for the civilian population."

There seems to have been a rapid cooling of generosity under the prospect of colossal sales. And the upshot of it was that, after all the hurrah, *the government really paid about 27 cents*.

What these figures mean, can be deduced from the fact that during the war the government bought 592,258,674 pounds of copper.

If the reader is not already staggered by the import of these facts, there remains one more for him to consider—

After the armistice the surplus copper was sold back to the copper producers. In April and May, 1919, the American Metals Selling Company received from the United States Government over 16,500,000 pounds of copper at a fraction over 15 cents. This was less than the boasted patriotic price of 16 2-3 cents at the beginning. Not counting what they had received from the government for the copper in the first place, their profits on the difference between the price they paid for the surplus copper and the price for which they sold it again, were beyond counting.

This is what occurred under the triple copper monarchy of the Baruchs, the Lewisohns and the Guggenheims, and their Jewish assistants and Gentile fronts. However, "Gentile fronts" were boldly dispensed with to a very large degree during the war. The real powers behind the throne themselves stood out, and did not hesitate to set their own people at every crossroads along the line of war business.

It is not to be supposed that the Baruch influence began or ceased with copper, nor with any of the multitudinous industrial powers which he possessed. A man like Baruch makes the most of such opportunities as were then his. In matters political, personal and even military, there were many openings for the use of his influence, and well-informed people about Washington did not doubt his facility in these things.

Once, however, Mr. Baruch felt he was skating on thin ice with regard to the law. He had gone ahead on his own plan, but in such a way that he would exercise the power without taking the responsibility. That seems to have been a very clear ideal with him—power without responsibility. Everything was fixed, all the conditions within which every contract would have to be made were carefully determined, but Mr. Baruch never permitted himself or his board to make a contract. After having consulted with numbers of his associates in business, an agreement was reached, and only then were the responsible officers of the government told, "Go ahead and make contracts." The officials took the responsibility, but the Baruch coterie made the conditions and then remained aloof.

Even this plan, however, had a questionable aspect which came to trouble Mr. Baruch, and the manner in which he manipulated the matter shows either a very shrewd mind or else very shrewd advice. The latter undoubtedly went with the former; there were plenty of Jewish advisors about.

85

To begin with, Mr. Baruch says: "The members of that committee *were picked out by myself; the industries did not pick them out.*" Which means, in fact, that Mr. Baruch picked out a group from a group that had previously been chosen by the producers, although plainly Mr. Baruch was desirous of modifying this impression. And again: "It is true that these great copper producers were on the committee, and I selected them because they were great men * * * "

Now, these men, as members of a government committee, were to all appearances selling to themselves as members of the government committee, and, apparently, buying from themselves as owners and controllers of the great producing combinations. Not necessarily in any discreditable way, but in a very unusual way.

In the face of this condition, Mr. Baruch had the coolness to say, "So you can see that the government was as much in the saddle as it was possible to be. "The producer-members of the committee, headed by Baruch, were the government, so far as this statement is concerned. Time and again it was shown that the responsible officials of the government were not even visible until this extra-government had determined all the conditions.

Mr. Garrett—"Did any troubles arise with the committees growing out of the legal situation, that you remember of?"

Mr. Baruch—"The committees of the trade, especially some of those that I had asked to serve, were very much disturbed about their standing in reference to the Sherman Anti-Trust Law. Is that what you refer to?"

Mr. Garrett—"Yes."

Mr. Baruch—"And also in regard to the Lever Act, on the point that 'no man could serve two masters.' * * * There was no basis for it * * * because these men were not serving two masters. They did not make trades with themselves, but, with the instrumentality provided, carried out the government's wishes or orders or suggestions with reference to the particular industry which they represented."

The "instrumentality" with which the copper men dealt, for example was the American Metals Selling Company which, together with the American Smelting and Refining Company, was represented at Washington by Mr. Mosehauer. The special copper committee, composed of Guggenheim employes, did business pertaining to the "instrumentality" which carried on the business of the combined copper companies.

It was dangerous. Some of the members seem to have felt it before Mr. Baruch did. Mr. Baruch never seems to have questioned anything that he did. Why should he? He "had more power than any other man in the war" and he had the most powerful and autocratic backing that a man ever had. But the others, the non-Jewish members, were thinking of the law.

So Mr. Baruch solved it very nicely. He took the committees comprising the same men, and had them named as committees of the United States Chamber of Commerce for their various industries, and although the process was not changed in the least, the legal aspect of it was changed. It was rather clever. It was more, it was typical.

And after that, Mr. Baruch who had previously insisted that he himself had picked those men and that the industries had not, thus clearly encouraging the inference that these men did not represent the industries' side, but the government side of the matter, he now insists that they represented the industry.

Mr. Graham—" * * * you changed and took these advisory committees and had the National Chamber of Commerce reappoint them, so that they then were direct representatives of the Chamber of Commerce and not of the officials of the United States or connected with any governmental machinery?"

Mr. Baruch—"I never considered them officials of the government, Mr. Graham."

Mr. Graham—"They were as much officials of the government as the rest of you, were they not?"

Mr. Baruch—"I do not think so * * * (after several questions) * * * I asked them to serve so that when the government wanted anything they could go to one small, compact body, rather than to send out to I do not know how many people. You see?"

Mr. Graham—"Let us see about that. They were serving under you, were they not? You were the head?"

Mr. Baruch—"I appointed them and asked them to do this so that I could have a compact body to deal with."

Mr. Graham—"You did not think for a minute that they were representing the government, but did you not think you were?"

Mr. Baruch—"I was doing the best I knew how."

Mr. Graham—"But you had authority to bring these men in, Mr. Baruch, and appoint them as committeemen under you, and you did so. Surely, if they were representing anybody it was the government, was it not?"

Mr. Baruch—"I do not think so."

Mr. Graham—"Am I right in assuming that you thought they represented the industries?"

Mr. Baruch—"Yes."

A great deal, of course, can be overlooked in men who were working under stress and endeavoring to do things the best way. It does not follow that because a business man serves the government in matters pertaining to his own business, he is necessarily dishonest. But so frequent is dishonesty under such conditions, or, if not dishonesty, then a loss to the government because of a divided interest, that laws have been framed to regulate such matters. These laws were on the books at the time.

This is a fact, whatever else may be true, that "copper" made tens and hundreds of millions out of the war and it is not at all inconceivable that if "copper" had not been so completely in control of the government operations of purchase, the profits might not have been so great, and the burdens which the people bore through taxation, high prices and Liberty bonds might not have been so heavy.

Mr. Baruch is but one illustration of the clustering of Jewry about the war machinery of the United States. If the Jews were the only people left in the United States who were able enough to be put in the important places of power, well and good; but if they were not, why were they there in such uniform and systematized control? It is a definite situation that is discussed. The thing is there and is unchangeably a matter of history. How can it be explained?

Issue of December 11, 1920

XXVIII.

Jewish Control of the American Theater

THE Theater has long been a part of the Jewish program for the guidance of public taste and the influencing of the public mind. Not only is the theater given a special place in the program of the Protocols, but it is the instant ally night by night and week by week of any idea which the "power behind the scenes" wishes to put forth. It is not by accident that in Russia, where they now have scarcely anything else, they still have the Theater, specially revived, stimulated and supported by Jewish-Bolshevists because they believe in the Theater just as they believe in the Press; it is one of the two great means of molding popular opinion.

Everybody has assumed offhand that the Theater is Jew-controlled. Few, if put to the test, could prove it, but all believe it. The reason they believe it is not so much what they see as what they feel; the American *feel* has gone out of the Theater; a dark, Oriental atmosphere has come instead.

Not only the "legitimate" stage, so-called, but the motion picture industry—the fifth greatest of all the great industries--is also Jew-controlled, not in spots only, not 50 percent merely, but entirely; with the natural consequence that now the world is in arms against the trivializing and demoralizing influences of that form of entertainment as at present managed. As soon as the Jew gained control of American liquor, we had a liquor problem with drastic consequences. As soon as the Jew gained control of the "movies," we had a movie problem, the consequences of which are not yet visible. It is the genius of that race to create problems of a moral character in whatever business they achieve a majority.

Every night hundreds of thousands of people give from two to three hours to the Theater, every day literal millions of people give up from 30 minutes to two hours to the Movies; and this simply means that millions of Americans every day place themselves voluntarily within range of Jewish ideas of life, love and labor; within range of Jewish propaganda, sometime cleverly, sometimes clumsily concealed. This gives the Jewish masseur of the public mind all the opportunity he desires; and his only protest now is that exposure may make his game a trifle difficult.

The Theater is Jewish not only on its managerial side, but also on its literary and professional side. More and more plays are appearing whose author, producer, star and cast are entirely Jewish. They are not great plays, they do not remain long. This is natural enough, since the Jewish theatrical interests are not seeking artistic triumphs, they are not seeking the glory of the American stage, nor are they striving to develop great actors to take the place of the old line of worthies. Not at all. Their interest is financial and racial—getting the Gentiles' money and Judaizing the Theater. There is a tremendous Judaizing movement on; the work is almost complete. Boastful articles are already beginning to appear in the Jewish press, which is always a sign.

Gentile attendants on the Theater are frequently insulted to their faces, and never know it. Recently one of the best known Jewish entertainers on the stage indulged in vulgar and sacrilegious references to Jesus Christ, whereat the Semitic portions of his audience went into loud laughter, while the Gentiles sat blank-faced—because the remarks were in Yiddish asides!

Time after time the Jewish entertainer did that thing, and it was very plain to one who knew that the Jewish portion of the audience was enjoying the insult to the Gentiles much more than they were enjoying the well-worn humor of the entertainer's remarks. It was a great thing for them that in several important American cities they could see and hear being done under cover, and to American Gentiles, what is being done openly to Russian Gentiles.

In the audiences referred to there was probably $4,500 to $5,000 in gate money represented. Of this the Jews present, at the very highest estimate, could not have contributed more than $500. Yet the Jewish star several times slapped the religious sensibilities of the major portion of his audience under cover of Yiddish. The Theater is felt by him and his ilk to be a Jewish institution.

Down to 1885 the American Theater was still in the hands of the Gentiles. From 1885 dates the first invasion of Jewish influence. It meant the parting of the ways, and the future historian of the American Stage will describe that year with the word "Ichabod." That year marks not only the beginning of the Jewish wedge of control, but something far more important.

It is not important that managers are now Jews whereas managers were formerly Gentiles. That is not important. The importance begins with the fact that with the change of managers there came also a decline in the art and morals of the stage, and that this decline has become accelerated as the Jewish control became widened. What Jewish control means is this: that everything has been deliberately and systematically squeezed out of the American Theater except its most undesirable elements, and these undesirable elements have been exalted to the highest place of all.

The Great Age of the American Theater is past. About the time that Jewish control appeared, Sheridan, Sothern, McCullough, Madame Janauschek, Mary Anderson, Frank Mayo, John T. Raymond, began to pass off the stage. It was natural that, life being brief, they should pass at last, but the appalling fact began to be apparent that they had left no successors! Why? Because a Hebrew hand was on the stage, and the natural genius of the stage was no longer welcomed. A new form of worship was to be established.

"Shakespeare spells ruin," was the utterance of a Jewish manager. "High-brow stuff" is also a Jewish expression. These two sayings, one appealing to the managerial end, the other to the public end of the Theater, have formed the epitaph of the classic era. All that remained after the Hebrew hand fell across the stage were a few artists who had received their training under the Gentile school—Julia Marlowe, Tyrone Power, R. D. McLean, and, a little later, Richard Mansfield, Robert Mantell, E. H. Sothern. Two of this group remain, and with Maude Adams they constitute the last flashings of an era that has gone—an era that apparently leaves no great exemplars to perpetuate it.

The present-day average of intelligence appealed to in the American Theater does not rise above 13 to 18 years. "The tired business man" stuff (another Jewish expression) has treated the theatergoing public as if it were composed of morons. The appeal is frankly to a juvenile type of mind which can be easily molded to the ideals of the Hebraic theatrical monopoly. Clean, wholesome plays—the few that remain—are supported mainly by the rapidly vanishing race of theatergoers who survive from an earlier day; the present generation has been educated by the narrowed compass of modern dramatic themes to support plays of an entirely different type. Tragedy is taboo; the play of character, with a deeper significance than would delight the mind of a child, is out of favor; the comic opera has degenerated into a flash of color and movement—a combination of salacious farce and jazz music, usually supplied by a Jewish song-writer (the great purveyors of jazz!) and the rage is for extravaganza and burlesque.

The bedroom farce has been exalted into the first place. With the exception of "Ben Hur," which is favored by Jewish producers apparently because it holds before the public a romantic picture of a Jew (a very un-Jewish Jew, by the way) the historical drama has given way to fleshly spectacles set off with over-powering scenic effects, the principal component of which is an army of girls (mostly Gentiles!) whose investment of drapery does not exceed five ounces in weight.

Frivolity, sensuality, indecency, appalling illiteracy and endless platitude are the marks of the American Stage as it approaches its degeneracy under Jewish control.

That, of course, is the real meaning of all the "Little Theater" movements which have begun in so many cities and towns in the United States. The art of the drama, having been driven out of the Theater by the Jews, is finding a home in thousands of study circles throughout the United States. The people cannot see the real plays; therefore they read them. The plays that are acted could not be read at all, for the most part, any more than the words of the jazz songs can be read; they don't mean anything. The people who want to see the real plays and cannot, because Jewish producers won't produce them, are forming little dramatic clubs of their own, in barns and churches, in schools and neighborhood halls. The drama fled from its exploiters and has found a home with its friends.

The changes which the Jews have made in the theater, and which any half-observant theatergoer can verify with his own eyes, are four in number.

First, they have elaborated the mechanical side, making human talent and genius less necessary. They have made the stage "realistic" instead of interpretative. The great actors needed very little machinery; the men and women on the pay rolls of the Jewish managers are helpless without the machinery. The outstanding fact about the vast majority of present-day performances of any pretension is that the mechanical part dwarfs and obscures the acting, however good. And this is the reason: knowing that good actors are growing scarce, knowing that the Jewish policy is death to talent, knowing perhaps most keenly of all that good actors constitute a running charge on his revenue, the Jewish producer prefers to put his faith and his money in wood, canvas, paint, cloth and tinsel of which scenery and costumes are made. Wood and paint never show contempt for his sordid ideals and his betrayal of his trust.

And thus we have, when we go to the theater today, bursts of color, ruffles of lace and linen, waving lines and dazzling effects of light and motion—but no ideas, a great many stage employes, but very few actors. There are drills and dances without end, but no drama.

93

There is one influence on the American Theater which the Jew claims, and the credit for which can be given to him in full. He has put in the iridescence, but he has taken out the profounder ideas. He has placed the American public in the position of being able to remember the names of plays without being able to recall what composed them. Like the "Floradora Girls," a Jewish creation, we remember the name of the group, but not of any individual in it. The Jew has done this to perfection, but no one will contend that it represents a forward step; taken by and large, it is part of a very serious and harmful retrogression.

Second, the Jews may be credited also with having introduced Oriental sensuality to the American stage. Not even the most ardent Jewish defender will deny this, for the thing is there, before the eyes of all who will see. Little by little the mark of the filthy tide has risen against the walls of the American Theater until now it is all but engulfed. It is a truism that there is more unrefined indecency in the higher class theaters today than was ever permitted by the police in the burlesque houses. The lower classes must be restrained in the vicarious exercise of their lower natures, apparently, but the wealthier classes may go the limit. The price of the ticket and the "class" of the playhouse seems to make all the difference in the world between prohibited and permissible evil.

In New York, where Jewish managers are thicker than they ever will be in Jerusalem, the limit of theatrical adventuresomeness into the realm of the forbidden is being pushed further and further. Last season's spectacle of "Aphrodite" seemed to be deliberately designed as a frontal attack on the last entrenched scruple of moral conservatism. The scenes are most Oriental in their voluptuous abandonment. Men in breech-clouts, leopard skins and buckskins, women in flimsy gowns of gossamer texture, slashed to the hips, with very little besides, made a bewildering pageant whose capstone was the unveiling of a perfectly nude girl whose body had been painted to resemble marble. Save that it was all designed, and all put through on schedule, it was almost the "limit" to which such exhibitions could go in real life. Its promoter, of course, was a Jew. As an entertainment it was infantile; the splendor of its insinuations, the daring of its situations, were the fruitage of long study of the art of seducing the popular mind.

It is said when "Aphrodite" first appeared that the police had moved against it, but some held that this was a clever press-agent stunt to excite public interest in the promised pruriency. It was also said that even had the police interference been the genuine result of outraged official minds, the fact that the Jews of New York are represented in the judiciary out of all proportion to their numbers, would have rendered the Jewish producer free from interference. In any event, the piece was not molested. The sale of narcotics is illegal, but the instilling of insidious moral poison is not.

The whole loose atmosphere of "cabaret" and "midnight frolic" entertainment is of Jewish origin and importation. Mention the best known and the worst known, they are all Jewish. The runway down which less than half-dressed girls cavort, fluttering their loose finery in the faces of the spectators, is an importation from Vienna, but a Jewish creation. The abuses of the runway will not bear description here. The Paris boulevards and Montemartre have nothing at all in the nature of lascivious entertainment that New York cannot duplicate. *BUT* neither New York nor any other American city has that *Comedie Francaise* which strives to counterbalance the evil of Paris.

Where have the writers for the Stage a single chance in this welter of sensuousness? Where have the actors of tragic or comic talent a chance in such productions? It is the age of the chorus girl, a creature whose mental caliber has nothing to do with the matter, and whose stage life cannot in the very nature of things be a career.

It is only occasionally that a great writer for the stage, a Shaw, a Masefield, a Barrie, an Ibsen, or any Gentile writer of merit, is permitted to get as far as actual production, and then only for a short period; the stream of colored electric lighting effects, of women and tinsel closes in behind them and they are washed away, to survive in printed books among those who still know what the Theater ought to be.

A third consequence of Jewish domination of the American stage has been the appearance of "the New York star" system, with its advertising appliances. The last few years of the Theater have been marked by numerous "stars" that really never rose and certainly never shone, but which were hoisted high on the advertising walls of the Jewish theatrical syndicates in order to give the public the impression that these feeble lantern-lights were in highest heaven of dramatic achievement.

The trick is a department store trick. It is sheer advertising strategy. The "stars" of yesterday, who did not even survive yesterday, were either the personal favorites of managers, or goods taken off the shelf and heaped into the window for the sake of giving the appearance of a new stock. In brief, whereas in normal times the public made the "star" by their acclaim, nowadays the Jewish managers determine by their advertisement who the star shall be. The "New York stamp," which frequently means nothing at all, is the one imperial hierarchy. It is just this "New York stamp," that the rest of the country protests against; and the "little theater" movement throughout the West and Central West is a significant protest.

A Mary Anderson or a Julia Marlowe would be impossible under the Jewish system. They were disciples of art, who later became artists, and then were rightfully acclaimed as stars. But their development was a tedious process. Their fame was based on the rising approval of the people, year after year. These actresses put in season after season traveling the same circuit, learning little by little, rounding out their work. They did not have nor did they seek the "New York stamp"; they worked first for the approval of the people of "the provinces," which is the contemptuous Jewish term for the rest of the United States. There was, however, no Jewish dictatorship of the Theater when Mary Anderson and Julia Marlowe were building their art and careers; which throws a light on the reason for there being no Mary Andersons or Julia Marlowes coming up to the succession.

The Jew seeks immediate success in all but racial affairs. In this breakdown of the Gentile theater, the process cannot be too swift for him. The training of artists takes time. It is far simpler to have the advertising bills serve as a substitute and, as the itinerant faker-dentist had a brass band blare loud enough to drown the anguished cries of his victims, so the Jewish manager seeks to divert attention from the dramatic poverty of the Theater by throwing confetti, limbs, lingerie and spangles dazzlingly into the eyes of his audience.

These three results of Jewish control in the Theater are all explainable by a fourth; the secret of the serious change which has occurred since 1885 is found in the Jewish tendency to commercialize everything it touches. The focus of attention has been shifted from the Stage to the box office. The banal policy of "give the public what they want" is the policy of the panderer, and it entered the American Theater with the first Jewish invasion.

About 1885 two alert Jews established in New York a so-called booking agency and offered to take over the somewhat cumbersome system by which managers of theaters in St. Louis, Detroit or Omaha arranged engagements of attractions for their houses for the ensuing season. The old process involved extensive correspondence with producing managers in the East and many local managers were obliged to spend several months in New York to make up a season's bookings. The advantages were that the booking agency, supplied with a list of the "open dates" of the houses they represented, were able to lay out a complete season's itinerary, or "route," for a traveling company and enabled the producer of a play to spend his vacation at the seashore instead of passing the sultry mid-season in New York, while the local manager was saved the trouble of much writing or even a trip East, and was content to let the booking concern attend to all details and send him his next season's bookings when completed.

In this manner was laid the foundation of the later-day Theatrical Trust. The booking firm was that of Klaw & Erlanger, the former a young Jew from Kentucky who had studied law, but drifted into theatrical life as an agent; the

97

latter a young Jew from Cleveland with little education but with experience as an advance agent.

The booking system was not of their devising. They borrowed the idea from Harry C. Taylor, who had established a sort of theatrical exchange where producers and local managers could meet, desks being provided them at a small rental, and who took over the booking in the smaller cities, without foreseeing—but probably scorning—the opportunity thus placed in his hands to club the whole theatrical world into submission to his dictates.

With characteristic shrewdness Klaw & Erlanger elaborated the idea they had borrowed from Taylor, opened competition against the latter and enlisted the support of a number of young Jewish advance agents who were beginning to recognize the lucrative opportunities which the theatrical profession afforded. Prominent among their earliest supporters was Charles Freeman, employed by J. H. Haverley. His brother, Daniel, had been business manager for the Mallorys at the Madison Square Theater since 1881, and though the Frohmans stand out in relief from the background of the *Polish Jewish* influence on the theater, they found it to their advantage to co-operate with the booking firm and subsequently became prominent members of the Trust.

The establishment of the Jewish booking agency system is the key to the whole problem of the decline of the American stage. The old booking system had the enormous advantage of the personal touch in the relationship between manager and company, and made possible the development of genius in accordance with the organic laws which determine its nurture, growth and fruition. Except in its highest form, acting is not an art; but heaven-born genius is no more vocal in an Edwin Booth without long training than a Bonaparte is necessarily a world conqueror without the technique of the artillery school. These two thoughts have the utmost bearing on giving the Jews the control of the theater.

There being no "syndicate," no pooling, among the Gentile managers of the 80's, they presented their stars or other attractions at rival theaters in competition as individual offerings, and at the end of a reasonable New York run, not forced for "road consumption," took their companies on a tour of the country. The manager's whole investment was probably tied up in his enterprise. He thus became a part of his group of artists, sharing their hardships of travel, their joys and sorrows. If business was good they shared the satisfaction; if otherwise, it was sink or swim for one as well as the other. In those days much was heard about troupes traveling "on their trunks." The stories were not exaggerated, but life had its better side, too. The manager and the actor were daily companions; there was a mutual absorption of ideas; the manager learned to know and appraise the "artistic temperament"—which is a tangible asset when not a form of artificial grouch or congenital ill-nature— and to respect the actor's point of view, while, reciprocally, the actor was abler to place himself in the manager's position and to get his point of view from close personal affiliation.

Issue of January 1, 1921.

XXIX.

The Rise of the First Jewish Theatrical Trust

I T HAS long been known among dramatic critics that the reason for the maintenance of "Ben Hur" in the theater for nineteen years is this: it is the most successful of all the vehicles for pro-Semitism now on the stage. That will appear to be a prejudicial statement in the minds of the thousands who have seen and enjoyed "Ben Hur," but there is truth in it. The point which should not be overlooked, however, is that *if* "Ben Hur" is useful in framing the public mind favorably toward the Jews, it is not because of a pro-Semitic intention in the story. That may be the intention of the producers, Messrs. Klaw and Erlanger, but it was not the intention of General Lew Wallace.

It would seem that art and fate conspire against the propagandist play, for in no other way can the failure of avowedly pro-Semitic drama be explained. Perhaps there was never such a serious and even strenuous attempt made to force the Jewish controlled theater into the service of pro-Semitism as has been made in recent months. And the attempts, with one possible exception, have been failures. Lavishly produced, heralded by an unbroken clacque of press announcement, swathed in an initial chorus of praise, sponsored by officialdom which had been dragged out to stand godfather to the productions, they have nevertheless failed.

Be it said to the credit of the American Jew that he has been one of the causes of the failure. A most significant and hopeful sign was the reaction of the intelligent Jewish community against the attempts to utilize the stage as a hustings to boost the Jew to an unreal eminence and desirability. Certain competent Jews wrote their opinions about this with much freedom and wisdom. And they evinced a spirit, which, if it could be made to permeate all Jewish activities, would quickly dispose of the Jewish Question in whatever phase it might be considered. It is this spirit of judging Jewish interests in the light of the whole which promises a helpful and lasting solution of all the differences which unfortunately have been permitted to arise between the people of Judah and the others.

The fact of Jewish control of the theater is not of it self a ground for complaint. If certain Jews, working separately or in groups, have succeeded in wrenching this rich business from its former gentile control, that is purely a matter of commercial interest. It is precisely on the same footing as if one group of Gentiles won the control from another group of Gentiles. It may be regarded as a business matter. In this, as in other business matters, however, there is the ethical test of *how the control was gained* and *how it is used*. Society is usually willing to receive the fact of control with equanimity, provided the control is not used for anti-social purposes.

The fact that the old-time Gentile producing managers usually died poor—Augustin Daly being about the only exception—while Jewish producing managers wax immensely wealthy (there being on this side the exception of the late Charles Frohman), would indicate that Gentile managers were better artists and poorer business men than the Jewish managers. At least poorer business men, perhaps; and in any case working on a system whose chief object was to produce plays not profits.

The advent of Jewish control put the theater on a more commercialized basis than it had previously known. It really represented applying the Trust Idea to the theater before it had been largely applied to industry. As early as the year 1896 the Theatrical Trust controlled 37 theaters in strategic cities. The men composing this alliance were Klaw and Erlanger, Nixon and Zimmerman, and Hayman and Frohman. All but Zimmerman were Jews, and his racial origin was a subject of dispute. This group was later joined by Rich and Harris, of Boston, and Joseph Brookes, all known as Jews.

Controlling these theaters, the Trust was able to assure a long season to both managers and playing companies. Outside the Trust, the managers and companies were left to make arrangements between each other, which resembled a species of barn-storming.

The effect on the independent theaters and managers was disastrous. The Trust boosted royalties on plays from $50 to $450 and eventually to $1,000 a week. This of itself cut off the material of the stock companies with which the independent managers endeavored to keep open their houses.

The running out of the stock companies by excessive charges for the use of plays that had already been used in the regular theaters of the Trust, really served Jewish interests in another way. The motion picture industry was coming to the front. It was a Jewish enterprise from the first. There never was any need to drive Gentiles out of that, because the Gentiles never had a chance to get in. Thus, the driving out of the stock companies threw the empty theaters over to the "movies," and the benefit was again confined to a particular racial group.

This will answer the question so frequently asked by people who wonder why the theaters they formerly saw offering plays at all seasons, are now devoting the larger part of the year to "movies."

It was not to be expected that this sort of thing could be put through without a struggle. There was a struggle and a severe one, but it is ended with what the public can see today.

The opposition offered by the artists was prolonged and dignified. Francis Wilson, Nat C. Goodwin, James A. Herne, James O'Neil, Richard Mansfield, Mrs. Fiske and James K. Hakett stood out for a time, all of them with the exception of Goodwin bound by a forfeit of $1,000 if they deserted the cause of a free theater.

Joseph Jefferson was always with the actors in this opposition and continued of the same mind to the end, playing in both Trust and anti-Trust houses.

It is a matter of record that Nat Goodwin was the first to give in. He was the head and front of the opposition, but he had his weaknesses which were well known to the Trust, and upon these they played. One of his weaknesses was for New York engagements, and he was offered a long engagement at the Knickerbocker Theater. He was also given the promise of dates wherever and whenever he wanted them. Goodwin thereupon deserted the alliance of stars and became the henchman of the Trust. (The "Trust" was the name by which the new control was known in these days. The racial name was not given although the racial nature was plainly discerned.)

Nat Goodwin's star began to decline from that day. He made a final essay as Shylock, and with that he was practically ushered out as a headliner of the serious stage.

Richard Mansfield and Francis Wilson were delivering nightly curtain speeches against the Trust wherever they appeared, and although the public was sympathetic it was very much like the present state of affairs—what could the public do? What can an unorganized public ever do against a small, organized, determined minority? The public hardly ever appears as a party in any of the movements that concern itself; the public is the prize for which the parties strive.

The Trust dealt strongly with Wilson. His dates were canceled. Neither his status nor his ability was of any avail to him. One of the Trust made an open statement: "Mr. Wilson is a shining mark, and we determined to make an example of him for the benefit of the lesser offenders."

Wilson's strong spirit was finally subdued to see "reason." In 1898 the Philadelphia members of the Trust offered him $50,000 for his business, and he took it.

In due time Richard Mansfield also surrendered, and Mrs. Fiske was left alone to carry on the fight.

The Theatrical Trust, which must be described as Jewish, because it was that, was at the beginning of the new century in full control of the field. It had reduced what was essentially an art to a time-clock, cash-register system, working with the mechanical precision of a well-managed factory. It suppressed individuality and initiative, killed off competition, drove out the independent manager and star, excluded all but foreign playwrights of established reputation, fostered the popularity of inferior talent which was predominantly Jewish, sought to debase the service of the dramatic critics of the public press, foisted countless "stars" of mushroom growth upon a helpless public while driving real stars into obscurity; it handled plays, theaters and actors like factory products, and now began a process of vulgarizing and commercializing everything connected with the theater.

If space permitted, a number of opinions could be presented here from men like William Dean Howells, Norman Hapgood and Thomas Bailey Aldrich, whose concern was for the theater, but who voiced no other observation as to the racial influences at work.

Their concern was justified. It is quite possible that many who read this article are not interested in the theater, and are, in fact, convinced that the theater is a menace. Very well. What principally makes it a menace? This—that the stage today represents the principal cultural element of 50 per cent of the people. What the average young person absorbs as to good form, proper deportment, refinement as contrasted with coarseness, correctness of speech or choice of words, customs and feelings of other nations, even fashions of clothes, as well as ideas of religion and law, are derived from what he sees and hears at the theater. The masses' sole idea of the homes and the life of the rich is derived from the stage and the movies. More wrong notions are given, more prejudices created by the Jewish controlled theater in one week, than can be charged against a serious study of the Jewish Question in a century. People sometimes wonder where the ideas of the younger generation come from. This is the answer.

As was just said, all the original opposers of this new control of the theater surrendered and left Mrs. Fiske to fight alone. She had, however, an ally in her husband, Harrison Grey Fiske, who was editor of the New York *Dramatic Mirror.*

Mrs. Fiske herself had said: "The incompetent men who have seized upon the affairs of the stage in this country have all but killed art, ambition and decency."

Her husband wrote in his paper: "What then should be expected of a band of adventurers of infamous origin, of no breeding and utterly without artistic taste? * * * Let it be kept in mind that the ruling number of these men who compose the Theatrical Trust are absolutely unfit to serve in any but the most subordinate places in the economy of the stage and that they ought not to be tolerated even in these places except under a discipline, active, vigorous and uncompromising. Their records are disreputable and in some cases criminal, and their methods are in keeping with their records." (First printed in the *Dramatic Mirror*, December 25, 1897; reprinted March 19, 1898.)

This attack was regarded, foolishly and wrongfully of course, as an attack on the whole House of Israel and, as is always the case when one Jew is censured for wrongdoing, all the Jews in the United States came to the rescue. Pressure was brought to bear on a famous news company which handled the circulation of the most important magazines in the United States. Leading hotels were induced to withdraw the *Dramatic Mirror* from their news stands. *Mirror* correspondents were refused admittance to theaters controlled by the Trust. Any number of underground influences were set in operation to "get" Fiske and his business.

Suit was brought against Fiske for $10,000 damages for the strictures he had printed upon the personal character of certain members of the Trust. Fiske replied in his answer, setting up various facts against specific members of the Trust, their records, actions, and so on. One he accused of carrying on business under a fictitious name ("cover name," as it is known in Jewish circles). Another he accused of charging managers for advertising expenses that were never incurred. Another he accused of issuing "complimentary" tickets in which he did a private speculative business of his own, selling them and pocketing the proceeds. Another he accused of specific crimes for which he had been arrested and convicted.

He charged that the Trust as a whole advertised in various cities that "the original New York company" would play, charging exorbitant admission fees on the strength of this advertisement, when in truth these were secondary companies and not the one advertised.

A strange court hearing was held in which the magistrate did not wish to hear any of Fiske's testimony, even forbidding him to enter official records of the criminal proceedings had against a certain member of the Trust. The Magistrate did not seem to want to hear what Fiske based his statements upon. There was a serious shooting scrape involving a woman, but the magistrate did not want to hear about it. There was even considerable difficulty on the part of Fiske's lawyer in procuring the attendance of Abraham L. Erlanger at court, although he was one of the complainants.

All the important questions asked of Klaw were overruled.

As to Al Hayman, the court overruled all questions relating to his real name and the circumstances under which he left Australia.

The facts were not brought out in this hearing, but the whole character of the hearing was made known to the public. Fiske was bound over to the Grand Jury, with $300 bail in every allegation of libel.

The Grand Jury lost no time in dismissing all the complaints against Fiske. The Trust members had come off badly because of their evident unwillingness to meet the case. They were revealed to be a much lower type of men than the American public had supposed was in charge of the American theater. They were shown to be a type that would not even stop at demanding the discharge of a local newspaper reporter whose critique of their plays did not please them.

The fight of the dramatic critics first against the bribery and then against the bludgeoning of the Theatrical Trust makes a story of which echoes have frequently come to the American public through the press. Conciliatory at first, with managers, actors, playwrights and critics, the Trust, as soon as it gained power, showed the claws beneath the velvet. It had the millions of dollars of the public coming its way, why should it care? Whenever a critic opposed its methods or pointed out the inferior, coarse and degrading character of the Trust productions, he was ordered barred from the Trust's theaters, and local managers were instructed to demand his discharge from his newspaper. It is with mingled feelings that an American is compelled to relate that in many, many cases the demand was complied with, the papers being threatened with the loss of Sunday advertising! But here and there courageous writers on the Stage held to the honor of their profession and refused to be bribed or intimidated.

Writers like James S. Metcalfe, of *Life;* Hillery Bell, of the New York *Press;* Frederick R. Schrader, of the Washington *Post;* Norman Hapgood, on the New York *Evening Globe;* James O'Donnell Bennett, of the Chicago *Record-Herald*, stood out against the Trust and made their fight. Metcalfe went so far as to bring suit against the Trust for unlawful exclusion from a place of public amusement. The courts were kind to the Trust. They decided that a theater may pick its patrons. Even in very recent years the Trust has followed blacklisted dramatic critics in an effort to prevent their employment by newspapers.

The Theatrical Trust does not exist in the form it did ten years ago. It grew arrogant and bred secret enemies among its own people. A new force arose, but it also was Jewish, as it originated in the Shubert brothers with David Belasco. Instead of one, the American people have now a dual dictatorship of the stage. The rage of the day is not plays, but playhouses. With not three plays of any character to distinguish them from the dregs of the stage, there are now building in New York alone a dozen new playhouses. The theatrical business has entered upon its real estate phase. There is money in renting chairs at the rate of $1 to $3 an hour. The renting of the chairs is a reality. The Stage is rapidly becoming an illusion.

Issue of January 8, 1921

XXX.

How Jews Capitalized a Protest Against Jews

T HE American stage is under the influence and control of a group of former bootblacks, newsboys, ticket speculators, prize ring habitues, and Bowery characters. At the present writing the most advertised man in the world of theatrical production is Morris Gest, a Russian Jew, who has produced the most salacious spectacles ever shown in America— "Aphrodite" and "Mecca." It is reported that the scent of nastiness has been so strongly circulated among theatergoers that tickets are sold a year ahead for the Chicago exhibition of one of these shows, the patrons being, of course, mostly Gentiles.

Now, it is a fair question, who is this Morris Gest who stalks before his fellow Jews as the most successful producer of the year? It is nothing against him to say that he came from Russia. It is nothing against him to say that he is a Jew. It is nothing against him to say that although success has favored him, his father and mother are still in Odessa, or were until recently. Yet, in a recent interview, in which the professional note of pathos was obtrusively present, he lamented that he was not able to bring his parents to America.

The story of Morris Gest is the last one in the world to use as a "success story" of the type of "the poor immigrant boy who became a great theatrical producer." He is not a great producer, of course, although he is a great panderer to the least creditable tastes of a public whose taste he has been no mean factor in debasing. Gest sold newspapers in Boston, and became property boy in a Boston theater. In 1906 he was a member of a notorious gang of ticket speculators who were the bane of the public until ticket-peddling on the sidewalks in front of theaters was suppressed by the police. There are still other stories told about him that link his name with another sort of traffic, but whether these stories are true or not, there is nothing in Gest's career to indicate that he would ever contribute anything to the theater's best interest. He is the son-in-law of David Belasco.

Then there is Sam Harris, long the junior partner of the firm of Cohen & Harris, who began his career in the arts by managing Dixon, the colored champion featherweight pugilist, and the redoubtable Terry McGovern, champion lightweight prize fighter. With tastes formed at the ringside, he launched into theatrical ventures, allying himself with Al Woods. He catered to the lower classes and made a fortune by producing atrocious melodramas in second and third class houses.

And yet this is the Sam Harris who commands the patronage of hundreds of thousands, yes, millions of theatergoers, some of whom go on innocently believing that when they invade the theater they also enter, by some mystical process, "the realms of art."

Al H. Woods has but one good eye. It is not this personal loss that matters, but the history of the misfortune which goes back to the time when Al was a member of an East Side gang. The common report was that he used to play the piano in a downtown place, east of Fifth Avenue. Mr. Woods is also a distinguished patron of dramatic art—he presented "The Girl from Rector's" and "The Girl in the Taxi," two of the most immoral and pointless shows of recent years. Several times he has secured the rights to certain Viennese operas, which were bad enough in themselves from a moral point of view, but which were at least constructed with true artistry; but even these he marred by an inept infusion of vulgarity and plague.

The public, of course, does not see and does not know these gods before whom they pour their millions yearly, nor does the public know from what source theatric vileness comes. It is amusing to listen to the fledgling philosophers discuss the "tendencies of the stage," or expatiate learnedly on the "divine right of Art" to be as flippant and as filthy as it pleases, when all the time the "tendency" is started and the "art" is determined by men whose antecedents would make Art scream!

The American Theater is a small group of Jewish promoters and a large group of Gentile gullibles, and it is only the latter who "kid themselves" that there is anything real about the matter.

It is perfectly natural, therefore, that the complete Judaization of the theater would result in its being transformed into "the show business," a mere matter of trade and barter. The real producers are often not culturally equipped for anything more than the baldest business. They can hire what they want, mechanicians, costumers, painters, writers, musicians. With their gauge of public taste and their models of action formed upon the race track and the prize ring; with their whole ideal modeled upon the ambition to pander to depravity, instead of serving legitimate needs, it is not surprising that the standards of the Theater should now be at their lowest mark.

As theatergoers are noticing more and more, the Jewish manager whenever possible employs Jewish actors and actresses. Gentile playwrights and actors are steadily diminishing in number for want of a market. At times the employment of Jewish actors has been so obtrusive as to endanger the success of the play. This was notably the case when the part of a young Christian girl of the early Christian Era was given to a Jewess of pronounced racial features. The selection was so glaringly inept, ethnically and historically, that it militated strongly against the impression the play was intended to produce.

The "cover-name" conceals from the theatergoing public the fact that the actors and actresses who purvey entertainment are, in large and growing proportion, Jewish.

Some of the more prominent Jewish actors, many of them prime favorites are Al Jolson, Charlie Chaplin, Louis Mann, Sam Bernard, David Warfield, Joe Weber, Barney Bernard, "Ed Wynne, or to mention his real name, Israel Leopold," Lou Fields, Eddie Cantor, Robert Warwick.

Among the prominent Jewish actresses are: Theda Bara, Nora Bayes, Olga Nethersole, Irene Franklin, Gertrude Hoffman, Mizi Hajos, Fanny Brice (wife of Nicky Arnstein), Bertha Kalisch,

Jose Collins, Ethel Levy, Belle Baker, Constance Collier. The Late Anna Held was a Jewess.

In addition to these there are others whose racial identity is not revealed by their names or any public knowledge about them. The Jewish press claims for the Jews, aside from the commercial control of the stage, the control of the fun-making business. "The greatest entertainers, vaudevillians and fun-makers are Jews," says an article in the Chicago *Jewish Sentinel,* commenting on the extent to which Jewish actors monopolized the Chicago stage that week.

Among the composers we once beheld Victor Herbert and Gustav Kerker in honorable places; but now the Irving Berlins have forced themselves into places hewn out and established by Gentiles who had a regard for art.

There are no great Jewish playwrights. Charles Klein wrote "The Lion and the Mouse," but never repeated. There is, of course, much commonplace work turned out for the stage; a commercialized stage needs a certain amount of "product." Among those engaged in such work are Jack Lait, Montague Glass, Samuel Shipman, Jules Eckert Goodman, Aaron Hoffman, and others.

The Jewish claim to exceptional genius is not borne out by the theater, although the Jewish will to power is therein amply illustrated.

Belasco's name comes to mind, perhaps, oftener than any; and Belasco is the most consummate actor off any stage. To understand Mr. Belasco is to understand the method by which the "Independents" fought the Jewish Theater Trust, and still retained the monopoly of the Theater for the Jews.

The old Trust was bowling along merrily, smashing everything in its way, thrusting honored "stars" into obscurity, blocking the path of promising playwrights, putting out of business all actors who would not prostitute art to commercialism, and there occurred what always occurs—for even the Jews are not superior to natural law—a bad case of "big head" was developed.

Klaw, Erlanger and their immediate associates felt themselves to be kings and began to exhibit a few supposedly royal idiosyncrasies.

There were some protests, of course, against the arrogance of the Czars of the Theater. The Vanderbilts and other New York millionaires embodied their protest in a movement toward a national theater which was erected at Grand Central Park, and for which $1,000,000 was spent. One of the members of the Trust proved his birth and breeding by saying that this attempt to cleanse the theater was really only a plan to provide a place of vice for the benefit of the millionaire backers. The remark inspired deep rancor, but was more revelatory of the Jewish Trust's essential conception of the theater, than anything else. Belasco came from San Francisco, where he had done various stunts, including those of an itinerant recitationist, illusionist and actor. James E. Herne took an interest in him as a youth and discovered him to be adept in helping himself to dialogues out of printed plays. Under Herne, Belasco learned much about stage effects, and soon became very successful in touching up defective plays. Coming to New York, Belasco fell in with DeMille, a Jewish writer for the stage, who only needed Belasco's "sense of the theater" to make his qualities effective.

Belasco became a factor in enlarging the Jewish control of the stage, in this way: he was connected with the Frohmans, but was unable to persuade them that Mrs. Leslie Carter, who had been the center of a sensational divorce suit and who had placed herself under Mr. Belasco's professional direction, was a great actress. The making of a star out of Mrs. Carter, and the gaining of public recognition for her, proved a long task. The Frohmans were unsympathetic.

Then, among the managers there was dissension too. The Shuberts had been compelled to take the leavings of the other Jewish magnates, especially the leavings of Charles Frohman, and the Shuberts revolted. The Shuberts were natives of Syracuse, and their preparation for the theater was not promising of their devotion to art. They were program boys and ushers. Then the haberdashery business claimed them as possibly a speedier course to wealth. Samuel Shubert eventually became a ticket seller in the box office. In due time, having learned a few marketable secrets of the theater, he launched a frivolous burlesque and comedy show. With this he floated into New York, and continued with his musical shows of a shallow kind, until the name Shubert has come to be descriptive of the productions. The Shuberts, of course, booked in Trust theaters.

About the year 1900, the Shuberts quarreled with the Trust and Belasco quarreled with the Frohmans, and the two hailed each other as fellow belligerents and proceeded to see what could be made of their belligerency. The public was showing signs of disgust with the Trust. Belasco and the Shuberts would play the part of injured independents; public sympathy would be aroused, and public patronage would boost the "Independents" into the strength of a new Trust. That is exactly what occurred.

Belasco's theatricalism helped to this end. He is an actor off, as well as on the stage. He affects the pose of a benevolent priest, and dresses the part, wearing a priestly collar, with clerical vest and coat. Although of Portuguese-Hebraic origin, Belasco dresses after this manner to honor, as he says, a tutor of his early days. Anyway, the costume is very effective, especially with the ladies. He has a tremulous, shy way about him, and he sits in his sanctum with the lights so arranged that his priestly face and splendid shock of silver hair seem to rise out of an encompassing and shadowy mystery. It is very effective—very effective. One woman declared, after being admitted to the presence and gazing on the face that rose out of the shadows into the light--"I have a better understanding of the divine humility of Jesus Christ since I have been privileged to meet Mr. Belasco."

Thus, "the master," as he is called, was well equipped to appeal to public sympathy. And he did appeal. There was no end to his appeal. He told stories of personal attacks made on him. He wrung his hands in desperate grief against the Trust's menace to the stage. His own productions, however, were not all immaculate. There was one, "Naughty Anthony" which brought the police censor down upon him. But there was a very clear conception in the public mind as to what the Trust had done to the stage; Belasco said he was against the Trust, and the rest was snap judgment.

The Shuberts and Belasco thus found themselves in a very favorable combination of circumstances. Their first financial aid came, strangely enough, through ex-Congressman Reinach, a Jew, "Boss" Cox, of Ohio, and others who were interested. These supplied the first money; the Shuberts supplied the wonderful impersonation of a Daniel come to call the Jewish Theater Trust to judgment. The campaign succeeded and the wealth rolled in. For a time Belasco did prove to the public that he could produce better plays than the old Trust had given to the public, and to that extent he justified public confidence in him.

The end of the old Trust came in a natural way. The Shuberts became rich and powerful, and the Trust was then willing to do business with them. Some of the Trust members died, and about 1910 the old Trust ceased to exist as the dominant factor in American theatrical affairs. But the rise of the "Independents" did not bring relief; it only captured for Jewish enterprise that part of the theater which might have become the prize of a legitimate body of protesters against the old cheapness and vulgarity. The pretended protest won. The theater was saved to Jewish control.

Jewish managers had created the public disgust in the first place. They knew what the public reaction would be, so they prepared to capitalize the reaction, and thus control the theatergoing public both going and coming. This they did with admirable strategy.

During the outbreak there was some genuine feeling of independence on the part of a few non-Jewish managers. John Cort organized a western theater circuit. Colonel Henry W. Savage swung loose from Klaw and Erlanger, as did also William A. Brady. But independence of the Jewish control has never flourished. Wherever it did keep up an independent front, it stood for the theater in its best sense, and served as the only channel of expression for the remaining few stage artists. The coming of the motion picture, however, gave true independence its quietus. The motion picture "industry"—and it is rightly named an "industry"—is entirely Jewish controlled, and as it is pushing its way into the legitimate theaters and crowding out human players for long periods every year, theater managers have to bow to it more and more.

It remained for the Shuberts, however, to give the theatrical business a most original twist. They made it a real estate speculation. Readers of this article may recall that recently they have read that in their own or a neighboring city the Shuberts are going to build one or two theaters. In one city, the announcement was made that two theaters were to be built. That particular city happens to need almost everything else but theaters. However it cannot get anything else that it needs, and there is no doubt it will get the theaters.

The Shuberts learned this trick when they were supposed to be "bucking the Trust." They went after any building they could get, and because of the public enmity to the Trust, they got better terms than otherwise could have possible. An old riding school in New York became the Winter Garden. The Great Hippodrome, the materialized dream of a non-Jew, Frederick Thompson, was taken over by the Shuberts. It soon dawned on the Shuberts that there was more money in theatrical real estate than in theatrical art.

Today, the Shuberts, while nominally theatrical managers, are really dealers in theatrical leases and buildings where theatrical productions are made. A theater, as a real estate proposition, pays amazingly well. Figure up the amount of space you occupy at a show, the length of time you occupy it, and the price you pay for it. It is rent raised to the *nth* degree; then the offices which make the bulk of the structure, and the stores in front. Really, "the show business" is the minor consideration.

What does it cost the Shuberts? Very little but the use of their name. When it is the matter of a new theater, outside capital supplies three-fourths of the money, but the lease and control are vested in the Shuberts. That is a rather handsome arrangement.

In the matter of producing plays, the same arrangement is often followed—the author, the star, or their backers supplying the larger part, sometimes all of the capital, while the Shuberts lend their name to the management and take their share of the booking fees and the rental of the theaters where the show is produced.

In October of last year (1920) a serious slump hit the theatrical business. Even in New York the theaters were experiencing the worst depression of years. More than 3,000 actors were idle and managers were compelled to resort to the cut-rate ticket agents to sell their seats. And yet, in the midst of it, Shubert announced six new theaters for New York alone. At the same time they announced the production of forty plays.

Forty plays! If a man announced that he was going to build six new art museums in one city and fit them up with the requisite number of oil paintings produced under his own direction, he would be considered crazy, especially if it were a matter of common repute that he knew nothing of art and was having the pictures painted merely to give value to his real estate!

It indicates how thoroughly accustomed the public has become to "the show business" and the "motion picture industry," that the announcement of these former haberdashers is taken so complacently. Forty plays!—when anyone can count on the fingers of both hands all the present-day American and English playwrights even remotely deserving of notice!

It is said that the Shuberts do not expect more than three out of forty plays to succeed. The success of a play, in the artistic sense, is not their business. To maintain enough plays on the road to keep alive their real estate investments is really the thing.

Thus it is now not strange where theatrical slang comes from. An actor who wins success is said to have "delivered the goods." An approved actress is "all wool and a yard wide." An author "puts it over" his audience. A girl of no particular class is a "skirt." A young chorus girl is a "broiler" or a "chicken." An actress who plays the part of an adventuress is a "vamp." A very successful play is a "knockout." Taken all together, it is "the show business." This is the effect of Jewish control of any profession—as any American lawyer will tell you.

The only protest now being offered is by the small dramatic clubs which, whether or not they know it, are the strongest "anti-Semitic" influence on the theatrical horizon.

Issue of January 22, 1921.

XXXI.

The Jewish Aspect of the "Movie" Problem

T here was once a man named Anthony Comstock, who was the enemy of public lewdness. No newspaper ever spoke of him without a jeer. He became the stock joke of the time—and it was not very long ago. He died in 1915. It is very noticeable that the men who mocked his life with banal jesting were non-Jews. It is also worth recording that the men who profited from the commercializing of much of the vice he fought, were Jews. It was a very familiar triangle—the morally indignant non-Jews fighting against public lechery, and the Jewish instigators of it hiding behind ribald Gentiles and Gentile newspapers.

Well, the fight is still going on. If you will subscribe to a clipping bureau, or if you will look over the press of the country, you will see the problem of the immoral show has been neither settled nor silenced. In every part of the country it is intensely alive just now. In almost every state there are movie censorship bills pending, with the old "wet" and gambling elements against them, and the awakened part of the decent population in favor of them; always, the Jewish producing films constituting silent pressure behind the opposition.

This is a grave fact. Standing alone this would seem to charge a certain Jewish element with intentional gross immorality. But this hardly states the condition. There are two standards in the United States, one ruling very largely in the production of plays, the other reigning, when it does reign, in the general public. One is an Oriental idea—"If you can't go as far as you like, go as far as you can." It gravitates naturally to the flesh and its exposure, its natural psychic habitat is among the more sensual emotions.

This Oriental view is essentially different from the Anglo-Saxon, the American view. And it knows this. Thus is the opposition to censorship accounted for. It is not that the producers of Semitic origin have deliberately set out to be bad according to their own standards, but they know their taste and temper are different from the prevailing standards of the American people; and if censorship were established, there would be a danger of American standards being officially recognized, and that is what they would prevent. Many of these producers don't know how filthy their stuff is—it is so natural to them.

Scarcely an American home has not voiced its complaint against the movies. Perhaps no single method of entertainment has ever received such wide-spread and unanimous criticism as the movies, for the reason that everywhere their lure and their lasciviousness have been felt. There *are* good pictures, of course; it were a pity if that much could not be said; we cling to that statement as if it might prove a ladder to lift us above the cesspool which the most popular form of public entertainment has become.

The case has been stated so often that repetition is needless. Responsible men and organizations have made their protests, without results. The moral appeal meets no response in those to whom it is made, because they are able to understand only appeals that touch their material interests. As the matter now stands, the American Public is as helpless against the films as it is against any other exaggerated expression of Jewish power. And the American Public will continue helpless until it receives such an impression of its helplessness as to shock it into protective action.

In a powerful indictment of the movie tendency and the National Board of Review of Motion Pictures, Frederick Boyd Stevenson writes in the Brooklyn Eagle:

"On the other hand the reels are reeking with filth. They are slimy with sex plays. They are overlapping one another with crime.

"From bad to worse these conditions have been growing. The plea is set up that the motion picture industry is the fourth or fifth in the United States, and we must be careful not to disrupt it. A decent photoplay, it is argued, brings gross returns of, say, $100,000, while a successful sex play brings from $250,000 to $2,500,000."

Dr. James Empringham was recently quoted in the New York World as saying; "I attended a meeting of motion picture owners in New York, and I was the only Christian present. The remainder of the company consisted of 500 un-Christian Jews."

Now, there is little wisdom in discoursing against evil in the movies and deliberately closing our eyes to the forces behind the evil.

The method of reform must change. In earlier years, when the United States presented a more general Aryan complexion of mind and conscience, it was only necessary to expose the evil to cure it. The evils we suffered from were lapses, they were the fruits of moral inertia or drifting; the sharp word of recall stiffened the moral fiber of the guilty parties and cleared up the untoward condition. That is, evil doers of our own general racial type could be shamed into decency, or at least respectability.

That method is no longer possible. The basic conscience is no longer present to touch. The men now mostly concerned with the production of scenic and dramatic filth are not to be reached that way. They do not believe, in the first place, that it is filth. They cannot understand, in the second place, that they are really pandering to and increasing human depravity. When there does reach their mentalities the force of protest, it strikes them as being very funny; they cannot understand it; they explain it as due to morbidity, jealousy or—as we hear now—anti-Semitism.

Reader, beware! if you so much as resent the filth of the mass of the movies, you will fall under the judgment of anti-Semitism. The movies are of Jewish production. If you fight filth, the fight carries you straight into the Jewish camp because the majority of the producers are there. And then you are "attacking the Jews."

If the Jews would throw out of their camp the men and methods that so continuously bring shame upon the Jewish name, this fight for decency could be conducted without so much racial reference.

An analysis of the motion picture industry in the United States will show:

That 90 per cent of the production of pictures is in the hands of 10 large concerns located in New York City and Los Angeles.

That each of these has under it a number of complete units, making up the large aggregate of companies seen in photoplays all over the world.

That these parent concerns control the market.

That 85 per cent of these parent concerns are in the hands of Jews.

That they constitute an invincible centralized organization which distributes its products to tens of thousands of exhibitors, the majority of whom are Jews of an inferior type.

That the independent motion pictures have no distributing center but sell in the open market.

It may come as a surprise to many people that there is no dearth of good pictures. The trouble is that there is no means by which good pictures can reach the public. One of the notable libraries of beautiful pictures, containing the cream of dramatic and educational films, has been rendered absolutely useless because of the impossibility of getting them before the public. The owners of these pictures achieved a little advance by engaging Jewish salesmen to push the pictures, but against them has always been the huge and silent force of that concentrated opposition which is apparently against the introduction of decency and delight into the screen world.

Once in a while an independent producer like David Wark Griffith or Charles Ray gives the world a screen production that is not only without offense or propaganda, but is a veritable delight and joy. These pictures, with their attendant success, are the strongest answers that can be made to the cry of some producers that the only profitable plays are the nasty ones.

That cry, of course, is based on fact. Without doubt, as things now go, the nasty pictures are the more profitable, because they are the most elaborately made and the most gorgeously advertised. The very lewdest of them have secured their patronage by advertising that they deal with "moral problems."

But all public taste is cultivated. Every city which can boast of public spirit has citizens who spend tens of thousands of dollars annually in an attempt to create a community taste for good music. They succeed to a certain extent, but very rarely do they make it pay. It appears that the work of demoralizing the public taste is far more profitable. And as our whole range of public entertainment, outside of the higher musical field, has fallen into the hands of groups who do not know what the term "art" means, it is evident how overwhelming the appeal of the dollar must be.

If the public taste is now so fixedly demoralized that the moving picture producers can confidently claim that "the public demands what we are giving it," the case is more damning than otherwise. For it is recognized by all detached observers that such a public taste is a most urgent reason why immediate and heroic remedies should be adopted.

Cocaine peddlers can easily establish a "public demand" for their drugs, and they do. But that demand is never considered to be an extenuation for the peddling of "coke." So with the psychic poison and visual filth of the ordinary movie—the demand it has created is morally lawless, and the further satisfaction of the demand is morally lawless too.

Carl Laemmle, one of the leading producers in America and head of the Universal Film company, testified before a congressional committee that he had sent a circular entitled "What Do You Want?" to the exhibitors who bought his pictures. At that time his company was in communication with about 22,000 exhibitors. Mr. Laemmle says that he expected about 95 per cent of the answers to favor clean, wholesome pictures, but "instead of finding 95 per cent favoring clean pictures, I discovered that at least one-half, or possibly 60 per cent, want pictures to be risqué, the French for smutty."

Laemmle himself is a German-born Jew, and did not state what percentage of the replies were from people of what is euphemistically termed his "faith."

It is a very noticeable fact that whenever any attempt is made to control the tumultuous indecency and triviality which the movies ceaselessly pour out day and night upon the American public, the opposition thereto is Jewish. Take, for example, the attempt to arouse the sober spirit of America to a proper appreciation of what is happening to Sunday, the Day of Rest. The opponents of the whole movement—a movement for the awakening of conscience, not for the passage of laws—are Jews, and they justify their opposition on Jewish grounds.

Whenever the movies are before the bar of public opinion, their defenders as they are, are Jews. In the Congressional hearing before referred to, the lawyers who appeared for the companies were all Jews, distinguished by the names Meyers, Ludvigh, Kolm, Friend and Rosenthal.

There was even a Jewish rabbi involved, who gave a most ingenuous explanation both of Jewish control of the movies and also of Jewish opposition to control of the character of the movies.

"I am a Jew," he said. "You know as well as I do that we have been the unfortunate victims of the nasty, biting tongue, and you know as well as I do that the movie first held us up to ridicule, and we have not only been disgraced in these movies, but we have had our religion traduced, and disgracefully traduced."

If this is true, it is chargeable to the Jews themselves, for Jews have always controlled the business. That it is true is probable, for the most zealous lampooners of the Jews have been Jewish comedians. Non-Jews fail abjectly in endeavoring to portray the character.

"We felt very much hurt," he continued, "and we felt there was a remedy, and that remedy was public opinion; and what did we do? We did not come to Congress. We organized a society--the Independent Order of B'nai B'rith which is the largest Jewish fraternal order in the world. It organized what is called the Anti-Defamation League with headquarters in Chicago; and the league for the defense of the Jewish name united with other people—in the Catholic Church, the Truth Society and Holy Name Society— and it wrote to all the movie manufacturers of the country asking them that they do not traduce the Jewish character and the

Jewish religion, and that they do not hold us up to ridicule; that we did not object to the depiction of Jewish character, but we did object to the caricature of Jewish character and the caricature of our name and religion; and after thus having explained to the manufacturers our position, we appointed a committee of men in every city in the country, asking them that they appeal to the municipal authorities that they permit not the presentation of pictures that were calculated to offend the Jewish character and the Jewish sensitiveness.

"What has been the result? There has been necessary not a protest, because movies in this country are not producing that class of movies any longer."

Of course! there are excellent reasons why the Jewish protests, if any really were necessary, should be instantly obeyed.

But why has not the continued and clamorous protest of decent America been equally heeded? Why not? Because the protest has come largely from non-Jews.

If the Jews can control the movies to the extent the rabbi claimed, why *cannot they control them for decency*—why *do not they control them for decency?*

The one weakness of the rabbi's statement is the charge that the Jewish religion was traduced. It would be most interesting to learn how this was done, and by whom. It is a religion which does not easily lend itself to that sort of treatment, picturesque as some of its forms may appear to alien eyes.

There is, however, a meaning hidden in this statement of the rabbi. The Jew considers any public expression of Christian character as being derogatory to his religion. For example: if the President of the United States or the governor of your state should make a specifically Christian allusion in his Thanksgiving Proclamation, or mention the name of Christ, that act would be protested as offensive to Jewish sensitiveness. Not only would be done, but has been done.

In the same hearing referred to, quotation was made from a letter written by Carl H. Pierce, special representative of the Oliver Morosco Photoplay Company, to the executive secretary of the Motion Picture Board of Trade, in which the following statement appeared:

"You and I have seen boards turn down such plays as the 'Life of the Savior' because they thought it might offend the Hebrews."

It is apparent that "Jewish sensitiveness" is a spoiled child which has been unduly coddled and that it has interfered to such an extent that the real question becomes one of non-Jewish rights.

The Jewish defenders have been asking, Why should a nation of 110,000,000 people be considered in danger from 3,000,000 Jews? and "Gentile fronts," with all the zest of a new idea, have shouted the same challenging question.

It might be advantageous to answer thus: Why should a country of 110,000,000 people, mostly of Christian faith and practice, be prevented from seeing the "Life of the Savior" portrayed on the screen because it is feared to offend the Jews?

The answer in both cases is not a comparison of numbers, but a recognition of the fact that, as in the motion picture world the Jews are at the neck of the bottle where they can absolutely control what goes to the public, so they are in other fields at corresponding places of control.

But whether the Jewish producer is qualified to do better than he is doing is a question. When you consider the conditions from which many of them sprang, you will be rendered rather hopeless of voluntary reform.

Why were not "Way Down East" and "The Shepherd of the Hills" put on the screen by Jews? Because the Jews in control of the movies have no knowledge of American rural life, and therefore no feeling for it. The Jew is a product of city life, and that peculiar phase of city life which is found in the ghetto. He sees in a farmer only a "hick" and a "rube." You may rest entirely assured that it was not the Yankee, himself a product of the farms, who turned the agriculturist into a joke, until today the joke has emptied our farms of men. The theatrical "hick" and "rube" of the gold-brick story and the hayseed play, were of Jewish origin. The Jew is a product of city life, and of that phase of city life where the "wits" play a large part. The America of the average Jew who caters to the entertainment of Americans is comprehended in a beaten path from the box-office, to backstage, and thence to an eating place. He doesn't know America as yet, except as a huge aphis which he may milk.

It follows, therefore, that in all probability he is equally ignorant of American home life. He has not as yet been able to understand what American domesticity means. The American home is an almost unknown quantity to foreigners of the Eastern races. An Armenian woman who has lived in America for five years says that she knows nothing of an American home save what she can see through the windows as she passes. This, of course, is a lack not easily to be bridged over. It may not be strictly true that the majority of movie producers do not know the interiors of American homes, but there is certainly every indication that they have not caught its spirit, and that their misrepresentation of it is more than a false picture, it is also a most dangerous influence.

It is dangerous to foreigners who gain their most impressive ideas of American life from the stage. It is dangerous to Americans who fancy that the life of the screen is the life that is lived by "the better classes." If we could map the community mind of whole sections of our cities, and trace the impressions of American people, American habits and American standards which those mind-groups hold, we should then see the dangerous misrepresentation which movie producers have given to things American. Falsity, artificiality, criminality and jazz are the keynotes of the mass of screen productions.

American life is bare and meager to the Eastern mind. It is not sensuous enough. It is devoid of intrigue. Its women of the homes do not play continuously and hysterically on the sex motif. It is a life made good and durable by interior qualities of faith and quietness—and these, of course, are ennui and death to the Orientally minded.

There lies the whole secret of the movies' moral failure: they are not American and their producers are racially unqualified to reproduce the American atmosphere. An influence which is racially, morally and idealistically foreign to America, has been given the powerful projecting force of the motion picture business, and the consequences are what we see.

The purpose of this and succeeding articles is not to lift hands in horror and point out how rotten the movies are. Everybody is doing that. The case against the movies is not contested at all. It is unanimous. Women's clubs, teachers, newspaper editors, police officers, judges of the courts, ministers of religion, physician, mothers and fathers—everybody knows just what the movies are.

What all these disgusted groups evidently do not know is this: their protests will be entirely useless until they realize that behind the movies there is another group of definite moral and racial complexion to whom the protest of non-Jews amounts to next to nothing at all, if they can possibly circumvent it.

As the rabbi previously quoted showed, the Jews got what they wanted from the producers as soon as they made their request.

What have the non-Jewish teachers, women's clubs, newspaper editors, police officers and judges, ministers of religion, physicians, and just plain parents of the rising generation—what have *they* obtained for all their complaints and protests?

Nothing!

And they can go on beating the air for a lifetime and still obtain no improvement, unless they face the unpleasant racial fact that the movies are Jewish. It is not a question of morals—that question has been settled; it is a question of management.

When the people know who and what is this intangible influence we call the "movies," the problem may not appear so baffling.

Issue of February 12, 1921.

XXXII.

Jewish Supremacy in the Motion Picture World

A LITTLE "Who's Who in the Motion Picture Industry" would make a valuable department in the movie theater's printed programs, but it is not pleasant to think of what would happen to the manager who should print one. There is a strange confusion in the Jewish mind, a struggle between a desire to remain unidentified and a desire to be known. Sometimes they measure friendship by the depth of the silence about their being Jews; sometimes by the amount of open laudation. To say a man is a Jew is sometimes to be vilified as an "anti-Semite," and sometimes to be honored as a "a friend of our nation."

In what is said now, the only purpose is to inform "movie fans" of the source of the entertainment which they crave and the destination of the millions of dollars which they spend. When you see millions of people crowding through the doors of the movie houses at all hours of the day and night, literally an unending line of human beings in every habitable corner of the land, it is worth knowing who draws them there, who acts upon their minds while they quiescently wait in the darkened theater, and who really controls this massive bulk of human force and ideas generated and directed by the suggestions of the screen.

Who stands at the apex of this mountain of control? It is stated in the sentence: The motion picture influence of the United States—and Canada—is exclusively under the control, moral and financial, of the Jewish manipulators of the public mind.

Jews did not invent the art of motion photography; they have contributed next to nothing to its mechanical or technical improvement; they have not produced any of the great artists, either writers or actors, which have furnished the screen with its material. Motion photography, like most other useful things in the world, is of non-Jewish origin. But by the singular destiny which has made the Jews the great cream-skimmers of the world, the benefit of it has gone not to the originators, but to the usurpers, the exploiters.

Who is who in the motion picture world? The names of the leading producing companies are widely known: The Famous Players; Selznick; Selwyn; Goldwyn; Fox Film Company; The Jesse L. Lasky Feature Play Company; United Artists' Corporation; The Universal Film Company; The Metro; Vitagraph; Seligs; Thomas H. Ince Studios; Artcraft; Paramount, and so on.

The Famous Players is headed by Adolph Zukor. Mr. Zukor is a Hungarian Jew. He was a fur dealer in Hester Street, and is said to have gone from house to house selling his goods. With his first savings he went into the "nickel" theater business with Marcus Loew. He is still in his forties and immensely wealthy. He is conceded to be the leader of the fifth largest industry in the world—an industry which is really the greatest educational and propagandist device ever discovered.

The reader will not be deceived by the use of the word "educational" in this connection. Movies are educational, but so are schools of crime. It is just because the movies are educational in a menacing way that they come in for scrutiny.

Zukor's control extends over such well-known names as Famous Players-Lasky Corporation, The Oliver Morosco Photoplay Company, Paramount Pictures Corporation, Artcraft Pictures, all of which have been absorbed within the past five years.

It is commonly supposed that the United Artists' Corporation is a non-Jewish concern, but according to an article in the American Hebrew, the head of this photoplay aggregation is Hiram Abrams. The United Artists' Corporation was formed several years ago by the Big Four among the actors—Mary Pickford, Douglas Fairbanks, Charlie Chaplin and David Wark Griffin, and notwithstanding the fact that Charlie Chaplin is a Jew, the company was regarded by the public as being non-Jewish. Hiram

Abrams is a former Portland, Oregon, newsboy, and graduated from that wholesome occupation into the position of manager of a "penny arcade." He was one of the founders of the Paramount Pictures Corporation, and became its president.

The Fox Film Corporation and the Fox circuit of theaters are under control of another Hungarian Jew who is known to the American public as William Fox. His original name is said to have been Fuchs. He also began his artistic and managerial career by running a "penny arcade." The penny arcade of 15 and 20 years ago, as most city-bred men will remember, was a "peep show" whose lure was lithographed lewdness but which never yielded quite as much pornography as it promised.

Fifteen years ago William Fox was in the clothes sponging business. He also is still in his early forties, is immensely wealthy, and one of the men who can pretty nearly determine what millions of movie fans shall think about certain fundamental things, what ideas and visions they shall entertain.

Marcus Loew also reached fame via the penny arcade and cheap variety vaudeville routes. He went into pictures and is now said to be the active head of 68 companies in various parts of the world. He is in the neighborhood of 50 years old. Loew controls the Metro Pictures Corporation.

The names of Marcus Loew and Adolph Zukor are closely linked in the history of the movies. Both were in the fur business, and both were partners in the first penny arcade venture. Zukor went the way of pictures exclusively, although he later made investments in Loew's enterprises, but Loew went into variety and vaudeville of the type which is now to be found in the less desirable burlesque houses. From this he developed great entertainment enterprises which have made him a name and a fortune. The theaters he personally controls now number 105.

At the head of the Goldwyn Film Corporation is Samuel Goldwyn who is described as having been engaged "along mercantile lines" until motion pictures won his attention. In company with Jesse Lasky and Cecil DeMille he organized a $20,000 corporation in 1912. In 1916 he had prospered so greatly that he organized a $20,000,000 corporation with the

Shuberts, A. H. Woods and the Selwyns, the purpose of this latter company being to screen the works of prominent non-Jewish writers—a matter of which more will be said presently.

The Universal Film Company, known everywhere through the name of Universal City, its studio headquarters, is under the control of Carl Laemmle. It would seem, from a reading of Who's Who, that Laemmle was his mother's name. His father's name is given as Julius Baruch. He is a Jew of German birth. He was manager of the Continental Clothing Company of Oshkosh until 1906, in which year he branched out into pictures, taking his first stand in a small Chicago motion picture theater. Laemmle conceived the idea of fighting the "trust." He bought an enormous tract of land near Los Angeles and built Universal City as the headquarters of his production work.

The Select Pictures Corporation is headed by Lewis Selznick, who is also head of Selznick Pictures, Incorporated. He was at one time vice-president of the World Film Corporation. With him are associated a number of members of his race.

This is but to name a few. These are the official heads. Penetrate down through the entire organizations, until you come to the last exhibition of the cracked and faded film in some cut-price theater in an obscure part of a great city, and you will find that the picture business, on its commercial side, is Jewish through and through.

In the above notes, reference has been made to the occupations out of which the present arbiters of photo-dramatic art have come to their present eminence. They are former news-boys, peddlers, clerks, variety hall managers and ghetto products. It is not urged against any successful business man that he formerly sold newspapers on the streets, or peddled goods from door to door, or stood in front of a clothing store hailing passers-by to inspect his stock. That is not the point at all. The point is here: men who come from such employments, with no gradations between, with nothing but a commercial vision of "the show business," can hardly be expected to understand, or, if they understand, to be sympathetic with a view of the picture drama which includes both art and morality.

Mr. Laemmle, it will be remembered from a former article, said of his company, "The Universal does not pose as a guardian of public morals or of public taste." This is probably the attitude of other producers, too. But though they avoid any responsibility for taste or morals, they consistently fight all attempts of the state to set up a public guardianship in those regions. A business that frankly brutalizes taste and demoralizes morals should not be permitted to be a law unto itself.

It is very difficult to see how the Jewish leaders of the United States can evade the point that Motion Pictures are Jewish. And with this being true, there is the question of responsibility upon which they cannot very well be either impersonal or silent.

The moral side of the movies' influence need not be discussed here because it is being discussed everywhere else. Everybody who has an active moral sense is convinced as to what is being done and as to what ought to be done.

But the propaganda side of the movies does not so directly declare itself to the public. That the movies are recognized as a tremendous propagandist institution is proved by the eagerness of all sorts of causes to enlist them. It is also proved by the recent threat of a New York "Gentile front," that the movies themselves could prevent any progress being made in the attempt to save Sunday to the American people.

But who is the propagandist? Not the individual motion picture exhibitor on your street. He doesn't make the films. He buys his stuff as your grocer buys his canned goods—and has a far narrower margin of choice. He has hardly any choice in the kind of pictures he shall show. In order to get any good pictures that may be distributed, he must take all of the other kind that may be distributed. He is the "market" of the film producers and he must take the good with the bad, or be cut off from getting any.

As a matter of fact, with the "movie bug" so rampant in the country, it is next to impossible to supply enough good pictures for the stimulated and artificial demand. Some people's appetite calls for two or more pictures a day. If working people, they see a show at noon, and several at night. If shallow-pated wives, they see several in the afternoon and several at night. With all the brains and the skill of the country engaged on the task it would be impossible to supply a fresh drama of quality, hot out of the studios every hour, like bread.

Where the Jewish controllers have overstepped themselves is here: they have overstimulated a demand which they are not able to supply, except with such material as is bound to destroy the demand. Nothing is more dangerous to the motion picture business than the exaggerated appetite for them, and this appetite is whetted and encouraged until it becomes a mania.

Like the saloon business, the movie business is killing itself by killing that quality in its customers on which it was built.

Now, as to propaganda, there is evidence that the Jewish promoters have not overlooked that end of it. This propaganda as at present observed may be described under the following heads:

It consists in silence about the Jew as an ordinary human being. Jews are not shown upon the stage except in unusually favorable situations. Among the scenes offered the public you never see Hester Street of lower Fifth Avenue at noontime. Recall if you have ever seen a large Jewish group scene on general exhibition. After a terrible fire in a clothing factory, the mayor of New York asked a certain motion picture company to prepare a film to be entitled, "The Locked Door," to show how buildings are turned into firetraps by ignorance and greed. The scenario was written by a fire official who knew the circumstances of many holocausts. As most of the fire victims had been sweatshop girls, the scenario included a sweatshop. The picture was made as true to life as possible, so the head of the sweatshop was depicted as a Hebrew. The gentleman who told this incident to a committee of Congress said: "It was no discredit to the Hebrew race. We all know they have been the fathers of the clothing industry; in fact, they made the first clothes." But all the same, the picture was declared taboo by Jewish leaders. It broke the cardinal rule of silence about the Jew except when he can be depicted under exceptionally favorable circumstances.

This ill-concealed propaganda of the Jewish movie picture control is also directed against non-Jewish religions. You never saw a Jewish rabbi depicted on the screen in any but a most honorable attitude. He is clothed with all the dignity of his office and he is made as impressive as can be. Christian clergymen, as any movie fan will readily recall, were subjected to all sorts of misrepresentation, from the comic to the criminal. Now, this attitude is distinctly Jewish. Like many unlabled influences in our life, whose sources lead back to Jewish groups, the object is to break down as far as possible all respectful or considerate thought about the clergy.

The Catholic clergy very soon made themselves felt in opposition to this abuse of their priestly dignity. You never see a priest made light of on the screen. But the Protestant clergyman is still the elongated, sniveling, bilious hypocrite of anti-Christian caricature. More and more the "free love" clergyman is appearing on the screen. He is made to justify his deeds by appeals to "broad" principles—which really kills two birds with one stone: it degrades the representative of religion in the eyes of the audience, and at the same time it insidiously inoculates the audience with the same dangerous ideas.

In the February *Pictorial Review*, Benjamin B. Hampton, a successful picture producer, throws a sidelight on this. He quotes a poster outside a movie show. The text says:

" 'I refuse to live with you any longer. I denounce you as my wife–I will go to HER–my free-lover.' Thus speaks the Rev. Frank Gordon in the greatest of all Free-Love dramas."

You may not depict a Hebrew as owner of a sweat shop—though all sweatshop owners are Hebrews; but you may make a Christian clergyman everything from a seducer to a safe-cracker and get away with it.

There may be no connection whatever, but beholding what is done, and remembering what is written in the Protocols, a question arises. It is written:

"We have misled, stupefied and demoralized the youth of the Gentiles by means of education in principles and theories, patently false to us, but which we have inspired."—Protocol 9.

"We have taken good care long ago to discredit the Gentile clergy."—Protocol 17.

"It is for this reason that we must undermine faith, eradicate from the minds of the Gentiles the very principles of God and Soul, and replace these conceptions by mathematical calculations and material desires."—Protocol 4.

Two possible views are open to choice: one, that this constant caricature of representatives of religion is simply the natural expression of a worldly state of mind; the other, that it is part of a traditional campaign of subversion. The former is the natural view among uninformed people. It would be the preferable view, if peace of mind were the object sought. But there are far too many indications that the second view is justified, to permit of its being cast aside.

The screen, whether consciously or just carelessly, is serving as a rehearsal stage for scenes of anti-social menace. There are no uprisings of revolutions except those that are planned and rehearsed. That is the most modern fruit of the study of history: that revolutions are not spontaneous uprisings, but carefully planned minority actions. Revolution is not natural to the people, and is always a failure. There have been no popular revolutions. Civilization and liberty have been set back by those revolutions which subversive elements have succeeded in starting.

But if you are to have your revolution, you must have a rehearsal. In England, the whole process of sovietizing the country has been set forth on the stage, as in vivid object lessons. In this country they have rehearsals by parades, by starting marches through factories and up to the offices, by importing lecturers who tell just how it was done in Russia, Hungary and elsewhere. But it can be done better in the motion pictures than anywhere else: this is "visual education" such as even the lowest brow can understand, and the lower the better.

Indeed, there is a distinct disadvantage in being "high-brow" in such matters. Normal people shake their heads and pucker their brows and wring their hands and say "we cannot understand it: we simply cannot understand it!" Of course they cannot. But if they understood the low-brow, they would understand it, and very clearly. There are two families in this world, and on one the darkness dwells.

Reformers, of course, heartily agree with this as far as criminal portrayals are concerned. Police protest against the technique of killing a policeman being shown with careful detail on the screen. Business men object to daily object lessons in safe-cracking being given in the pictures. Moralists object to the art of seduction being made the stock motif no matter what the subject. They object because they recognize it as evil schooling which bears bitter fruits in society.

Well, this other kind of education is going on too. There is now nothing connected with violent outbreaks which has not been put into the minds of millions by the agency of the motion picture. It may, of course, be a mere coincidence. But coincidences also are realities.

There are several developments proceeding in screendom which are worthy of notice. One is the increasing use of non-Jewish authors to produce the Jewish propaganda. Without using names, it will be easy for each reader to recall for himself the more popular non-Jewish authors whose books have been screened by the Jewish producers, and who are soon after announced to have a new photoplay in preparation. In several cases these new photoplays have been sheer Jewish propaganda. They are the more effective because they are backed by non-Jewish names famous in the literary world. Just how this state of affairs comes about it is not possible now to say. How much of it is due to the authors' desire to enter the field of pro-Semitic propaganda, and how much of it is due to their reluctance to refuse amiable suggestions from movie magnates who have already paid them liberal sums and are likely to pay them more is a question. It is not difficult to bring oneself to believe that "anti-Semitism" is wrong. Everybody knows it is. It is not difficult to bring oneself to an admiration of Israel. Every writer is happy in idealizing an individual or a nation; it is a pleasure to write about an altogether admirable Jewish hero or heroine. And so the non-Jews are writing Jewish propaganda ere they are aware.

The flaw, of course, is here: in avoiding anti-Semitism, they fall into the snare of pro-Semitism. And one is as inconclusive as the other.

Another development is one which movie fans have doubtless noticed: it is the abolition of the "star" system. Readers of this series will recall that it was this same sort of thing which marked Jewish ascendancy in the control of the legitimate stage. Not long ago the full glare of movie publicity was thrown upon names and personalities—the Marys and Charlies and Lulus and Fatties of screen fame. The name was headlined; the star was featured; it did not matter what the theme of the play was—suffice it that it was "a Chaplin film." or a "Pickford film," or whatever it might be.

The motion picture "industry" has reached its present importance because of the exaltation of the "star." But this has its inconveniences, too. Educate the public to demand a star, and that demand will eventually rule the business. Jewish control will not permit that. The way to break the control which the public may exercise through such a demand, is to eliminate the stars. Then all pictures will be on the same plane.

This is occurring now in filmdom. Some of the stars have taken the hint and have set up their own studios. But steadily the doctrine is preached throughout fandom that "the play's the thing," not the star. You don't see so many star names before the theaters; you see more and more the lurid names of plays. The star is being sidetracked.

There is a triple advantage in this. The bloated salaries of the stars can be eliminated. The public can be deprived of a point on which to focus a demand. Exhibitors can no longer say, "I want this or that," even within the narrow margin they recently had; they will have no choice because there will be no choice; the business will be a standardized "industry."

These, then, are some of the facts of the American motion picture world. They are not all the facts, but each of them is important. Not one can be overlooked by students of the influence of the theater. Many a perplexed observer of everyday affairs will find in these facts a key which explains many things.

Issue of February 19, 1921.

XXXIII.

Rule of the Jewish Kehillah
Grips New York

A RE the Jews organized? Do they consciously pursue a program which on one side is pro-Semitic and on the other anti-Gentile? How can a group so numerically inferior wield so large an influence upon the majority of the world?

These are questions which have been asked and which can be answered. The clan solidarity of the Jew, the ramifications of his organizations, the specific purpose which he has in view, are themes upon which there is any amount of "say so," but very little authoritative statement. It may therefore be useful and informing to study one or two of the more important Jewish organizations in the United States.

There are Jewish lodges, unions and societies whose names are well known to the public, and which seem to be the counterpart of similar groups among the non-Jewish population, but these are not the groups upon which to focus attention. Within and behind them is the central group, the inner government, whose ruling is law and whose act is the official expression of Jewish purpose.

Two organizations, both of which are as notable for their concealment as for their power, are the New York Kehillah and the American Jewish Committee. By concealment is meant the fact that they exist in such important numbers and touch vitally so many points of American life, without their presence being suspected.

If a vote of New York could be taken today it is doubtful if one per cent of the non-Jewish population could say that it had ever heard of the New York Kehillah, yet the Kehillah is the most potent factor in the political life of New York today. It has managed to exist and mold and remold the life of New York, and very few people are the wiser. If the Kehillah is mentioned in the press, it is most vaguely, and the impression is, then there is any impression at all, that it is a Jewish social organization like all the rest.

The Kehillah of New York is of importance to Americans everywhere because of two facts: it not only offers a real and complete instance of a government within a government in the midst of America's largest city, but it also constitutes through its executive committee, through which pro-Jewish and anti-Gentile propaganda is operated and Jewish pressure brought to bear against certain American ideas. That is to say, the Jewish government of New York constitutes the essential part of the Jewish government of the United States.

Both of these societies began at about the same time. The records of the Kehillah state that the immediate occasion of its organization was to make a protest against the statement by General Bingham, then police commissioner of the City of New York, that 50 per cent of the crime of the metropolis was committed by Jews. There had been a government investigation into the "White Slave Traffic," the result of which was a direct set of public opinion into channels uncomplimentary to the Jewish name, and a defensive movement was begun. There is no intention to rake up past scandals, unless it shall become necessary; it is enough to say here that, very soon afterward, General Bingham disappeared from public life, and a national magazine of power and influence which had embarked on a series of articles setting forth the government's findings in the White Slave investigation was forced to discontinue after the printing of the first article. This was in the year 1908. The American Jewish Committee, to whose influence the Kehillah really owes its existence, came into being in 1906.

The word "Kehillah" has the same meaning as "Kahal," which signifies "community," "assembly" or government. It represents the Jewish form of government in the dispersion. That is to say, since destiny has made the Jews wanderers of the earth, they have organized their own government so that it might function regardless of the governments which the so-called "Gentiles" have set up. In the Babylonian captivity, in Eastern Europe today, the Kahal is the power and protectorate to which the faithful Jew looks for government and justice. The Peace Conference established the Kahal in Poland and Rumania. The Kahall itself is establishing its courts in the city of New York. The Kahal issues laws, judges legal cases, issues divorces—the Jews who appeal thereto preferring Jewish justice to the justice of the courts of the land. It is, or course an agreement among themselves to be so governed; just as citizenship in the United States assumes an agreement to be governed by institutions provided for that purpose.

The New York Kehillah is the largest and most powerful union of Jews in the world. The center of Jewish world power has been transferred to that city. That is the meaning of the heavy migration of Jews all over the world toward New York. It is to them what Rome is to the devout Catholic and what Mecca is to the Mohammedan. And by that same token, immigrant Jews are more freely admitted to the United States than they are to Palestine.

The Kehillah is a perfect answer to the statement that the Jews are so divided among themselves as to render a concert of action impossible. That is one of the statements made for Gentile consumption, that the Jews are hopelessly divided among themselves. Hundreds of thousands of Americans have had opportunity during recent weeks to see and hear for themselves that when an anti-Gentile purpose is in view, Jews of all classes make the same threats and the same boasts. They are either going to "get" somebody, or they have "got" somebody.

A recent Jewish writer attempted to raise a laugh about the very idea of the members of the Jewish needle-workers' unions of New York having anything in common with the needle-work bosses. He made his attempt in confidence that the public knew little or nothing about the Kehillah. But the public can find all groups and all interests in that body, for there they meet as Jews. The capitalist and the Bolshevik, the rabbi and the union leader, the strikers and the employers struck against, are all united under the flag of Judah. Touch the conservative capitalist who is a Jew, and the red anarchist who is also a Jew will spring to his defense. It may be that sometimes they love each other less, but altogether they hate the non-Jew more, and that is their common bond.

The Kehillah is an alliance, more offensive than defensive, against the "Gentiles." The majority of the membership of the New York Kehillah is of an extremely radical character, those seething hundreds of thousands who carefully organized on the East Side the government which was to take over the Russian Empire, even choosing in the Jewish Quarter of New York the Jew who was to succeed the Czar—and yet, in spite of this character of membership, it is officered by Jews whose names stand high in government, judiciary, the law and banking.

It is a strange and really magnificent spectacle which the Kehillah presents, of a people of one racial origin, with a vivid belief in itself and its future, disregarding its open differences, to combine privately in a powerful organization for the racial, material and religious advancement of its own race to the exclusion of all others.

The Kehillah has mapped New York just as the American Jewish Committee has mapped the United States. The city of New York is divided into 18 Kehillah districts which comprise a total of 100 Kehillah neighborhoods, in accordance with the population. The Kehillah District Boards administer Kehillah affairs in their respective districts in accordance with the policy and rules laid down by the central governing body.

Practically every Jew in New York belongs to one or more lodges, secret societies, unions, orders, committees or federations. The list is a prodigious one. The purposes interlace and the methods dovetail in such a manner as to bring every phase of New York life not only under the watchful eye, but under the swift and powerful action of experienced compulsion upon public affairs.

At the meeting which organized the Kehillah a number of sentiments were expressed which are worthy of consideration today. Judah L. Magnes, then rabbi of Temple Emanu-El, chairman of the meeting, set forth the plan.

"A central organization like that of the Jewish Community of New York City is necessary to create a Jewish public opinion," he said.

Rabbi Asher was loudly applauded when he said: "American interests are one, Jewish interests are another thing."

The delegates at this meeting represented 222 Jewish societies, as follows: 74 synagogues, 18 charitable societies, 42 mutual benefit societies, 40 lodges, 12 educational societies, 9 communal federations, 9 literary and musical societies, 9 Zionist societies and 9 religious societies.

At a meeting somewhat more than a year later the number of organizations under the jurisdiction of the Kehillah aggregated 688. These included 238 constituent organizations, 133 congregations, 58 lodges, 44 educational and benevolent societies, and 3 federations. These three federations were made up of 450 societies.

The affiliation now numbers more than 1,000 organizations.

The Kehillah has produced a map of New York City on which the varying densities of the Jewish population are represented by varying densities of shade. In order to comprehend the power of the Kehillah, the Jewish population of New York must be considered. Three years ago, according to Jewish figures (there are no others) there were 1,500,000 Jews in the city alone. Since that time the number has considerably increased—even the Government of the United States cannot say how much.

In 1917-18 the Jews resident in the five boroughs of New York City were estimated—again by Jewish officials—as follows:

Manhattan, 696,000; Brooklyn, 568,000; Bronx, 211,000; Queens, 23,000; Richmond, 5,000; making a total of 1,503,000.

The Kehillah districts form distinct and segregated parts of the City's population, and are 18 in number. These 18 in turn comprise 100 neighborhoods, or little ghettos. The districts, with the number of neighborhoods in each, are represented in the following table:

			Neighborhoods
No.	1	North Bronx District	7
No.	2	South Bronx District	7
No.	3	West Side and Harlem District	7
No.	4	East Harlem District	7
No.	5	Yorkville District	5
No.	6	Central Manhattan District	4
No.	7	Tompkins Square District	6
No.	8	Delancey District	8
No.	9	East Broadway District	8
No.	10	Williamsburg District	7
No.	11	Bushwick District	6
No.	12	Central Brooklyn District	6
No.	13	Brownsville District	6
No.	14	East New York District	7
No.	15	Borough Park District	6
No.	16	West Queens District	1
No.	17	East Queens District	1
No.	18	Richmond District	1

Districts such as the Delancey Street and East Broadway sections cover the Great Ghetto of the East Side, while the West Side and Harlem Districts represent the neighborhoods which are the residential goals of the prosperous Jews of New York.

It has been stated that there are districts in which the density of Jewish population is more than 300,000 per square mile, which is more than 2,150 to the usual square city block. There are 19 neighborhoods in which the density is more than 200,000 to the square mile (1,430 to the square block); and 36 neighborhoods in which the density is more than 100,000 to the square mile (715 to the square block).

The average density of the general population for New York City both Jewish and non-Jewish, in 1915, was about 16,000 to the square mile, or 107 to the square block. More than one-third of the Jews, about 38 per cent, that is, 570,000 Jews, live on one per cent of the area of New York. If all New York's population were as dense as is the Jewish population of the congested districts, the City would have almost as many inhabitants as the whole United States, or about 95,000,000.

These figures dimly portray the overcrowding which has resulted from the terrific influx of Russian-Polish Jews of the ghetto type, who have settled in the Metropolis and steadfastly refused to go any farther, resulting in problems which are probably unparalleled in the history of civilization.

Yet it is out of such conditions that the far-reaching power of the Kehillah is derived.

When the aggressive program of the Kehillah to make New York a Jewish city, and through New York the United States a Jewish country, was announced, some of the more conservative Jews of New York were timorous. They did not expect that the American people would stand for it. They thought the American people would immediately understand what was afoot and oppose it. There were others who doubted whether the same Kehillah authority could here be wielded over the Jews as was wielded in the old country ghettos. As an official of the Kehillah wrote:

"There were those who doubted the ultimate success of this new venture in Jewish organization. They based their lack of belief on the fact that no governmental authority could possibly be secured; in other words, that the Kehillah of New York could not hope to wield the same power, based on governmental coercion, as the Kehillahs of the Old World."

There is much in that paragraph to indicate the status of the Kehillah in Jewish life. Add to this the fact that the vast majority of adult Jews in New York lived under the Kehillahs of the Old World, whose power was based on coercion, and you have an interesting situation.

What the doubt consisted in, however, is not as stated there. No doubt existed as to what it would be possible to do with the Jews. The entire doubt consisted in how far the Americans would let the thing go on. The program of the Kehillah was ostensibly "to assert Jewish rights." No Jewish rights have ever been interfered with in America. The expression is a euphemism for a campaign to interfere with non-Jewish rights.

Just how the free exercise of American rights by an American may be construed and is construed by the Jew to be an interference with his rights, will be shown in a separate article.

The doubters felt that when the Jews began to make such demands as that Christmas carols should be suppressed in the schools, as "offensive to the Jews"; and that Christmas trees should be banished from police stations in poor neighborhoods as "offensive to the Jews"; and that the Easter holidays should be abolished, as "offensive to the Jews";—the business class of Jews felt that the American would not stand for it.

The American has never interfered with any man's religious observances; would he stand to have his own prohibited in his own institutions and in his own country?

However, the Jews' misgivings were not justified. The Americans made no protest. The Kehillah went ahead with its campaign, and the native population submitted. New York is Jewish. It is actually an offense, an offense speedily though unofficially punished, to intimate in any public way that New York may possibly be other than Jewish. New York is the answer to those who ask, "How can a numerically inferior group dictate the terms of life for all the rest?" Go into a New York school, and see. Go into a New York newspaper office, and see. Stand anywhere in New York, and see.

But with it all one gets a sense of the insecurity of this usurpation of power. It doesn't belong to those who have seized it; it doesn't belong either by right of numbers, or by right of superior ability, or yet by right of a better use made of the power thus taken. They have taken it by audacity; they have taken it in such a way as to make resentment of it seem like an anti-racial movement—and that is why they have held it as long as they have.

That is the only way to explain the meekness of the American in this matter, and it also accounts for the sense of insecurity which even the Jews feel in the position they hold. The American is the slowest person in the world to act on any line that savors of racial or religious prejudice. Even when his justifiable act is taken without the slightest prejudice, he is extremely sensitive even to the charge that he is prejudiced. This makes for a seeming aloofness from matters like the Jewish Question. This also leads men to sign protests against "anti-Semitism" which are really designed to be protests against the publication of Jewish facts.

But it would be a serious mistake to believe that the Americans have accepted within their minds the fact of Jewish supremacy in any field, for they have not. And the Jews know that they have not. Present Jewish importance in American affairs threatens to become as precarious as Bolshevik rule in Russia; it may fall at any time. The Jews have overplayed their hand. They have threatened too wildly and boasted too loudly. The very weight of the importance of the Kehillah and the American Jewish Committee is to be one of the factors in the fall. The Jews may live among us, but they may not live upon us.

These things are better known to the Jew than to the non-Jew, for the Jew knows the Jewish Question better than anyone else, and he knows better than any Gentile when a statement hits the bull's-eye of the truth. The American Jews are not now protesting against lies; they are roused to protest by the power of the truth, and they are the best judges of the truth with reference to themselves.

The situation is not one that calls for expulsion, or resistance, but simply exposure to the light—for to vanquish darkness, what is better than light?

The Jews had a great opportunity in the New York Kehillah. They had an opportunity to say to the world, "This is what the Jew can do for a city when he is given freedom to work." They have the city government, the police department, the health department, the school board, the newspapers, the judiciary, financiers—every element of power.

And what have they to show for all this? The answer is,—New York.

New York is an object lesson set in the sight of the whole world, as to what the Jew can do and will do when he exalts himself to the seat of rule. It is inconceivable that even the Jewish spokesmen will defend Jewish New York.

Lest the New York Kehillah—in view of statements yet to be made concerning it—should be disregarded, or its importance minimized, by the feeling that, after all, it only represents the more radical elements, "the apostate Jews" which seems to be a

145

recent favorite designation for them, a partial view is here given of its leaders.

Present at the 1918 convention were Jacob H. Schiff, banker; Louis Marshall, lawyer, president of the American Jewish Committee and frequent visitor to Washington; Otto A. Rosalsky, judge of the General Sessions, who has taken part in several affairs of interest both to Jews and Gentiles; Adolph S. Ochs, proprietor of the New York *Times*; Otto H. Kahn, of the banking house of Kuhn, Loeb & Company—AND—Benjamin Schlesinger, who is lately returned from Moscow where he had a conference with Lenin; Joseph Schlossberg, general secretary of the Amalgamated Clothing Workers of America, with 177,000 members; Max Pine, also recently a consultant with the Bolshevik rulers of Russia; David Pinski; Joseph Barondess, labor leader.

The high and the low are here; Judge Mack, who headed the War Risk Insurance Bureau of the United States Government, and the little leader of the reddest group in the East End—they all meet in the Kehillah, as Jews.

As to the Kehillah being officially representative, it may be added that the Kehillah has in it representatives of the Central Conference of American rabbis, Eastern Council of Reform rabbis, Independent Order of B'nai B'rith, Independent Order of B'rith Sholom, Independent Order Free Sons of Israel, Independent Order B'rith Abraham, Federation of American Zionists—orthodox Jews, reform Jews, "apostate Jews," Zionist Jews, Americanized Jews, rich Jews, poor Jews, law-abiding Jews and red revolutionary Jews—Adolph Ochs of the great New York *Times*, together with the most feverish scribbler on a Yiddish weekly that calls for blood and violence—Jacob Schiff who was a devoutly religious Jew of strong faith and obedience, and Otto H. Kahn, of the same banking house, who professes another religion—all of them, of all classes, bound together in that solidarity which has been achieved by no other people so perfectly as by Judah.

And these are banded together for the purpose of "protecting Jewish rights." From what? If Americans were not large in their liberal-mindedness the very statement of purpose would be an offense. Who in this country is interfering with anyone's rights?

The American wants to know, for that is the kind of thing he wants to put down, and always has put down, and will put down again wherever or from whatever quarter it arises. Therefore it will occur to him sooner or later to demand particulars of these rights that need protection, and from what they need to be protected.

What rights have Americans that Jews in America do not possess? Against whom are the Jews organized, and against what?

What basis is there for the cry of "persecution"? None whatever, except the Jews' own consciousness that the course they are pursuing is due for a check. The Jews always know that. They are not in the stream of the world, and every little while the world finds out what Judah always knows.

Rabbi Elias L. Solomon has been quoted as saying:

"There is no thinking Jew outside of America whose eyes are not turned toward this country. The freedom enjoyed by the Jews in America is not the outcome of emancipation purchased at the cost of national suicide, but the natural product of American civilization.

Of course. Then where is the "protection" needed? What are the "rights" which the Kehillahs of this country are organized to "defend"? What are the meanings of these committees in every city and town of the land, spying upon American activities and bringing protests to bear to keep those activities within well-defined channels acceptable to the Jews?

These questions have never been answered by the Jewish spokesmen. Let them prepare a Bill of Rights, as they conceive their rights to be. Let them name every right they desire and claim. They have never done so. Why? Because the rights they dare name in public are such as they already possess in abundance, and further, because the rights that in their hearts they most desire are such that they cannot state to the American public.

A Jewish Bill of Rights, such as could be published, would be met by the American people thus: "Why, you have all these things already. What more do you want?" And that is the question which lies at the core of the entire Jewish Problem—What more do they want?

A further penetration of Kehillah activities may help to answer that question.

_____

Issue of February 26, 1921

XXXIV.

The Jewish Demand for "Rights" in America

D URING the twelve years of its existence the New York Kehillah has grown in power and influence until today it includes practically the entire Jewish population in its operations. Among its direct of affiliated leaders and supporters are the owners of powerful newspapers, officials in the state, Federal and city administration; influential officeholders on public boards, such as the department of health, the board of education and the police department; members of the judiciary; financiers and heads of banking houses, mercantile and manufacturing establishments, many of which exert a controlling influence in certain industries and financial combinations.

But the New York Kehillah is more than a local organization. It is the pattern and parent Jewish community in the United States, the visible entourage of the Jewish government, the dynamo which motivates those "protests" and "mass meetings" which are frequently heralded throughout the country, and the arsenal of that kind of dark power which the Jewish leaders know so well how to use. Incidentally it is also the "whispering gallery," where the famous whispering drives are originated and set in motion and made to break in lying publicity over the country.

The people of the United States have a deeper interest than they realize in the New York Kehillah.

The liaison between this center of Jewish power and the affairs of the people of the United States is made by the American Jewish Committee. The Committee and the Kehillah are practically identical as far as the national Jewish program is concerned. It may be added that through their foreign associations they are also identical as far as the world program is concerned.

The United States is divided into 12 parts by the American Jewish Committee. The remark that this division is after the Twelve Tribes of Israel may be disregarded. Suffice it to say that every state belongs to a district, and that District No. XII includes New York, and that the District Committee of District No. XII is chosen by the New York Kehillah, and is by weight of wealth, authority and continuous effort in behalf of Judah justly recognized as the center of Jewish power in America, and it may be in the world also. This committee, some of the names of whose members are impressive, represents the focusing point of the religious, racial, financial and political will of Jewry. This committee, it should be remembered, is also the executive committee of the New York Kehillah. New York Jewry is the dynamo of the national Jewish machinery. Its national instrument is the American Jewish Committee.

There are certain announced purposes of these associations, and there are certain purposes which are not announced. The announced purposes may be read in printed pages; the purposes not announced may be read in the records of attempted acts and achieved results. To keep the record straight let us look first at the announced purposes of the American Jewish Committee, then of the Kehillah; next at the line which binds the two together; and then at the real purposes as they are to be construed from a long list of attempts and achievements.

The American Jewish Committee, organized in 1906, announced itself as incorporated for the following purposes:

1. To prevent the infraction of the civil and religious rights of the Jews in any part of the world.

2. To render all lawful assistance and to take appropriate remedial action in event of threatened or actual invasion or restriction of such rights, or of unfavorable discrimination with respect thereto.

3. To secure for the Jews equality of economic, social and educational opportunities.

4. To alleviate the consequences of persecution wherever they may occur, and to afford relief from calamities affecting Jews.

It will thus be seen to be an exclusively Jewish program. There is nothing reprehensible about it. If it meant only what it said, and was observed only as to its ostensible purpose, it would be not only unobjectionable but commendable.

The charter of the Kehillah empowers it, among other things, to establish an educational bureau, to adjust differences between Jewish residents or organizations by arbitration or by means of boards of mediation or conciliation; while the Constitution announces the purpose to be:

"to further the cause of Judaism in New York City and to represent the Jews in this city with respect to all local matters of Jewish interest."

Where the American Committee and the Kehillah join forces is shown as follows:

"Furthermore, inasmuch as the American Jewish Committee was a national organization, the Jewish community (Kehillah), of New York City, if combined with it, would have a voice in shaping the policy of Jewry *throughout the land.*

1. It is expressly understood that the American Jewish Committee shall have exclusive jurisdiction over all *questions of a national or international character* affecting the Jews generally.

2. The membership of the American Jewish Committee is to be increased, so that the Twelfth District shall have allotted to it 25 members.

3. These 25 members are to be elected by the Jewish Community (Kehillah), of New York City.

4. These 25 men shall at the same time constitute the Executive Committee of the Community (Kehillah).

It will be seen, therefore, that the Kehillah and the principal body of the American Jewish Committee are one. The capital of the United States, in Jewish affairs, is New York. Perhaps that may throw a side-light on the desperate efforts which are being continually made to exalt New York as the spring and source of all the thoughts worth while today. New York, the Jewish capital of the United States, has also been sought to be made the financial center, the art center, the political center of the country. But its art is Aphrodite, Mecca and Afgar; its politics are those of a Judaized Tammany. Tell it not to the American Jewish Committee, nor yet to the Kehillah, but let all Americans know that most of the United States lies west of New York. The country has come to view that strip of eastern coast as a miasmatic place whence rises the fetid drivel of all that is subversive in public thought. It is the home of anti-American propaganda, of pro-Jewish hysteria, a mad confusion of mind that passes in some quarters as a picture of America. But America is west of the "metropolis"; New York is an unassimilated province on the outskirts of the nation.

As nine-tenths of all the Jews in the United States live in allegiance to organizations which look to the American Jewish Committee as their overlord, the influence of the New York Kehillah on the nation is not hard to measure. In every town, large and small, even where the Jewish community consists of a few, 30 or 75 souls, there is a leading Jew, be he rabbi, merchant or public officeholder, who is in constant touch with headquarters. What is done in New Orleans or Los Angeles or Kansas City is known in New York with surprising dispatch.

Incidentally, it would interest some clergymen to know that their names are listed among those who can be depended on to play the Jewish hand whenever required.

Now, the public statement of purpose on the part of these Jewish bodies has just been shown. It is seen that the protection of Jewish rights is the ostensible program—against which no one can say a word. Perhaps the term "Jewish rights" is unfortunately chosen. If Jewish rights coincide with American rights, then more than the Jews are protecting them—the whole American nation is engaged in that work.

But it is not true that "Jewish rights" are the same as "American rights." Unfortunately the Jews have adopted an attitude which could only have sprung from the belief that it is a "Jewish right" to Judaize the United States. This is one of the dangerous doctrines being preached today, and most assiduously by Jews and those who have been influenced by Jewish thought, namely, that the United States is not any definite thing as yet, but that it is yet to be made, and it is still the prey of whatever power can seize it and mold it to its liking. It is a favorite Jewish view that the United States is a great unshapen mass of potentiality, of no particular character which is yet to be given its definite form. It is in the light of this view that the Jewish activity must be interpreted.

That doctrine with which so large a mass of Americans are inoculated is making havoc with the whole Americanization program today. It is "broadening" America out of all semblance to its distinctive self and blurring those determining ideals and ideas on which American institutions are based. The attempt, first to give the people to understand that the United States is "nothing particular" as yet, and second to make it something different spiritually from what it has always been, is peculiarly agreeable to the philosophy which sways the internationally-minded Hebrew. We are not making Americans; we are permitting foreigners to be educated in the theory that America is a free-for-all, the prize of whatever fantastic foreign political theory may seize it.

There you have the secret of the great refusal of the foreign population to change themselves into conformity with America; why should they, when they are taught that America may be changed into conformity with them?

It is time to limit our "broad-mindedness" until it will fit within the limits of the Constitution and the traditions which made America what it is—the desired haven, even in preference to Palestine, of the Jews and every other race.

So, then, what is this conception of "Jewish rights" which the Kehillah and the American Jewish Committee are organized to defend? It is only by deductions from the acts of these bodies that the answer can be formulated.

In the Jewish records for the year 5668 (1907-1908) we read:
"Perhaps the most noticeable feature of the year in America has been the demand in certain quarters for *the complete secularization of the public institutions* of the country, *what may be deemed the demand of the Jews* for their full constitutional rights."

Let the reader notice that the only time he finds the religious note struck in this series of studies of International Jewish activity, it is struck by the Jews. Honest non-Jews have been nonplused by the Jewish charge that any scrutiny of Jewish action is "religious persecution," even when religion has never been thought of or mentioned. The explanation is not far to seek. In the above quotation the religious note is struck at once: the "full constitutional rights" of Jews demands that we effect "the complete secularization of the public institutions of the country."

That is worth thinking of. But to continue the quotation:
"Justice Brewer's article asserting that this is a Christian country has been challenged more than once, and the idea was formally combated in papers by Dr. Herbert Friedenwald, of New York, Isaac Hassler, of Philadelphia, and Rabbi Ephraim Frisch, of Little Rock, Arkansas.

"The legal and theoretical argument was supplemented in a practical way by widespread opposition to Bible readings and Christmas carols in public schools, an opposition specifically derided upon by the Central Conference of American Rabbis.

"In New York the agitation against the carols produced a counter-demonstration in their favor, and the matter seems to have been left to the discretion of the individual teacher.

"In Philadelphia, Cincinnati, St. Paul and maybe elsewhere, there were similar movements and counter-movements, and the question may yet return to plague us."

There you have, in officially authorized Jewish statement, what the Jews conceive to be a part of their Jewish rights.

A careful examination of the intensive propaganda conducted by the Kehillah and the American Jewish Committee will not only reveal that the whole United States is considered to be the legitimate field for Jewish interference, but also that a very wide diversity of "rights" is insisted upon by them.

In dozens of states and hundreds of towns and cities this program has been plied, but always with too little publicity to appraise the people what is going on. In any number of cases the Jews win their contentions because of the local pressure they are able to produce, usually by their very forehanded way of selecting and obligating public officials. In other instances they have lost, but every loss they credit to a beginning of their "educational" campaign. A loss enables them to "teach a lesson" to somebody by means of a boycott or a changed attitude on the part of the local bank, or in some other way equally effective in creating "the fear of the Jews."

The Jews have evidently convinced themselves that the Constitution of the United States entitles them to change the character of many of the time-honored practices obtaining here, and if this is true, American citizens should take cognizance of these things and prepare to adjust themselves to further changes. If they do not take kindly to further changes at the behest of Jewry, they owe it to themselves to know what the Jewish program is, that they may meet it with a higher type of weapon than that to which the Jew naturally resorts.

It is intended in this and the following article to indicate, by the actual program, what the real objective of Jewry is in the United States. When you collect and summarize all the demands that have been made by the New York Kehillah alone, you gain an idea of what is afoot. A few of these demands are referred to now, subject to further illustration in another article.

1. *The unrestricted admission of Jewish immigration to this country from any part of the world.*

Heads of Kehillah labor unions in New York demand that the Jews in Europe be exempted from the operation of whatever American immigration law may be passed. The Kehillah is many times on record to this effect. No matter where the Jews may come from—Russia, Poland, Syria, Arabia or Morocco—they are to be let in no matter who may be kept out.

Note: As one pursues the study of "Jewish rights," the quality of "exemption" seems to appear in most of them. Nowhere do the Jews proclaim their separateness as a people more than in their unceasing demands that they be treated differently than any other people and given privileges that no other people would dream of asking.

2. *The official recognition by City, State, and Federal governments of the Jewish Religion.*

The Kehillah in its reports describe its efforts to obtain special recognition of Jewish holidays, in some cases going so far as to demand the continuance of pay to public employes who absent themselves at Yom Kippur, at the same time, opposing the continuance of pay to Catholic public employes who desired to observe the chief Lenten days. This is a peculiarly inconsistent form of the demand for "exemption" which has led to some interesting situations, to be dealt with later.

3. *The suppression of all references to Christ by City, State and Federal authorities, in public documents or at public gatherings.*

Kehillah records show that the Jews of Oklahoma addressed a petition to the convention which formulated the first state constitution, protesting that the acknowledgment of Christ in the instrument would be repugnant to the Constitution of the United States. The record also shows that a Jewish rabbi protested against a governor of Arkansas using "a Christological expression" in his Thanksgiving Day proclamation.

4. *Official recognition of the Jewish Sabbath.*

The educational, cultural, business and industrial life of the United States is regulated with reference to Sunday as the legal day of rest. For over ten years the Kehillah has sought legislative recognition for Saturday. In the absence of official recognition, however, much public business is held up on account of jurors and others refusing to serve on Saturday. Jewish lawyers in the trial of cases are frequently "ill" on Saturdays. There is, of course, no objections to Jews recognizing their own Sabbath. This is their American privilege. But to make their Sabbath the Sabbath of all the people is another question. The Jews' chief objection to the observance of Sunday is that it is "a Christological manifestation."

5. *The right of the Jews in this country to keep open their stores, factories and theatres, and to trade and work on the Christian Sunday.*

The Kehillah, through the Jewish Sabbath Alliance (Rabbi Bernard Drachman, president), is "promoting the observance of the Holy Sabbath in every possible way," through propaganda made to promote Sabbath sentiment, and the distribution of circulars and pamphlets to the Yiddish populations of New York City. Sabbath sentiment is unobjectionable, but it becomes anti-Sunday sentiment. The Sunday laws of the city are, therefore, often broken. Much agitation and ill feeling result. Kehillah records are full of the disagreeable conditions which this demand promotes.

6. *Elimination of Christmas celebrations in public schools and public places, police stations, and so on, public displays of Christmas trees, singing of Christmas carols and Christian hymns.*

Kehillah compelled the Council of University Settlement in New York City to adopt a resolution that in holiday celebrations held annually by the Kindergarten Association, Christmas trees, a Christmas program for celebration and the singing of Christmas songs be eliminated.

Kehillah records show that Jews petitioned the Chicago School Board, demanding that sectarian teachings in public schools and the singing of Christian hymns be discontinued.

Also that at the demand of a Jewish rabbi, three public school principals were compelled to omit all Christmas celebrations and the use of the Christmas tree in public schools.

7. *The removal from office or prosecution of all public persons who criticize the Jewish race, even where such action is in the public interest.*

Judge Otto A. Rosalsky, member of the Kehillah, announces that he will try to put through a bill for the prosecution of all persons who criticize the Jewish race.

Kehillah leaders at public meeting condemn City Magistrate Cornell for criticizing the East Side Yiddish Community because of the increase in criminality of Jewish youth, and demand his impeachment.

Leaders of New York Jewry succeed in having Police Commissioner Bingham removed from office by the Mayor because of his criticism of criminality among Russian-Polish Jews of New York City.

8. *The establishment of Bet Dins, or Jewish courts, in public courthouses.*

The Kehillah has succeeded in the establishment of a Bet Din in the Criminal Courts Building, New York, at which there presides the Rev. Dr. Aaron A. Yudelovitch, Chief Rabbi of the United States.

Kehillah records show that prominent Jews of Jersey City, Paterson, Newark, Bayonne and Hoboken have organized to establish Bet Dins in New Jersey.

9. *The right to eliminate from all schools and colleges all literature that is objected to by Jews.*

Kehillah records show that Jews have prohibited the reading of the "Merchant of Venice" and Lamb's "Tales from Shakespeare" from schools throughout the country, including those in Galveston and El Paso, Texas; Cleveland, Ohio, and Youngstown, Ohio.

At the present time a cleaning of public library shelves is proceeding in a number of cities to prevent the public securing books which public money has bought—the objection to the books being that they discuss Jews as they are. All works in praise of Jews are spared.

10. *Prohibition of the term "Christian" or the use of the phrase "state, religion and nationality" in any public advertisement, as being an invasion of Jewish rights and a discrimination against Jews.*

Louis Marshall, as president of the American Jewish Committee, obtained apologies from Charles M. Schwab, as director of the United States Shipping Board; Benjamin Strong, governor of the Federal Reserve Bank and head of the Liberty Loan Committee; Secretary McAdoo and Secretary of War Baker, because of the use of the term *"Christian"* in help wanted advertisements inserted in newspapers by their subordinates.

The Jews succeeded in obtaining the withdrawal of the Junior Plattsburg Manual, used by students in officers' training camps, because it contained the phrase "the ideal officer is a *Christian* gentleman," which the Jews construed to be an infringement of their rights.

The Kehillah in its report for 1920 stated that several important New York newspapers, having been informed by it that the term *"Christian"* had appeared in the help wanted advertisements of mercantile firms, the owners of the newspapers sent in their apologies, and promised stricter censorship in the future.

The Jews do not consider the use of the term "Jews" in help wanted advertisements as a discrimination against non-Jews, and Jewish mercantile houses continue its use in their advertisements in the New York *Times* and other Jewish-owned dailies.

These are "Jewish rights" as they are indicated by Jewish demands. But they are by no means all; they are merely typical of all the so-called "rights" and all the insistent demands.

To go still further: the Kehillah condemned the use of the term "Americanization," because of the implication that there is no distinction between "Americanization" and "Christianization." "Americanization" is claimed by the Jews to be a mere cloak for proselytizing.

The Kehillah is behind demands on public funds for the support of Jewish educational, charitable, correctional and other institutions. One important point about the great influx of Jewish immigration is that tens of thousands of these people come from lands where Jewish government has been established by order of the Peace Conference, and where public funds support Jewish activities. Their attitude toward America in this respect may therefore be accurately gauged.

It is a common practice in New York for the Jews to force themselves into juries which try Jewish cases. Jewish law students, with which the city swarms, "work their way through college" partly or wholly by jury duty.

Another "Jewish right" is that the Associated Press shall print what the Jews want printed and in exactly the tone the Jews desire. This is perhaps one of the factors in the loss of luster on the part of the Associated Press of late years, the feeling that it is too much under the influence of certain groups, which are not non-Jewish groups. Newspapermen all sense this; A.P. men throughout the country sense it; but they express it in newspaper terms; they say "The A. P. gives a New York coloring to everything." But the ingredients of the New York coloring are 85 per cent Jewish.

From a survey of the demands, these appear to be some of the "Jewish rights" which Kehillah and the American Jewish Committee are organized to secure. And how far they say they have succeeded, we shall next see.

Issue of March 5, 1921

XXXV.

"Jewish Rights" Clash With American Rights

I T IS well that the public should understand that the present study of the Jewish Question in the United States is not based upon religious differences. The religious element does not enter except when it is injected by the Jews themselves. And it is injected in three ways; First, in their allegation that any study of the Jews is "religious persecution"; second, by their own records of what their activities in the United States consist of; third, by the impression which is very misleading if not corrected, that the Jews are the Old Testament people of the Old Testament religion which is so highly regarded in the Christian world. The Jews are not the Old Testament people, and the Old Testament, their Bible, can be found among them only with difficulty. They are a Talmudical people who have preferred the volumes of rabbinical speculation to the words of their ancient Prophets.

The note of religion does not enter this discussion until the Jews place it there. In this series of articles we have set aside every non-Jewish statement on this question, and have accepted only that which proceeds from recognized Jewish sources. It has been more than a surprise, in studying the proceedings of the New York Kehillah and the American Jewish Committee and their affiliated organizations, as represented by their activities throughout the country, to learn how large a part of these activities have a religious bearing, as being directly and combatively anti-Christian.

That is to say, when the Jews set forth in the public charters and constitutions of their organizations that their only purpose is to "protect Jewish rights," and when the public asks what are these "Jewish rights" which need protection in this free country, the answer can be found only in the actions which the Jews take to secure that "protection." The actions interpret the words. And thus interpreted, "Jewish rights" seem to be summed up in the "right" to banish everything from their sight and hearing that even suggests Christianity or its Founder. It is just there, from the Jewish side, that religious intolerance makes its appearance.

What follows in the course of this article is nothing less nor more than a group of citations form Jewish records covering a number of years. It is given here partly as an answer to the charge that this series of articles is "religious persecution," and partly to help interpret by official actions the official Jewish program in the United States.

An important fact is that previous to the formation of the Kehillah and the Jewish Committee, this sort of attack on the rights of Americans was sporadic, but since 1906 it has increased in number and insistence. Heretofore it has gone unheeded by the public as a whole because of our general tolerance in this country, but from this time forth the country will possess information that what it has been tolerating is intolerance itself. Under cover of the ideal of Liberty we have given certain people liberty to attack liberty. We ought at least to know when that is being done.

Look rapidly down the years and see one phase of that attack. It is the attack on Christianity.

That is rather a hard thing to set down in writing in this country, and it would not be set down did not the facts compel it. Jewish writers nowadays show a great deal of anxiety that non-Jews should follow certain Christian doctrines. "We gave you your Savior, and he told you to love your enemies; why don't you love us?" is the implication with which their statements usually come.

However, here are a few items from the record: They are recorded according to the Jewish calendar (our modern calendar is "Christian," and therefore taboo) but here both calendar dates shall be supplied.

5661 (A. D. 1899-1900) The Jews attempt to have the word "Christian" removed from the Bill of rights of the State of Virginia.

5667 (A. D. 1906-1907) The Jews of Oklahoma petition the Constitutional Convention protesting that the acknowledgment of Christ in the new state constitution then being formulated would be repugnant to the Constitution of the United States.

5668 (A.D. 1907-1908) Widespread demand by the Jews during this year for the complete secularization of the public institutions of this country, as a part of the demand of the Jews for their constitutional rights.—Supreme Court Justice Brewer's statement that this is a Christian country widely controverted by Jewish rabbis and publications.

5669 (A.D. 1908-1909) Protests made to governor of Arkansas against "Christological expressions" employed by him in his Thanksgiving Day proclamation, 1908.—Professor Gotthard Deutsch protest against "Christological prayers" at the high school graduating exercises at Cincinnati.

5673 (A.D. 1912-1913) The alarming growth of the Jewish population in New York makes it necessary for business men advertising for clerks or secretaries, or housewives advertising for help, to specify where Jewish help was not desired, otherwise the flood of Jewish applicants was overwhelming. The expressions "Christian preferred," or "Jews please do not apply" are used. This year the New York Kehillah takes the matter in hand stating that "these advertisements indicate an alarming growth of discrimination against the Jews and it is remarkable that many firms which cater to the trade of Jews display this form of prejudice."

5679 (A.D. 1918-1919) The American Jewish Committee took up the alleged discrimination against Jews by army contractors. Louis Marshall, president of the Committee, notified Newton D. Baker, Secretary of War, that advertisements had appeared calling for carpenters to work in government camps, and that the advertisements required the applicants to be Christians. Secretary Baker replied that he had made an order prohibiting contractors from making this discrimination. (On the whole, this special form of advertisement may appear rather stupid: how many Jewish carpenters are there? Not enough to discriminate against. But there were doubtless other reasons.)

Provost Marshal Crowder, in charge of the Selective Draft, had issued an order to all medical examiners, under direction of the Surgeon General, stating "The foreign-born, especially Jews, are more apt to malinger than the native-born," and Louis Marshall again telegraphed both the Provost Marshal and the Surgeon General demanding that "the further use of this form shall be at once discontinued; that every copy of it that has been issued should be recalled by telegram; and the proper explanation be made, so as to expunge from the archives of the United States the unwarranted stigma upon three millions of people."

It was President Wilson, however, who eventually ordered the excision of this paragraph.

The United States Shipping Board sent an advertisement to the New York Times calling for a file clerk and stating that a "Christian" (by which is always meant a non-Jew) was preferred. The ad was not published as written; it was changed so that it requested applicants to state their religion and nationality. This last form would seem to be far more objectionable than the other. In the first instance the employer states fairly what he wants. In the second instance the applicant is compelled to divulge certain facts about himself in utter ignorance of the employer's preference. In the first instance, only the two classes that can do business get together; in the second instance there is no clearness about the situation until much useless effort is undertaken. Why? Because the Kehillah demands it. And why does the Kehillah demand it? Because, while it is all right for a Jew to remember that he is a Jew, it is not all right for you to remember it.

So, Louis Marshall got into action again with the Shipping Board, this time with certain drastic demands. Strangely enough, the protest was lodged through Bainbridge Colby, who was Woodrow Wilson's last Secretary of State. Mr. Marshall demanded: "Not because of any desire for inflicting punishment, but *for the sake of example and the establishment of a necessary precedent, this offense should be followed by a dismissal from the public service of the offender, and the public should be informed of the reason.*"

Attention is particularly called to the tone which Mr. Marshall adopts when addressing high American officials in the name of the Jewish Committee. It is not to be duplicated in the addresses of any other representatives of other nationalities or faiths.

Unfortunately for Mr. Marshall's plan of punishment, the object of his wrath was found to be a woman, and she was not discharged, although the Jewish Committee got an apology from Charles M. Schwab.

The Federal Reserve Bank and Liberty Loan Committee also got in wrong when an advertisement was printed calling for a "Stenographer for the Liberty Loan Committee (Christian)." Protest was made to Benjamin Strong, governor of the Federal Reserve Bank and chairman of the Liberty Loan Committee, and the advertisement was withdrawn. But this was not enough. Secretary of the Treasury McAdoo was also drawn in to express his "reprobation for an unpatriotic act."

An officer in the Quartermaster's Department replied to a young woman who applied for the position of secretary to him that he preferred not to have Jews on his office staff. He was reprimanded upon the request of Mr. Marshall.

The Plattsburg Manual, published for officers in the United States officers' training camps, contained the statement that "the id d officer is a Christian gentleman." Mr. Marshall at once made the standard protest against all "Christological manifestations," and the Manual was changed to read "the ideal officer is a courteous gentleman."

5680 (A.D. 1919-1920) In this year the Kehillah was so successful in its New York campaign that it was possible for a Jewish advertiser in New York to say that he wanted Jewish help, but it was not possible for a non-Jewish advertiser to state his non-Jewish preference. This is a sidelight both on Jewish reasonableness and Jewish power.

One gathers that a few people are still hugging the delusion that there is no Jewish Question in the United States. But another glance down the records will show the most prejudiced person that there is such a Question. If space permitted, the few details added below could be matched by a sufficient number to overflow all the pages of this paper.

5668 (A.D. 1907-1908) Jews agitate in many cities against Bible reading, Christmas celebration or carols. In Philadelphia, Cincinnati, St. Paul and New York the Jewish opposition to the carols is met with strong counter-movements.

5669 (A.D. 1908-1909) Jewish Community at Tamaqua, Pennsylvania, defeats resolution providing daily Bible reading in the schools.—Jews attempting same compulsion in New Jersey are met with decision that pupils may absent themselves from devotional exercises.—Jewish agitation in Louisiana stirs ministerial association to defend the right of the school to the Bible.— Local council of Jewish Women of Baltimore petitions school board to prohibit Christmas exercises.—On demand of Edwin Wolf, Jewish member, Philadelphia school board prohibits Christmas exercises.—Jews present bills asking that New York Hebrews be permitted to ply trades and businesses on Sunday. Interdenominational Ministers' Conference takes official action and Rev. Dr. David J. Burrell, of the Marble Collegiate Church, states that the attempts of Jews to undermine the sanctity of Sunday are ethically unjustified.

5670 (A.D. 1909-1910) On demand of Jews the school board of Bridgeport, Pennsylvania, votes to discontinue the recitation of The Lord's Prayer in the schools.—In Kentucky State Senate, Jews defeat the Tichenor Bill making the Bible a book eligible for the schools.

5671 (A.D. 1910-1911) Jews oppose Bible reading and singing of hymns in Detroit schools.—New York State Federation of Labor opposes Jewish Bill to exempt Jews from prosecution for violating Sunday laws. (The workingman knows that it means a 7-day week for the Goy!)—New York Kehillah does two contradictory things; favors bill to permit Jews to do all kinds of business on Sunday, and pledges itself to co-operate in the strict enforcement of the Sunday laws.

5672 (A.D. 1911-1912) Upon the urgence of two Jews the Hartford, Connecticut, school board votes on the question of abolishing all religious exercises in the schools. The motion is lost by 5 to 4.—Jewish pupils in a Passaic, New Jersey, school petition the board of education to eliminate the Bible and all Christian songs from the school.—At the request of a rabbi, three principals of Roxbury, Massachusetts, public schools agree to banish the Christmas tree and omit all references to the season in their schools.—Jewish pupils of Plainfield, New Jersey, petition the abolition of the Bible and Christian songs from the schools.—The council of the University Settlement, at the request of the New York Kehillah and the Federation of Rumanian Jews, adopts this resolution: "That in holiday celebrations held annually by the Kindergarten Association at the University Settlement every feature of any sectarian character, including Christmas trees, Christmas programs and Christmas songs, and so on, shall be eliminated."—Philadelphia Kehillah demands that Jews be exempted from operation of the Sunday laws.—In the *Outlook,* Dr. Lyman Abbott advises an inquiring schoolmaster that he is under no moral obligation to admit Jews to his private school.—A Jewish delegate to the Ohio Constitutional Convention suggests that the constitution be made to forbid religious references in the schools.—Jewish merchants of Paterson, New Jersey, petition for exemption from the Sunday laws.—Board of education of Yonkers, New York, denies Jewish request to forbid singing of Christian songs in the schools.

5673 (A.D. 1912-1913) Annual Convention Independent Order of B'nai B'rith at Nashville, Tennessee, adopts resolution against reading the Bible and singing Christian songs in public schools.—Jews at Jackson, Tennessee, seek an injunction to prevent the reading of the Bible in city schools.—Jews of Nashville, Tennessee, petition board of education against Bible and Christian songs.—Richmond, Virginia, school board restores Bible reading in the schools.—Bill introduced into Pennsylvania legislature providing for Bible reading in schools and the discharge of teachers omitting to do so. Jewish rabbis protest against bill. Jewish Kehillah of Philadelphia sends telegram to governor urging him to veto bill. Governor approves bill.—Chicago board of education, scene of much Jewish agitation, approves recommendation of subcommittee to remove Christmas from the list of official holidays in public schools.—In response to demands of Jews the Revere, Massachusetts, school board consents to remove references to Jesus from Christmas exercises in the public schools. This action, however, was rescinded at a special meeting.—California Jews appeal before Senate Committee on Public Morals to protest against a proposed Sunday law.—At Passaic, New Jersey, 29 Jewish members of the senior high school class walk out of class election, alleging "racial discrimination." — At Atlantic City, New Jersey *during the national convention of the United States War Veterans, the proposal to restore the Cross as part of the insignia of chaplain,* was defeated by Jews.

5674 (A.D. 1913-1914) This year the energies of the Jewish powers were concentrated on the task of preventing the United States from changing the immigration laws in a manner to protect the country from undesirable aliens.

5675 (A.D. 1914-1915) Jewish rabbi demands of California state superintendent of public instruction that some verses appearing in school readers be eliminated.—New York Kehillah concerns itself with attempts to secure modification of the Sunday laws.

5676 (A.D. 1915-1016) This year occupied by opposition to various movements toward making the schools free to use the Bible, and in opposition to the Gary system. The Gary system receives a great deal of attention from the Jews this year.

5677 (A.D. 917) Jews are busy carrying out an immense campaign against the "literacy clause" of the immigration bill.

And so it goes on. The incidents quoted are typical, not occasional. They represent what is transpiring all the time in the United States as the Jews pursue their "rights." There is no interference whatever with Jewish ways and manners. The Jew may use his own calendar, keep his own days, observe his own form of worship, live in his own ghetto, exist on a dietary principle all his own, slaughter his cattle in a manner of which no one who knows about can approve—he can do all these things without molestation, without the slightest question of his right in them. But the non-Jew is now the "persecuted one." He must do everything the way the Jew wants it done; if not he is "infringing on Jewish rights."

Americans are very sensitive about infringing on other people's rights. The Jews might have gone on for a long time had they not overplayed their hand. What the people are now coming to see is that it is American rights that have been interfered with, and the interference has been made with the assistance of their own broad-mindedness. The Jews' interference with the religion of others, and the Jews' determination to wipe out of public life every sign of the predominant Christian character of the United States, is the only active form of religious intolerance in the country today.

But there is still another phase of this matter. Not content with the fullest liberty to follow their own faith in peace and quietness, in a country where none dares make them afraid, the Jews declare—we read it in their activities—that every sight and sound of anything Christian is an invasion of their peace and quietness, and so they stamp it out wherever they can reach it through political means. To what lengths this spirit may run is shown in the prophecies of the Talmud, and in the "reforms" undertaken by the Bolsheviki of Russia and Austria.

But even that is not all; not content with their own liberty, not content with the "secularization," which means the de-Christianization of all public institutions, the third step observable in Jewish activities is the actual exaltation of Judaism as a recognized and specially privileged system. The program is the now familiar one wherever the Jewish Program is found: first, establishment; second, destruction of all that is non-Jewish or anti-Jewish; third, exaltation of Judaism in all its phases.

Put the Lord's Prayer and certain Shakespeare plays out of the public schools; but put Jewish courts in the public buildings—that is the way it works. Secularization is preparatory to Judaization.

The New York Kehillah is an illustration of how it is all done, and the American Jewish Committee is an illustration of the type of men who do it.

Now for illustrations of the third phase of the program of "defending Jewish rights."

The year 5669 (A.D. 1908-1909) was marked by an effort to introduce the idea of the Jewish Sabbath into public business. Jews refused to sit as jurors in court, thus postponing cases.

Boycotts were instituted in New York against merchants who opened on Saturday. That this campaign has borne fruit is known by all travelers in eastern cities who notice that even large department stores are closed on Saturday.

The year 5670 (A.D. 1909-1910) was dedicated apparently to the work of introducing the idea of Jewish national holidays into public life. This question lately rose in New York in a threatening way, but was withdrawn just before the breaking point. Only temporarily withdrawn, however. The feint revealed the identity and number of those who are still on guard against the complete Judaization of their city.—Jewish members of stock exchanges endeavored to have these institutions recognize Yom Kippur by closing; in Cleveland this was done.— The Council of Jewish Women appealed to the Civil Service Commission at Washington for recognition of Jewish holidays.— In Newark, New Jersey, the rabbis ask the night schools to discontinue Friday evening sessions, because the Jewish Sabbath begins at sundown on Friday.

In 1911 an attempt to have Hebrew officially recognized was frustrated by Supreme Court Judge Goff who refused incorporation of "Agudath Achim Kahal Adath Jeshurun" on the ground that the title should be in English.—Chicago Jews have election day changed because the official date fell on the last day of the Passover.

In 1912-1913 a number of special recognitions of the Saturday Sabbath were obtained, including Jersey City, Bayonne, Hoboken, Union Hill. In the Ohio legislature the Jews defeated a bill fixing a certain Saturday as the date of a primary election.

In 1913-1914 the United States Bureau of Immigration granted the request of Simon Wolf, long-time Jewish lobbyist at Washington, that instructions be given the Immigration Commissioners that no Jews be deported on Jewish holidays.— The Women's Party of Cook County, Illinois, passes resolutions against allowing Jewish holidays.—In this year also the question of the Jews' method of slaughtering animals—the Shehitah— was brought forward. The American Jewish Committee thought this question of sufficient importance to engage its full interest.

This series of facts could also be pursued at length. Kosher food for the children of public schools because there were Jewish children in the schools; protest against the Daylight Saving Ordinances because they were prejudicial to Jewish merchants who close their businesses on Saturday and open them after nightfall on that day. This is an illustration of the large number of small points at which Jewish life conflicts with community life. And, of course, each of these divergences is ground for an imperious "demand."—Harvard University was severely criticized in 1917-1918 for refusing to set aside an entrance examination date that conflicted with a Jewish holiday. Since that time, however, eastern universities have become more pliable. But the whole course of the Christian year would have to be changed and all the traditional seasonal customs of the country broken up if the Jews are to be given the full measure of "liberty" which they demand.

Of course, the work of the Kehillah is claimed to be "educational." It certainly is that. The best educated members are those who come from the ghettos of Galatia where the Kehillah idea is fully understood and the Jewish community government exercises unrestricted sway.

Whatever other phase of education the Kehillah may be interested in, it certainly stresses most *the education to separateness.* The New York *Times* especially likes to emphasize this matter of "education." It is a convenient description and somewhat aids the effort to minimize Kehillah's importance when it is under scrutiny. Nevertheless in the New York *Times* an article appeared about the Kehillah in which Dr. S. Benderly, director of the Bureau of Education, is quoted as describing the objects of the education:

"The problem before us was to form a body of young *Jews who should be on the one hand true American, a* part of this Republic, with an intense interest in upbuilding American ideals; *and yet, on the other hand, be also Jews* in love with the best of their own ideals, and *not anxious merely to merge with the rest and disappear among them.*

"That problem confronts Orthodox and Reform Jews alike. It is *not merely a religious but a civic problem."*

171

That is separatism and exclusivism as an educational program, and its results cannot help being a cloud of difference such as this article has in part disclosed. The New York Kehillah, through its Bureau of Education, is giving "a purely religious training to 200,000 Jewish children," the religious training being, of course, not what is generally understood by that term, but a training in ideas of racial superiority and separateness.

This difference is strikingly illustrated in Jewish fiction recently. To love a Christian maiden is sinful; this is the theme of all sorts of stories, sketches and editorials appearing these days. But James Gibbons Huneker, in a sketch extravagantly praised by Jewish critics, shows how deep this idea of separateness is when he makes Yaankely Ostrowicz say: "As a child I trembled at the sound of music and was taught to put my finger in my ears when profane music, Goy music, was played." This is the root idea: All Gentile life and institutions are "profane." It is the Jews' unceasing consciousness of the Goy that constitutes the disease of Judaism, this century-long tradition of separateness.

There is no such thing as anti-Semitism. There is, however, much anti-Goyism. In England, Germany, France, America, Russia, there is no anti-Arab sentiment of which anyone knows. None of the Semite peoples have been distinguished by the special dislike of any other people. There is no reason why anyone should dislike the Semites.

It is very strange, however, that the Semitic people should be a unit in disliking the Jews. Palestine, which still has only a handful of Jews, is peopled by Semites who so thoroughly dislike the Jews that serious complications are threatening the Zionistic advances being made there. This surely is not anti-Semitism. Semites are not against Semites. But they are at odds with Jews.

When Aryan and Semite are kept conscious through many centuries that the Jew is another race, and when it is known that neither Aryan nor Semite are touchy on the race question, what is the answer? Only this, that the whole substance of such a situation must be supplied by the Jews.

There is no such thing as anti-Semitism. There is only a very little and a very mild anti-Jewism. But a study of Jewish publications, books, pamphlets, declarations, constitutions and charters, as well as a study of organized Jewish action in this and other countries, indicated that there is a tremendous amount of anti-Goyism, or anti-Gentilism.

Not that it is anything to fear. It is, however, something to know. Knowledge is a good defense. The New York Kehillah, having as its executive committee the same committee which is also the ruling group of Jews known as District XII of the American Jewish Committee, is worth consideration, not only as an illustration of the interlaced organization which combines all classes of Jews in one group, but also as an illustration of what is meant by "Jewish rights."

It is worth remembering that every "demand" voiced in Washington before officials and committees, that every high personage that appears there on Jewish matters—the Louis Marshalls and the Wises, the Goldfogles, the Rosalskis, besides many others, like the Kahns and the Schiffs, who keep out of the committee limelight and away from the protesting parties—are all linked up, through this Jewish interest or that, with the main interest which is based on the Kehillah and expresses itself through District XII of the American Jewish Committee.

Issue of March 12, 1921

XXXVI.

"Jewish Rights" to Put Studies
Out of Schools

THE organizations of Jewry are numerous and widespread, all of them being international in tone whether so chartered or not. The Alliance Israelite Universelle is, perhaps, the world clearing house of Jewish policy, with which every national aggregation of Jewish societies has affiliation.

The Independent Order of B'nai B'rith, which is now hopeful of reaching the 1,000,000 membership mark, is frankly international. It has divided the world into 11 districts, seven of which are in the United States. Its lodges at last report numbered 426. The four members of its executive committee who do not reside in the United States, reside in Berlin, Vienna, Bucharest and Constantinople, respectively. Its lodges have been set up in the United States, Europe, Asia and Africa. Henry Morgenthau's name appears in the 1919-1920 Jewish year book as a member of this executive committee. Mr. Morgenthau will be remembered as the American Minister to Turkey, later talked of as Ambassador to Mexico, then chosen by President Wilson to mediate between the Turks and the Armenians. Mr. Morganthau also investigated for the President the reports of Polish pogroms.

In studying the executive committees of Jewish societies it is strikingly evident that the same minds guide all the important ones. A few names recur again and again. They are the names one meets at all Senate hearings, at various strategic places in the War Government of the United States, and at every stage of Jewish interference with American foreign policy. Everything centers at last, apparently, in the American Jewish Committee and the executive committee of the New York Kehillah. Judge Mack, Judge Brandeis, the Warburgs, the Schiffs, Morgenthaus, Wolf, Kraus, Elkus, Straus, Louis Marshall—these names appear over and over again, in offensive and defensive action, in all big affairs.

There are now in the United States 6,100 reported Jewish organizations. Of these, 3,637 are in New York City. This figure is offered from the 1919-1920 year book, although the statement was recently made that the New York Kehillah is the clearing house of 4,000 organizations.

Enough is shown to indicate how fully organized the Jews are, how they are linked together by every conceivable bond, the material of every bond being their racial likeness.

The organization about which the public has heard most is the Independent Order of B'nai B'rith. Its headquarters are not in New York, strange to say, but in Chicago. Its origin, however, as might be expected, was in New York.

This interesting order, without a reference to which no survey of Jewry is complete, came into existence in the back room of an Essex street saloon in 1843. Strangely enough, its most moving spirit at the beginning was a Henry Jones, although his colleagues retained their Hebraic names.

Because most of the founders were from Germany the name was given in German, Bundes Bruder, which is in Hebrew, B'nai B'rith (Brothers of the Covenant). The executive committee was known as The Elders. The order spread first to Cincinnati, apparently taking the course of German immigration through the country, and it is recorded that the second lodge in that city is the first where the English language was used in discussing lodge affairs. The first leap of the order abroad, was to Berlin where in 1885 Grand Lodge No. 8 was installed, followed soon after by Grand Lodges in Rumania and Austria. The order's literature lays stress on the work of inculcating patriotism which is said to be one of B'nai B'rith's special interests. It is perhaps not meant, however, that the head office at Chicago could undertake, especially during recent years, to guide the patriotism of all the districts throughout the world. It would have been rather awkward for District No. 6, which includes Illinois, to encourage District No. 8 to loyalty, seeing that District No. 8 embraced Germany.

The Order has not avoided the political field. The diplomatic history of the United States in the last 70 years is dotted all over with indications of B'nai B'rith activities. Oscar Straus, writing from the Legation of the United States at Constantinople in 1889, tells Secretary of State Blaine that the Jerushalaim Lodge of B'nai B'rith at Jerusalem was quite satisfied with the way in which the State Department had attended to a certain matter at the lodge's request. Mr. Morganthau in the midst of his investigation of the false pogrom rumors on Poland, goes to a B'nai B'rith lodge. In 1870 Brother Benjamin R. Piexotto was appointed "as United States consul at Bucharest for the express purpose of securing an amelioration of the condition of the shockingly persecuted Jews in Rumania." The "persecution" in Rumania was the protest of the Rumanian peasantry against the two greatest menaces to the peasant farmers—the Jew controlled liquor and mortgage traffics.

But this special appointment was made "in pursuance of suggestions made by the Order, and the negotiations were carried on chiefly by Brother Simon Wolf."

Simon Wolf has been the official Jewish lobbyist at Washington, on fixed post, for fifty years. He could write an informative story of the relation of B'nai B'rith to diplomatic appointments, if he would. It was he who suggested to William Jennings Bryan, when the latter was Secretary of State, that a Jew be appointed Minister to Spain to show Spain that the United States did not approve Spain's act of expulsion back in the fifteenth century. Jews are also suggesting to President Harding that a Jew be appointed Ambassador to Germany to rebuke the Germans' resentment against Jewish control of finance, industry and politics. This conception of the United States Diplomatic Service as a convenient agency for the transaction of Jewish world affairs has been in existence a long time, and has accounted for some of the strange appointments which have puzzled the people.

It is worth noting that while American Jews are crowding the eastern diplomatic posts with as many Jews as possible, British Jews are doing the same thing in the Judaization of the Persia, India and Palestine governments, so that the whole mid-Orient is now under Jewish control, and the Mohammedan World is given to understand that the Jews are merely coming back from their conquest of the white races. To those who have observed the Jewish attempt to seek a rapprochement between the followers of Moses and Mohammed, the situation is one of the keenest interest.

The B'nai B'rith is made up mostly of the more liberal Jews, religiously speaking, and doubtless includes a large number who are also liberal, racially speaking. The time when it stood as spokesman of Jewish ideals is now long past; it stands today the center of certain Jewish activities. It does not supersede the American Jewish Committee by any means, but it is the encircling arm, with fingers everywhere, through which the committee can get its will carried out. When there is anything to be *done,* the B'nai B'rith is the organization which takes the lead in putting it over. It may be described as a *freemasonry exclusively for Jews.* This brings up another characteristic that people have noticed and discussed: the Jew demands as his right entrance into other Orders; into his own he admits none but Jews. This one-sided policy is found everywhere.

Chief among the B'nai B'rith's activities in so far as they directly relate to the rest of the people, is the work of the Anti-Defamation League. This inside committee in every lodge attends to the espionage work necessary to keep the Grand Lodges informed as to what is going on with reference to Jewry in the United States. In its work, the Anti-Defamation League always takes the offensive and works along pretty well defined lines.

Ordinarily the head of the Anti-Defamation League in each city is a man competent to bring pressure to bear on the public press. Sometimes he is the head of an advertising agency which, as a rule, pools the Jewish department store advertising of that city, so that the newspapers may be controlled from that angle. Sometimes he is himself a heavy advertiser, pledged the co-operation of other advertisers in whatever he undertakes to do. The Anti-Defamation League is the instrument through which all boycotting tactics make their appearance. This league not only makes its protest from without, but directs reprisals from within. It is an exceedingly militant body and does not always depend upon "the rule of reason" in its activities.

Many quaint tales could be told of the operations of the Anti-Defamation League in various American cities, but as the present articles attempt to give no more than a bird's-eye view of widespread Jewish activities, mere story-telling will have to wait.

But perhaps the most notable accomplishment of the league has been the suppression of the word "Jew" in the public prints in any but the most laudatory connections. For a long time in the United States the people did not know how to refer to the Jews, whether as Hebrews of Israelites or what, because the fear of giving offense had been so diligently cultivated in all quarter.

The result was that other nationalities were laden with all the undesirable publicity which the Jews had evaded through the efforts of the Anti-Defamation League. Recently a Jew was on trial for the murder of his wife. The newspapers referred to him as "a pert little *Englishman.*" The Russians in the United States, and the Poles also, have been filled with indignation by the extent to which their national names have been used in police and newspaper reports to conceal the identity of Jews. The Russians resident in this country have several times been compelled to remonstrate with the press for it misrepresentative practice in this matter.

For this state of affairs the Anti-Defamation League receives the credit. Whenever a newspaper printed the word "Jew" as an identifying noun after the name of anyone who had been discredited, the Anti-Defamation League was instantly on the job in protest. The stock argument is, "If he had been a Baptist or an Episcopalian you would not have told it, and why should you say that he is a Jew—'Jew' being a mere religious denomination." City editors are obliging and the rule became established. In principle it is right, although it is urged on wrong grounds; but in practice it has turned out to be a great injustice to other nationalities and, more than all, it has curtailed the freedom of American speech. It has concealed the Jew where he most wishes to be concealed, and it cannot be hid that he has made the best use of this privilege.

It is this fixed policy of the B'nai B'rith's Anti-Defamation League which imperils the hope that the B'nai B'rith might have come to the front as one of the most useful influences in the solution of the Jewish Question. It includes a body of men sufficiently acquainted with the general point of view to be able to see where corrections and concessions are necessary as a ground, not to mere polite tolerance, but to reconciliation. There is no country in the world more propitious for the settlement of the world's Jewish Problem than is the United States, but it cannot be settled along the old line of the Judaization of the Untied States, nor by its de-Christianization either. The work of the Anti-Defamation League is positive to Judaization and negative to settlement.

There is nothing that Jewry, acting through the B'nai B'rith, does so well as to hold Mass Meetings and attack "The Merchant of Venice."

Mass Meetings may be described as the Jews' great American pastime. The New York Kehillah, that is, The American Jewish Committee, can on one day's notice organize Mass Meetings in every city in the United States. They are mechanical devices, of course; they are not so much expressions of the Jewish mind as they are attempts to impress the non-Jewish mind. There is a great deal of theatrical calculation in them. This column could be filled with the dates and places of Mass Meetings held within any seven days on any question in which the Jews had decided to coerce or accelerate public or, as it usually is, official opinion. The Mass Meeting, it appears, can still be made to seem real to the political official whose vote is sought.

It was by Mass Meetings that Congress was coerced into breaking off our commercial treaty with Russia.

It was by Mass Meetings that the literacy test was defeated.

It was by Mass Meetings that every attempt to restrict immigration has been defeated.

In 100 important cities a Mass Meeting could be held tomorrow night if President Harding should attempt to remove a Jewish official, or if the census bureau should attempt to record Jews under their proper racial name.

It is a very perfect system, even if a little antiquated. Doubtless its main purpose is to let the Jewish masses believe that they too have something to say in Jewish affairs. Jewish leadership of the Jews is never quite what the Jews think it is, and its weakness was never more apparent than today. There has not been any "persecution" of the Jews in the United States and never will be any, but all that the Jews have had to carry in the way of misunderstanding has been the result of the leadership which has misled them into paths of bloated ambition, instead of substantial human achievement. At this moment there is trembling, not among the Jewish masses, but among their leaders. The Jewish people will presently take their own affairs in their own hands, and then their affairs will go better. There are too many "committees," too many "prophets," too many "wise men," who think that two minutes with a President constitutes greatness, and that a busy bustling overseas and back constitutes statesmanship. The Jews have suffered from the personal ambitions and pathetic incapacity of some of their most advertised men.

The B'nai B'rith has this much in its favor: its leadership has always been progressive. Only when it has lent itself as local agent for the "leaders" of the New York Kehillah has it set up in its neighborhoods those influences which tend toward division instead of a better understanding.

Under whose inspiration it was that the B'nai B'rith undertook to bring its great power to bear against one of Shakespeare's plays, cannot now be said; but it has been most unfortunate for Jewish influence in all directions. Successful—oh, yes; but such a success as serious people could well do without.

Merely to glance over the record is interesting:

1907—Jews force "The Merchant of Venice" to be dropped from public schools in Galveston, Texas, Cleveland, Ohio; El Paso, Texas; Youngstown, Ohio.

1908—Jews have "The Merchant of Venice" eliminated from the English course in the high school at El Paso, Texas.

1910—Apparently the "Merchant" slipped back into Cleveland schools, for in April the superintendent of public schools issued an order that it was not to be used again.

1911—Rabbi Harry W. Ettleson and Solomon Elsner request the Hartford, Connecticut, school board to have "The Merchant of Venice" dropped from the reading list of the schools. The board complies.

1912—Jewish residents of Minneapolis, Minnesota, inaugurate a movement to have "The Merchant of Venice" dropped from the public schools.—In Boston, Massachusetts, the superintendent of schools refuses to withdraw "The Merchant of Venice" as a textbook, on the demand of Rabbi Phineas Israeli.

1916—On demand of Jews the New Haven, Connecticut, board of education votes to prevent the reading of "The Merchant of Venice," and extends the prohibition to "Lamb's Tales from Shakespeare" until an edition is published which omits the play.

And so on down the list of cities. A diversion was created by the Jewish attack on Sargent's painting entitled "The Synagogue" in an art scheme of the Boston Public Library. Many denunciatory resolutions were adopted throughout the country with regard to that, but the painting is still there.

It is all part of one mistaken program, to prohibit free speech, with reference to the Jew. It is utterly at one side of all that American principles mean. Shut him up! Boycott him! Tear down his painting! Bar his words from the mails and public library!—what a waste of energy and what a self-judgment such an attitude is!

And it has become pretty general. Last Christmas most people had a hard time finding Christmas cards that indicated in any way that Christmas commemorated Someone's Birth. Easter they will have the same difficulty in finding Easter cards that contain any suggestion that Easter commemorated a certain event. There will be rabbits and eggs and spring flowers, but a hint of the Resurrection will be hard to find. Now, all this begins with the designers of the cards. And even in this business one comes upon that same policy of declaring Anti-Semitic everything that is Christian. If Rabbi Coffee says the New Testament is the most Anti-Semitic book ever written, what must be the judgment on an Easter card that is truly an Easter card?

In November, 1919, the Anti-Defamation Com-mittee claimed that 150 American cities had excluded "The Merchant of Venice" from the public schools. The newspapers at this writing are announcing that David Warfield, the great Jewish actor, is going to play "Shylock" in the manner which, as he believes, represents the true Shakespeare conception. The Anti-Defamation League may yet find itself to have expended much energy beating the wind, especially as the best Shakespearean critics declare that "The Merchant of Venice" is not about a Jew at all, but about Usury as a vicious practice which gripped both Jew and non-Jew and brought division.

There was, however, a certain finesse in the manner of the Anti-Defamation League in approaching the matter of the exclusion of the "Merchant." It was not an incapacity to appreciate the fine work of Shakespeare. On, no, anything but that. Nor was it a confession of thin-skinned sensibility on the part of Jews. Not at all. No, it was really for the benefit of the Gentile children that the Anti-Defamation League wanted them kept away from that play in their reading lessons.

Here are excerpts from one of the letters sent out from the Anti-Defamation League in Chicago to the superintendent of public schools in an important city. The italics are ours:

"We have just been advised that the * * * * *high schools* still retain "The Merchant of Venice" in the list of required readings * * * *

"We do not base our request because of the embarrassment which may be caused to the Jewish students in class, nor is our attitude in this regard based on thin-skinned sensitiveness. It is the result of mature consideration and investigation. Our objection is made *because of its effect upon the non-Jewish children* who subconsciously will associate in their own minds the Jew as Shakespeare portrayed him with the Jew of today. Children are not analysts. A character in the past vividly portrayed exists for them in the present. The Jew of Shakespeare lives in the mind of the child as the Jew of New York, or the Jew of Chicago, or the Jew of Newark. Your teachers of literature might say much in favor of Shylock's good qualities, but our experience has been that only very seldom are Shylock's good qualities brought out strongly before children. Those traits of his character which are brought out most vividly in the study of the play are Shylock's greed, hatred, revenge and cruelty.

"The fact that the College Entrance Requirements Board realized the justice of our stand and struck the play off from the list as required readings for entrance to our universities and colleges indicates clearly that it is a most serious problem. * * * *

" * * * * We believe that when you realize the great harm which might be caused to hundreds and thousands of law-abiding Jewish citizens of this country, you will grant our request that the reading of 'The Merchant of Venice' be discontinued from your schools."

And in this case it was. Notwithstanding the fact that the play was used in the *high school,* and the argument of the letter was addressed to the effect of the play on *children,* it was discontinued. A study of the schedule of just what occurred showed that everything had been make ready even before the letter was written.

Does this frittering away of Jewish influence strike the Jewish leaders as a wise policy?

Is there any hope whatever of doing away with "The Merchant of Venice"?

Do they not know that it is the observation of teachers of literature that even if non-Jewish children are going to read it anyway, since it is the Jewish children who most heartily enjoy it because they more clearly understand it?

183

Do not the Jewish leaders know that non-Jews do not read the "Merchant" for Shylock, except perhaps his noble defense of the Jew as a human being? Whoever hears Shylock quoted in anything but this, which numerous Jewish writers delight to quote?—

"I am a Jew. Hath not a Jew eyes? Hath not a Jew hands, organs, dimensions, senses, affections, passions?"

To effect its purpose the Anti-Defamation League will have to perform an excision on our common English tongue. The wise and witty sayings of this Shakespearean play have passed into the permanent coinage of daily speech.

"I hold the world a stage where every man must play his part; and mine a sad one."

"* * * I am Sir Oracle,
And when I ope my lips let no dog bark!"

"If to do were as easy as to know what were good to do, chapels had been churches, and poor men's cottages princes' palaces."

"The Devil can cite Scripture for his purpose."

"A goodly apple rotten at the heart:

O, what a goodly outside falsehood hath!"

"Truth will come to sight; murder cannot be hid long."

"All that glitters is not gold."

"A harmless necessary cat."

"The quality of mercy is not strained,
It droppeth as the gentle rain from heaven
Upon the place beneath. It is twice blest:
It blesseth him that gives and him that takes.
* * * * * * * * * *

It is an attribute of God himself;
And earthly power doth then show likest God's,
When mercy seasons justice."

This is beyond the power of the Anti-Defamation League to destroy. Shylock may be forgotten, but not these living lines. It is true, however, that in 150 American cities, according to the league's claim, school children are prevented reading and hearing these words in school.

But is it worth it? Is it a part of "Jewish Rights" that an admittedly great play, taught in all the English courses of all the universities, should be prohibited to the children of the people in the public schools?

From the prohibition of the Bible to the prohibition of Shakespeare, the whole Jewish course has been a colossal mistake, the reaction from which will be to belittle Jewish public judgment in the future.

It is all very well said by a correspondent to the Newark *Evening News*, January 13, 1920:

"To the Editor of the *News:*

"Sir—Protests have been made by the representatives of the Jewish, Scotch and colored races against Shakespeare's being used in the public schools, the former because of the portrayal of Shylock in 'The Merchant of Venice.' Some Scotch folk have protested, as I understand it, to the Newark Board of Education, on account of the character given Macbeth. The colored folks, judging from the letter printed in the *News* from Washington, do not like the character of Othello, owing to his despicable treatment of Desdemona. As a descendant of the Welsh race, I enter my protest in behalf of that ancient people in regard to Shakespeare's ridicule in Henry V, of the Welshman, Captain Fluellen, who is made to look as if he did not know anything about war.

"I have no doubt that others could find fault with Shakespeare's penchant for holding up the weak side of some of his characters, so I think that Shakespeare and the Bible might well be kept out of the public schools because both books are rough on certain people whose identity is clearly shown. The board of education is to be congratulated for taking action in the matter, which promises at this late date to place the Newark educational system in a class all by itself."

Issue of March 19, 1921

XXXVII.

Disraeli—British Premier, Portrays the Jews

THE Jews have complained that they are being mis-represented. It is their usual complaint. They are always being "misrepresented" and "persecuted" except when they are being praised for what they are not. If the Jews were fully understood by the Gentiles, if the Christian churches, for example, were freed from their delusion that the Jews are Old Testament people, and if the churches really knew what Talmudic religion is, it is likely the "misrepresentation" would be still stronger.

The downfall of Russia was prepared by a long and deliberate program of misrepresentation of the Russian people, through the Jewish world press and Jewish diplomatic service. The name of Poland has been drawn in filth through the press of the United States under Jewish instigation, most of the signers of the latest Jewish protest against THE DEARBORN INDEPENDENT'S articles being leaders in the vilification of Poland whose sole crime is that she wishes to save herself from the Jews. All this real misrepresentation is regarded as the Jew's privilege.

But wherever a hand has been raised to prevent the Jews overrunning the people and secretly securing control of the major instruments of life, the Jews have raised the cry of "misrepresentation." They never meet the question outright. They are not meeting it now. They cannot meet it without confession. False denials, pleas for sympathy, and an unworthy attempt to link others with them in their fall, constitute their whole method of defense.

Freemasons may wonder how they come into this affair, as they see the name of their ancient order coupled with that of the Jews in the latest Jewish defense. It is all very easily understood by those who are acquainted with Jewish strategy during the two centuries which comprise modern Masonic history.

Twice in the history of the United States, the people have been aroused by a sense of strange influences operating in their affairs, and each time the real power behind the influences was able to divert suspicion to the Freemasons. Once in George Washington's time, once in President Adams' time this occurred. Books were written, sermons preached, newspapers took up the search, but none of the observers saw the Jewish influence there. George Washington knew that the disloyal influence was not Masonic, but he saw signs of the concealed power trying to operate under the guise of Masonry. President Adams had not so clear a view of the matter.

Masonry emerged unstained because it was guiltless of subversive purposes. A pseudo-Masonry, of French origin, given to atheistic and revolutionary purposes, strongly patronized by Jews, was the disturbing element, but all that the public was able to see was the Masonic similitude and not the Jewish hand. A recrudescence of this misrepresentation of the Masons occurred also in 1826, and from then until the other day, when the Leaders of American Jewry linked the name of Freemasonry with their own, the name of the Order has been unscathed.

This is to serve notice on the leaders of American Jewry that this time they will not be permitted to hide behind the name of Masonry, nor will they be permitted to hold up the name of Masonry as a shield to blunt the darts or as an ally to share the shafts aimed at their subversive purposes. That game has succeeded twice in the United States; it will never succeed again. Freemasonry is not and never was implicated in what the Jewish cabal has had in mind. And Freemasons everywhere are aware of the facts.

It is a curious fact that just as the Jews have sought to operate through the Masons and then leave that Order to take the brunt of the ensuing assault, so also have they at times sought to operate through the Jesuits, playing the same trick with that name and Order. If the Jesuits and the Masons would compare notes, they could both report the same thing. Jews have sought to use both, and have been frustrated, although in consequence the names of both Orders have suffered for a time.

This is one of the coincidences between the Protocols and the facts: the Protocols express themselves as against both the Masons and the Jesuits, but willing to use both to attain Jewish purposes.

Both these orders are well able to take care of themselves, once they know the key to the Jewish plan. But there is much information on these matters of which the public is not aware, and at a future date a study may be made of the historical efforts of the Jews to use and destroy Freemasonry. Such a study will be useful in showing how Jewish influence operated in a day when the people had no means of identifying it as Jewish. The people attacked the thing they saw, but what they saw was not the source of the element they opposed. Progress has been made at least to this extent, that nowadays, more than at any previous time, the world plan of the Jews is known and recognizable.

The main purpose of the present article, however, is to show the reader that the Jews have not been misrepresented, the means of showing this being a presentation of the Jews by a notable Jew whom the Jews are delighted to honor.

Benjamin Disraeli, who was Earl of Beaconsfield and prime minister of Great Britain, was a Jew and gloried in it. He wrote many books, in a number of which he discussed his people in an effort to set them in a proper light. The British Government was not then so Jewish as it has since become, and Disraeli was easily one of the greatest figures in it.

In his book, "Coningsby," there appears a Jewish character named Sidonia, in whose personality and through whose utterances, Disraeli sought to present the Jew as he would like the world to see him.

Sidonia first announces his race to young Coningsby by saying, "I am of that faith that the Apostles professed before they followed their Master," the only place in the whole book where the "faith" is mentioned. Four times, however, in the brief preface to the fifth edition, written in 1849, the term "race" is used in reference to the Jews.

In the first conversation between these two, Sidonia reveals himself as a great lover of power, and discourses charmingly of the powerful men of history, ending in this way:

"Aquaviva was General of the Jesuits, ruled every cabinet in Europe and colonized America before he was thirty-seven. What a career!" exclaimed the stranger (Sidonia), rising from his chair and walking up and down the room; *"the secret sway of Europe!"* (p. 120. The references are to Longman's edition published in 1919. The italics are ours.)

Taking up a study of the character of Sidonia the Jew, Disraeli the Jew begins to refer to the Jews as *"Mosaic Arabs."* If a modern writer were to describe the Jews thus, virtually as Arabs of the Mosaic persuasion, it would be denounced as another attempt at "persecution," but Disraeli did this a number of times, his purpose evidently being to give the Jew his proper setting as to his original position among the nations. Again he refers to them as *"Jewish Arabs."* Both of these terms may be found on page 209.

Disraeli also gives voice to the feeling, which every Jew has, that whoever opposes the Jew is doomed. This is a feeling which is strongly entrenched in Christians also, that somehow the Jews are the "chosen people" and that it is dangerous to oppose them in anything. "The fear of the Jews" is a very real element in life. It is just as real among the Jews as among non-Jews. The Jew himself is bound in fear to his people, and he exercises the fear of the curse throughout the sphere of religion—"I will curse them that curse thee." It remains to be proved, however, that opposition to the destructive tendencies of Jewish influences along all the principal avenues of life is a "cursing" of the Jews. If the Jews were really Old Testament people, if they were really conscious of a "mission" for the blessing of all the nations, the very things in which they offend would automatically disappear. If the Jew is being "attacked," it is not because he is a Jew, but because he is the source and life of certain tendencies and influences, which, if they are not checked, mean the destruction of a moral society.

The persecution of the Jew to which Disraeli refers is that of the Spanish Inquisition, which rested on religious grounds. Tracing the Sidonia family through a troubled period of European history, our Jewish author notes:

"During the disorders of the Peninsular War * * * a cadet of the younger branch of this family *made a large fortune by military contracts,* and supplying the commissariat of the *different armies.*" (p. 212.) Certainly. It is a truth unassailable, applicable to any period of the Christian Era, that "persecuted" or not, "wars have been the Jews' harvests." They were the first military commissaries. If this young Sidonia in supplying "the different armies" went so far as to supplying the opposing armies, he would be following quite perfectly the Jewish method as history records it.

"And at the peace, prescient of the great financial future of Europe, confident in the fertility of his own genius, in his original views of fiscal subjects, and his knowledge of natural resources, this Sidonia * * * resolved to emigrate to England, with which he had, in the course of years, formed considerable commercial connections. He arrived here after the peace of Paris, with his large capital. He stakes all that he was worth on the Waterloo loan: and the event made him one of the greatest capitalists in Europe."

"No sooner was Sidonia established in England than he professed Judaism * * * "

"Sidonia had foreseen in Spain that, after the exhaustion of a war of twenty-five years, Europe must require capital to carry on peace. He reaped the due reward of his sagacity. Europe did require money and Sidonia was ready to lend it to Europe. France wanted some; Austria more; Prussia a little; Russia a few millions. Sidonia could furnish them all. The only country which he avoided was Spain * * * " (p.213.)

Here the prime minister of Great Britain, from the wealth of his traditions as a Jew and the height of his observation as prime minister, describes the method of the Jew in peace and war, exactly as others have tried to describe it. He puts forward the same set of facts as others put forth, but he does it apparently for the Jews' glorification, while others do it to enable the people to see what goes on behind the scenes in war and peace. Sidonia was ready to lend money to the nations. But where did he get it, in order to lend it? He got it from the nations when they were at war! It was the same money; the financiers of war and the financiers of peace are the same, and they are The International Jews, as Benjamin Disraeli's book for the glorification of Jewry amply testifies. Indeed, he testifies on the same page just quoted:

"It is not difficult to conceive that, after having pursued the career we have intimated for about ten years, Sidonia had become one of the most considerable personages in Europe. *He had established a brother, or a near relative, in whom he could confide, in most of the principal capitals. He was lord and master of the money market of the world, and of course virtually lord and master of everything else.*"

This comes as near being The International Jew as anything can be, but the Jews glory in the picture. It is only when a non-Jewish writer suggests that perhaps it is not good for society of the money market of the world," and as a consequence "lord and master of everything else," that the cry of "persecution" arises.

Strangely enough, it is in this book of the British premier that we come upon his recognition of the fact that Jews had infiltrated into the Jesuits' order.

"Young Sidonia was fortunate in the tutor whom his father had procured for him, and who devoted to his charge all the resources of his trained intellect and vast and various erudition. *A Jesuit before the revolution; since then an exiled Liberal leader; now a member of the Spanish Cortes; Rebello was always a Jew.* He found in his pupil that precocity of intellectual development which is characteristic of the *Arabian* organization." (p. 214.)

Then followed in young Sidonia's career an intellectual mastery of the world. He traveled everywhere, sounded the secrets of everything, and returned with the world in his vest pocket, so to speak—a man without illusions of any sort.

"There was not an *adventurer* in Europe with whom he was not familiar. No minister of state had such communication with *secret agents and political spies* as Sidonia. He held relations with all *the clever outcasts* of the world. The catalog of his acquaintances in the shape of Greeks, Armenians, Moors, *secret Jews*, Tartars, Gypsies, wandering Poles and Carbonari, would throw a curious light on *those subterranean agencies of which the world in general knows so little,* but which exercise so great an influence on public events * * * *The secret history of the world* was his pastime. His great pleasure was *to contrast the hidden motive, with the public pretext,* of transactions." (pp. 218-219.)

Here is The International Jew, full dress; he is the Protocolist too, wrapped in mystery, a man whose fingers sweep all the strings of human motive, and who controls the chief of the brutal forces—Money. If a non-Jew had limned a Sidonia, so truthfully showing the racial history and characteristics of the Jews, he would have been subjected to that pressure which the Jews apply to every truth-teller about themselves. But Disraeli could do it, and one sometimes wonders if Disraeli was not, after all, writing more than a romance, writing indeed a warning for all who can read.

The quotation just given is not the description of Sidonia only; it is also a description—save for the high culture of it—of certain American Jews who, while they walk in the upper circles, have commerce with the "adventurers" and with "the secret agents and political spies," and with the "*secret Jews*," and with those "subterranean agencies of which the world in general knows so little."

This is the strength of Jewry, this commerce between the high and the low, for the Jew knows nothing disreputable within the circle of Jewishness. No Jew becomes an outcast, whatever he may do; a place and a work await him, whatever his character.

There are highly placed persons in New York who would rather not have it known what they contributed to the "adventurer" who left New York to overturn Russia; there are other Jews who would rather not have it printed how much they know of "secret agents and political spies." Disraeli did more than draw Sidonia; he portrayed The International Jew as he is found also in America.

Thus far Sidonia is described from the outside. But now he begins to speak for himself, and it is in behalf and praise of the Jews. He is discussing the discrimination practiced against his people in England.

It is the old story. Everywhere, even in the United States, the same story. Crying for pity while usurping power! "We poor Jews" wails a New York multli-millionaire at whose finger legislatures quail and even Presidents of the United States grow respectful.

The following quotation was written in 1844: Britons must be impressed with its uncanny parallel to their affairs today: it is Sidonia speaking—

" * * * yet, since your society has become agitated in England, and powerful combinations menace your institutions, you find *the once loyal Hebrew invariably arrayed in the same ranks as the leveller and latitudinarian,* and *prepared to support the policy which may even endanger his life and property,* rather than tamely continue under a system which seeks to degrade him."

Consider that. "Latitudinarianism" is the doctrine of the Protocols in a word. It is a break-up by means of a welter of so-called "liberal "*ideas* which construct nothing themselves, but have power to destroy the established order.

Note also Disraeli's answer to the question sometimes asked, "If the Jews suffer under Bolshevism, why do they support it?" or the Jewish spokesmen's form of it—"If we are so powerful, why do we suffer in the disorder of the world?" The disorder is always a step to a new degree of Jewish power: Jews suffer willingly for that. But even so, they do not suffer as the non-Jews do. The Soviets permit relief to enter Russia for the Jews. In Poland, the "starving war-sufferers" are able to glut all available ships in taking high-priced passage to America. They are not suffering as other people are, but, as Disraeli sees, they are willing to suffer because they see in every breakdown of

Gentile society a new opportunity for the Jewish power to dig nearer the central seat of power.

Just how the Jew works to break down the established order of things, by means of *ideas*, as the Protocols claim, is shown in this same conversation of Sidonia:

"The Tories lose an important election at a critical moment; 'tis the Jews come forward to vote against them. The Church is alarmed at the scheme of a latitudinarian university, and learns with relief that funds are not forthcoming for its establishment; a Jew immediately advances and endows it."

If these words had been written by a non-Jew, the cry of anti-Semitism would ring through the land. They are true, neither more nor less true, because written by a Jew, And Sidonia adds:

"And every generation they must become more powerful and more dangerous to the society that is hostile to them." (These quotations from page 249.)

Well, several generations have passed since these words were written. The Jew still regards every form of non-Jewish society as hostile to him. He organizes strongly against society. And, if Disraeli is to be taken as a prophet, his words remain— "they must become more powerful and more dangerous." They have become more powerful. Whoso would measure the danger, look around.

Let the charming Sidonia proceed with his revelations:

"I told you just now that I was going up to town tomorrow, because I always made it a rule to interpose when affairs of state were on the carpet. Otherwise I never interfere. I hear of peace and war in newspapers, but I am never alarmed, *except when I am informed that the Sovereigns want treasure; then I know that monarchs are serious.*"

It will be remembered that Sidonia held no governmental position. The time had not come for that. Power was exercised behind the scenes long before the craving for the spotlight was gratified. But whether there be Jews in office or not, the power they exercise behind the scenes is always greater than the power they show in the open. It can be seen, therefore, that the more numerous they are in office, the greater their secret power. Sidonia continues:

"A few years back we were applied to by Russia. Now there has been no friendship between the Court of St. Petersburg and my family. It has Dutch connections which have generally supplied it; and our representations in favor of the Polish Hebrew, a numerous race, but the most suffering and degraded of all the tribes, have not been very agreeable to the Czar. However, circumstances drew to an approximation between the Romanoffs and the Sidonias. I resolved to go myself to St. Petersburg, I had, on my arrival, an interview with *the Russian Minister of Finance, Count Cancrin; I beheld the son of a Lithuanian Jew.*

"The loan was connected with the affairs of Spain; I resolved on repairing to Spain from Russia. I traveled without intermission. I had an audience immediately on my arrival with *the Spanish Minister, Senor Mendizabel; I beheld one like myself, the son of a Nuevo Christiano, a Jew of Aragon.*

"In consequence of what transpired at Madrid, I went straight to Paris to consult *the President of the French Council; I beheld the son of a French Jew,* a hero, an imperial marshal * * * "

If Sidonia were traveling today he would find whole groups of Jews, where, in his day, he found one, and he would find them in exalted places. Suppose Disraeli were alive today and should revise "Coningsby," including the United States in the tour of this money-master of the world! What a host of Jewish names he could gather from official circles in Washington and New York—such a host, indeed, as makes the occasional Gentile look like a foreigner who had been graciously permitted to come in by the Jews!

"The consequence of our consultations was, that some northern power should be applied to in a friendly and mediative capacity. We fixed on Prussia; and the President of the Council made an application to the *Prussian Minister, who attended a few days after our conference. Count Arnim entered the cabinet, and I beheld a Prussian Jew.*"

Sidonia's comment upon all this is offered as an address to every reader of this article:

"So, you see, my dear Coningsby, that *the world is governed by very different personages from what is imagined by those who are not behind the scenes.*" (pp. 251-252.)

It is indeed! Why not let the world see behind the scenes for a little?

And now for the most illuminating lines Disraeli ever wrote —lines which half compel the thought that maybe, after all, he was writing to warn the world of Jewish ambition for power:

"You never observe a great intellectual movement in Europe in which the Jews do not greatly participate. *The first Jesuits were Jews. That mysterious Russian Diplomacy* which so alarms Western Europe *is organized and principally carried on by Jews. That mighty revolution which is at this moment preparing in Germany,* and which will be, in fact, a second and greater Reformation, and of which so little is yet known in England, *is entirely developing under the auspices of Jews.*" (p. 250.)

American Jews say that the Protocols are inventions. Is Benjamin Disraeli an invention? Was this Jewish Prime Minister of Great Britain misrepresenting his people? Are not his portrayals taken as true history? And what does he say?

He shows that in Russia, the very country where the Jews complained they were least free, the Jews were in control.

He shows that the Jews know the technique of revolution, foretelling in his book the revolution that later broke out in Germany. How did he foreknow it? Because that revolution was developing under the auspices of Jews, and though it was then true that "so little is yet known in England," Disraeli the Jew knew it, and knew it to be Jewish in origin and development and purpose.

One point is sure: *Disraeli told the truth.* He presented his people before the world with correctness. He limns Jewish power, Jewish purpose and Jewish method with a certainty of touch that betokens more than knowledge—he shows racial sympathy and understanding. He sets forth the facts which this series is setting forth. "Why did he do it? Was it boastfulness, that dangerous spirit in which the Jew gives up most of his secrets? Or was it conscience, impelling him to tell the world of Judah's designs?

No matter; he told the truth. He is one man who told the truth without being accused of "misrepresenting" the Jews.

Issue of December 18, 1920

XXXVIII.

Taft Once Tried to Resist Jews— and Failed

WILLIAM HOWARD TAFT is an amiable gentleman. There is so much to agree within the world that he seldom finds it possible to disagree with anything. It is a very comfortable attitude for one to assume, but it doesn't push the world along. Real harmony is wrung out of discord by laboring against disagreeable facts; it is not achieved by mere pit-pats on the back of untoward conditions.

There is no doubt that had one approached William Howard Taft a year ago and said: "Mr. Taft, you know there are evil forces in the world which ought to be resisted," he would have replied, "Certainly, by all means."

If one had said, "Mr. Taft, some of this evil is just ignorant inclination, which can be dealt with by various means of enlightenment, but some of it represents a deliberate philosophy which has gathered about itself a definite organization for action," he would have responded: "I am afraid it is true."

And then had one said: "Mr. Taft, the people should be made aware of this, given a key to it, that they may keep their eyes open and learn the meaning of certain tendencies that have puzzled them," he would in all likelihood have replied, "I believe in enlightening the public mind that it may take care of itself."

Suppose you had added: "Mr. Taft, if you found a written program setting forth the steps to be taken to fasten a certain control on society, and if on looking about you observed a definite set of tendencies which seemed to parallel the program at every point, would it appear to you significant?"

Mr. Taft would, of course, answer, Yes. There is no other answer to make. No other answer has been made by anyone who has compared the two things.

If Mr. Taft had been approached first on that side of the question, he would have uttered words very valuable to those who would attach value to his words.

But what has Mr. Taft's "testimonial" to do with either side of the case? Does his support strengthen it, or does his opposition weaken it? If it came to a battle of names, THE DEARBORN INDEPENDENT could present a very imposing list of men who acknowledge the importance of the studies being made, and who agree with most of the observations presented. But such a list would add nothing to the facts in the case, and facts must stand on their own foundation regardless of the attitude of Mr. Taft, or even Mr. Arthur Brisbane.

But there is a very interesting story about Mr. Taft and the Jews. M. Taft knows it and can verify it. A number of American Jews also know it. And it may perhaps be useful to tell it now.

However, that we may not seem to desirous of evading Mr. Taft's latest defense of the Jews, we shall begin with that.

Unduly stirred by this series of studies, the leading Jews of the United States indicated by their perturbation that the truth in these articles made it impossible to ignore them. Perhaps as many people have been inclined toward agreement with the articles by the attitude of the Jews themselves as by the statements made in the articles. Jewish defense has been made with great formality and show of authority, but without the hoped-for effect. The Jews of the United States, evidently finding that their own statements have failed to carry, are making a wholesale conscription of Gentiles for purposes of defense. As in Russia, the Gentiles are being pushed into the firing lines.

Mr. Taft was therefore approached with a proposition. That was some time ago, probably about November first.

Now, according to Mr. Taft's own signed statement made on November 1, he had not even read THE DEARBORN INDE-PENDENT'S *articles but was taking the Jews' word for their character and contents. And yet, on December 23, we find Mr.*

Taft in Chicago at the La Salle Hotel, delivering an oration before the B'nai B'rith, uttering his statements with all the finality of a man who had made a deep study of the Jewish Question and had at last attained a mature conclusion.

On November 1, Mr. Taft wrote to a New York Jew deprecating these articles as "a foolish pronouncement *which I understand has been issued* through THE DEARBORN INDEPENDENT " The expression, *"which I understand,"* is equivalent in ordinary speech to "which I have heard." He had not read them. He was taking *hearsay* on which to base his opinion. There are signs that he had not read them even at the time of his speech in Chicago, for he did not so much as allude to one of the startling parallels which have weighed on the minds of many important men in this country.

The Jews wanted Mr. Taft's name, they wanted "a Gentile front," and they got it. The speech contributes nothing to the discussion; it proves nothing, it disproves nothing. In parts it is a rehash of a speech delivered by a New York rabbi. Indeed, one of William Howard Taft's most telling points was the almost verbal repetition of a point made by that rabbi.

Mr. Taft's business now is the delivery of addresses. Between November 1, at which time he had not read the Jewish Question at all, until December 23, when he presumed to pronounce judgment on it for all time, he had been away a great deal on the road. Indeed, he reached Chicago without having done any of his Christmas shopping. He explained that he had "been traveling over the country so fast" that his time had all been taken up. When he found time to study the Jewish Question does not appear. It is most probable that he had no time and did no studying. If he did, he carefully concealed the fruits of it when delivering his address.

Before his address was delivered, the newspapers had announced that it was to be made against "anti-Semitism," and this series of articles was specified. It was apparently foreknown, therefore, that not a judicial pronouncement was to be expected from Mr. Taft, but a partisan plea. The newspapers indicated that Mr. Taft had not even dictated his speech until he reached

Chicago. The material he had at hand during his dictation was the printed propaganda with which the Jews have been flooding the country. Taft's speech reeks with it. There isn't an original idea in it. He was the human megaphone whom the Jews retained for one night through whom to voice their words. The real purpose of the speech was, of course, to secure its publication throughout the country as the voice of the people on the Question. But nothing whatever excuses the fact that the speech contains absolutely no contribution to the Question.

Mr. Taft is against religious prejudice. So is everybody else. Mr. Taft wants concord and good will. So does everybody else. But what have these to do with the facts which comprise the Jewish Question?

The real story of Mr. Taft and the Jews begins back in the time when Mr. Taft lived in the White House. The Jews maintain a lobby in Washington whose business it is to know every President and every prospective President, and, of course, Mr. Taft was known to them a long while before he was made President, but whether they did not foresee his political future or whether they considered his opinions as having too little force for them to bother about, is not clear, but the fact seems to be that very little fuss was made about him. There are no indications that he ran after the Jews or the Jews after him in the days before his presidency.

As President, Mr. Taft once stood out against the Jews, was strongly denounced as unfavorable to the Jews, was soundly beaten by the Jews in a matter on which he had taken a firm stand, and has ever since shown that he has learned his lesson by accommodating the Jews in their desires.

The story involves a portion of that voluminous history which consists of the quarrels between the United States and other nations on account of the Jew. Readers interested in this phase of the history of the United States can find it fully set out by Jewish writers. There seems to be a certain pride taken in recounting the number of times the nations have been compelled to give diplomatic recognition to the Jewish Question. From 1840 until 1911, the United States had special diplomatic trouble concerning the

Jews. The trouble that culminated during 1911, in an unparalleled act by the United States, involved William Howard Taft, who then was President.

For centuries, Russia has had her own troubles with the Jews and, as the world knows, has at last fallen prostrate before the Jewish power which for centuries has been working to undermine her. Even Disraeli was not blinded to the fact that Jews had a control over Russia which the rest of the world never knew. The biggest hoax in modern times was the propaganda against Russia as the persecutor of the Jews. Russia devoted to the Jews a large part of the most favored section of the land, and was always so lax in those laws which prohibited Jews from settling in other parts of the country that the Jew was able to create an underground system throughout the whole of Russia which controlled the grain trade, controlled public opinion and utterly baffled the czar's government. The cry of "persecution" arose because the Jews were not permitted to exploit the peasants as much as they desired. They have, however, gained that privilege since.

Now, when the United States appeared as "the new Jerusalem," its Jewish citizens conceived the idea of using the American Government to achieve for the Jews what other means had failed to achieve. Russian and German Jews would come to the United States, become naturalized as quickly as possible, and go back to Russia as "Americans" to engage in trade. Russia knew them as Jews and held them to be subject to the laws relating to Jews.

Protest after protest reached the State Department as more and more German or Russian Jews went back to Russia to circumvent the Russian laws. At first the matter was not serious, because it was shown in many cases that these naturalized "Americans" did not intend to return to the United States at all, but had acquired "American citizenship" solely as a business asset in Russia. In these cases, of course, the United States did not feel obligated to bestir herself.

The time came, however, when American ministers to Russia were requested to look into the situation. Their reports are accessible. John W. Foster was one of these ministers and he reported in 1880 that "Russia would be glad to give liberal treatment to bona fide American citizens, *not disguised German Jews.*"

During all this time the "Russian Question" was being sedulously propagated in the United States. It appeared first in the aspect of the "Russian persecutions." The Jews represented that their life in Russia was a hell. John W. Foster, later Secretary of State, father-in-law of Robert Lansing, the recently resigned Secretary of State under President Wilson, was at that time representing the United States in Russia, and he reported as follows on the status of the Russian Jews:

" * * * in all the cities of Russia the number of Jewish residents will be found more or less in excess of the police registry and greater than the strict interpretation of the law authorizes. For instance, persons who have given the subject close attention estimate the number of Jewish residents in St. Petersburg at 30,000, while it is stated that number registered by the police authorities is 1,500. From the same source I learn that * * * while only one Hebrew school is registered by the police, there are between three and four thousand children in unauthorized Jewish schools of this capital. As another indication of the extent of Jewish influence, it is worthy of note that one or more Jewish editors or writers are said to be employed on the leading newspapers of St. Petersburg and Moscow almost without exception * * * "

At every turn the United States government discovered that the Jews were exaggerating their difficulties for the purpose of forcing government action.

Presently, after years of underground work and open propaganda against Russia in the daily press, until the American conception of Russia was fixed almost beyond correction, the agitation took the form of the "Russian passport question." Russia insults the government of the United States! Russia degrades American citizens! And so forth and so on.

Jews in the United States demanded nothing less than that the United States break all treaty relations with Russia. They *demanded* it! James B. Blaine desired one thing more than another, which was this: that something, anything, be done to block the flood of Jewish immigration then beginning to flood the country. *"The hospitality of a nation should not be turned into a burden,"* he wrote.

There was then the strange situation of the United States itself making complaints about the Jews and at the same time being asked to question Russia's right to handle similar complaints in her own domain. The minister of foreign affairs for Russia appreciated this point, and when the American minister told him that 200,000 Jews had emigrated to the United States from Russia, he rejoined: "If such a number of people had gone to the United States as *workers* to aid in developing the country he supposed they would be acceptable, *but if they went to exploit the American people, he could understand how objectionable it was.*" Of course, the whole point with Russia was that the Jews were exploiting her. They were milking Russia, not feeding her.

If space permitted, much rich material could be presented here. The attitude of the American statesmen of 25 to 40 years ago, on questions of immigration and racial propaganda, was eminer 'y wise and sound.

So, ᴜntil the days of William Howard Taft, this Jewish propaganda continued, always aimed at Russia, always planning to use the United States as the club with which to strike the blow.

It must be borne in mind at all times that the Jews maintain a lobby at Washington, a sort of embassy from the Jewish Nation to the Government of the United States, and this lobby is in the hands of a principal "ambassador." It was, of course, this ambassador's business to get hold of President Taft as firmly as possible.

But President Taft was not at that time so "easy" as the people have since been taught to regard him. There was a commercial treaty between Russia and the United States, and it had existed since 1832, and President Taft behaved as if he thought the Jewish demand that the treaty be broken was rather too much. The Jewish demand was that the United States denounce a treaty which had existed between the two countries for almost 80 years, and during the life of which Russia had repeatedly proved herself to be a reliable friend of this country.

The Jews wanted just two things from William Howard Taft: the abrogation of the Russian treaty and the veto of what Congress has repeatedly tried to do, namely, put a literacy test on immigrants. Jewish immigration into the United States being so important an element of Jewish plans, American Jews have never cared what kind of human riffraff filled the country as long as the Jewish flood was not hindered.

Presently, President Taft had undergone the persistent nagging characteristic of such campaigns and had asked, perhaps impatiently, what they wanted him to do.

"Have a conference with some of the leaders of American Jewry" was the proposal made to him, and on February 15, 1911, there walked into the White House, Jacob H. Schiff, Jacob Furth, Louis Marshall, Adolph Kraus and Judge Henry M. Goldfogle. They had lunch with the President's family and adjourned to the library.

The President was fairly wise in the matter. There was no chance whatever for him in an argument. His guests had come prepared to talk, to "tell" him, as some of the same men lately "told" an eastern publisher, pounding the table and uttering threats. The President was to be overwhelmed, his good nature carried with a rush.

But, instead of anything like that, the President as soon as they gathered in the library, took out a paper and began to read his conclusions! That staggered the Jewish ambassadors at once—the President was reading his *conclusions*! He was "telling" *them* !

The President's statement is really worth reading, but it is far too lengthy to present here. He called attention to the right which this country exercised to say who shall and who shall not sojourn here, and also to the conflicting interpretations which American secretaries of State had given the Russian treaty. He contrasted with that Russia's consistent interpretation from the beginning. He then said that the treaty was sacred because under it for more than 50 years the citizens of the United States had made their investments in Russia—resting solely on their faith in the United States' and Russia's treaty honor. He said that if it were a new treaty that was being written, the case would be different; he would then consider the Jewish argument of weight. But, he said, we had other treaties with other countries who did not always share our views as to what certain sections of the treaties meant, but we have lived and worked under them. He instanced the Italian treaty with regard to the extradition of criminals. He wished to impress on the Jewish ambassadors that they wanted to make an exception of their case, which , of course, they did.

The President then said he would be willing to consider taking some action if he did not believe that in taking action he would be endangering the status the Jews already enjoyed in Russia. If this treaty were denounced, large American interests would be jeopardized (here the President mentioned certain interests, all Gentile).

He said he liked to see Russian Jews come into the country, but added "the more we spread them out in the West, the better I like it." He ended with a plea for the Jewish ambassadors there present to consider the plight which denunciation of the treaty might involve Russian Jews, and ended with the words—"That is the way it has struck me, gentlemen. That is the conclusion I have reached."

The Jewish group was plainly taken aback. Simon Wolf, who was always on guard at Washington, said, "Please, Mr. President, do not give to the Press such conclusions," but Jacob H. Schiff broke in with a voice vibrant with anger—"I want it published. I want the whole world to know the President's attitude."

The discussion then opened, with the President cool and self-contained. Finally, after some useless talk, and having other business to attend to, he gave them a letter just received form the American Ambassador at St. Petersburg, Mr. Rockhill. Mr. Rockhill presented in that letter to the President the whole Russian contention about the Jews—statements which have been confirmed a thousand times by the events that have since occurred.

They then renewed their expostulations and arguments, but to no avail. The President expressed regret, but said he could see no other course to pursue; he had studied the question in all its lights, and his conclusion was as stated.

On leaving the White House, Jacob Schiff refused to shake the President's hand, but brushed it by with an air of offended power. "Wasn't Mr. Schiff angry yesterday!" exclaimed the President the next day.

But the President did not know what was going on. When Jacob Schiff was descending the White House steps he said, "This means war." He gave orders to draw on him for a large sum of money. He wrote a curt letter to President Taft. The President sent Mr. Schiff's letter and the reply to the Secretary of Commerce and Labor, Charles Nagel, who replied to the President with these words: "I am very much impressed with the patience which you exhibit in your answer."

Neither did the President know what was behind it all. Look at most of the names of the men who represented American Jewry in the White House that 15th of February, 1911. And then consider that the abrogation of the Russian treaty would throw all the vast business between the United States and Russia into Germany, unto the hands of German Jews. The Frankfort bankers and their relatives in the United States knew what that meant. It meant that German Jews would be the intermediaries of trade between Russia and the United States. The business itself meant money, but the relation meant power over Russia—and Jacob Schiff lived to overthrow Russia. The neutrality of the United States was torn to shreds by a movement organized and financed on American soil for the overthrow of a friendly nation, and the organizers and financiers were Jews! They used their internal power to deflect the policy of the United States to assist their plans.

The game was financial and revolutionary. It was decreed. It was the then part of the program to be accomplished, and the United States was to be used as the crowbar to batter down the walls.

When the Jewish ambassadors left the White House, orders flew from Washington and New York to every part of the United States, and the Jewish "nagging" drive began. It had a center in every city. It was focused on every Representative and Senator— no official, however, was too mean or unimportant to be drafted.

American editors may remember that drive; it was operated on precisely the same lines as the one which is proceeding against the press today. The Jews have furnished absolute proof in the last two months that they control the majority of the American press. There are signs, however, that their control does not mean anything, and will not last long.

Jacob Schiff had said on February 15, "This means war." He had ordered a large sum of money used for that purpose. The American Jewish Committee, B'nai B'rith and others of the numerous organizations of Jewry (how well organized they are the signatories of the recent Jewish defense prove) went to work and on December 13 of that same year—almost 10 months to a day after Jewry had declared war on President Taft's conclusions—both houses of Congress ordered President Taft to notify Russia that the treaty with Russia would be terminated.

Frankfort-on-the-Main had won!

In the meantime, of course, the Jewish press of the United States berated President Taft with characteristic Jewish unreserve. It would be an eye-opener if, at every speech which William Howard Taft makes for his Jewish clients, there could be distributed copies of the remarks printed about President Taft by those same clients nine years ago.

The methods by which the Jews set forth to force Congressional action are all known, and the glee with which Jewry hailed the event is also known. Two governments had been beaten—the American and the Russian! And an American President had been reversed!

Whether this had anything to do with the fact that William Howard Taft became that unusual figure—a one-term President—this chronicle does not undertake to say.

There was quite a scurry for cover at that time. Taft had been beaten, and all the men who had stood beside him ran in out of the storm. John Hays Hammond was represented as having been sympathetic with the Russian view of the Jews—as most of the American representatives were. As late as 1917, William Howard Taft, then a private citizen, wrote to the principal Jewish lobbyist at Washington asking that Mr. Hammond be not held up in

Jewish histories as one who had opposed the breaking of the Russian treaty.

The President had really done what he could to prevent the Jewish plan going through. On February 15, 1911, he withstood them face to face. On December 13, 1911, they had whipped him.

And yet in the next year, 1912, a peculiar thing occurred; the high officials of the B'nai B'rith went to the White House and there pinned on the breast of President Taft a medal which marked him as "the man who had contributed most during the year to the welfare of the Jewish cause."

There is a photograph extant of President Taft standing on the south portico of the White House, in the midst of a group of prominent Jews, and the President is wearing his medal. He is not smiling.

But even after that, the Jews were not sure of President Taft. There was a fear, expressed by private letters between prominent Jews, and also in the Jewish press, that President Taft, while officially abrogating the treaty, would consent to some working agreement which would amount to about the same thing. There were cables from Jews in Russia, stating that Taft would do that. The President was closely watched. Whenever there was an open chink in his daily program, he was approached on the matter. It was made utterly impossible for him to do anything to patch up the differences. Frankfort was to have the handling of American trade with Russia, and Jewry was to have that club over Russia. Money, more and more money, always accompanies every Jewish plan for racial or political power. They make the world pay for them subjugating it. And their first cinch-hold on Russia they won in the United States. The end of that American influence was the rise of Bolshevism, the destruction of Russia, and the murder of Nicholas Romanoff and his family.

That is the story of William Howard Taft's efforts to withstand the Jews, and how they broke him. It is probably worth knowing in view of the fact that he has become one of those "Gentile fronts" which the Jews use for their own defense.

Issue of January 15, 1921

XXXIX.

When Editors Were Independent of the Jews

THE first instinctive answer which the Jew makes to any criticism of his race coming from a non-Jew is that of violence, threatened or inflicted. This statement will be confirmed by hundreds of thousands of citizens of the United States who have heard the evidence with their own ears. Of recent months the country has been full of threats against persons who have taken cognizance of the Jewish Question, threats which have been spoken, whispered, written and passed as resolutions by Jewish organizations.

If the candid investigator of the Jewish Question happens to be in business, then "boycott" is the first "answer" of which the Jews seem to think. Whether it be a newspaper, as in the case of the old New York *Herald*; or a mercantile establishment, as in the case of A. T. Stewart's famous store; or a hotel, as in the case of the old Grand Union Hotel at Saratoga; or a dramatic production, as in the case of "The Merchant of Venice"; or any manufactured article whose maker has adopted the policy that "my goods are for sale, but not my principles"—if there is any manner of business connection with the student of the Jewish Question, the first "answer" is "boycott."

The technique is this: a "whispering drive" is first begun. Disquieting rumors begin to fly thick and fast. "Watch us get him," is the word that is passed along. Jews in charge of ticker news services adopt the slogan of "a rumor a day." Jews in charge of local newspapers adopt the policy of "a slurring headline a day." Jews in charge of the newsboys on the streets (all the street corners and desirable places downtown are pre-empted by Jewish

211

"padrones" who permit only their own boys to sell) give orders to emphasize certain news in their street cries—"a new yell against him every day." The whole campaign against the critic of Jewry, whoever he may be, is keyed to the threat, "Watch us get him."

Just as Mr. Gompers and Justice Brandeis believe in "the secondary strike," as a recent Supreme Court decision reveals, so the Jews who set out to punish the students of the Jewish Question believe in a secondary boycott. Not only do they pledge themselves (they deny this, but the newspaper reports assert it, as do unpublished telegraphic dispatches to some of the newspapers) not to use the specific product in question, but they pledge themselves to boycott anyone else who uses it. If the article is a hat (it is unlikely to be a hat, however, hats being largely Jewish) not only do the Jews pledge themselves to refrain from buying that kind of hat, but also to refrain from doing business with anyone who wears such a hat.

And then, when anything seems to occur at the hat works which indicates slackness, the Jews, forgetting all about their denial of a pledged boycott, begin to boast—"See what we did to him?"

The "whispering drive," "the boycott," these are the chief Jewish answers. They constitute the bone and sinew of that state of mind in non-Jews which is known as "the fear of the Jews."

They do not always notify their victim. Recently the young sales manager of a large wholesale firm spoke at a dinner whose guests were mostly the firm's customers. He is one of those young men who have caught the vision of a new honor in business. He believes that the right thing is always practicable, and, other things being equal, profitable as well. Among the guests were probably 40 Jewish merchants, all customers of the firm. In his address the young sales agent expressed his enthusiasm for morality by saying, "What we need in business is more of the principles of Jesus Christ." Now, as a matter of fact, the young man knows very little about Jesus Christ. He has caught fire from the Roger Babson idea of religious principle as a basis of business, but he expressed it in his own way, and everybody knew what he meant; he meant decency, not sectarianism. Yet, because he used the expression he did, he lost 40 Jewish customers for his firm, and he doesn't yet know the reason why. The agents of the firm which got the new trade know the reason. It was a silent, unannounced boycott. This article is the story of a boycott which lasted over a number of years. It is only one of numerous stories of the same kind which can be told of New York. It concerns the New York *Herald,* one newspaper that dared to remain independent of Jewish influence in the metropolis.

The *Herald* enjoyed an existence of 90 years, which was terminated about a year ago by an amalgamation. It performed great feats in the world of news-gathering. It sent Henry M. Stanley to Africa to find Livingstone. It backed up the Jeanette expedition to the Arctic regions. It was largely instrumental in having the first Atlantic cables laid. But perhaps its greatest feat was the maintenance during many years of its journalistic independence against the combined attack of New York Jewry. Its reputation among newspapermen was that neither its news nor its editorial columns could be bought or influenced.

Its proprietor, the late James Gordon Bennett, had always maintained a friendly attitude toward the Jews of his city. He apparently harbored no prejudice against them. Certainly he never deliberately antagonized them. But he was resolved upon preserving the honor of independent journalism. He never bent to the policy that the advertisers had something to say about the editorial policy of the paper, either as to influencing it for publication or suppression.

Thirty years ago the New York press was free. Today it is practically all Jewish controlled. This control is variously exercised, sometimes resting only on the owners' sense of expediency. But the control is there and, for the moment, it is absolute. One does not have to go far to be able to find the controlling factor in any case. Newspapermen do not glory in the fact, however; it is a condition, not a crusade, that confronts them, and for the moment "business is business."

Thirty years ago there were also more newspapers in New York than there are today. There were eight or nine morning newspapers; there are only five today. The *Herald,* a three-cent newspaper, enjoyed the highest prestige, and was the most desirable advertising medium due to the class of its circulation. It easily led the journalistic field.

At that time the Jewish population of New York was less than one-third of what it is today, but there was much wealth represented in it.

Now, what every newspaperman knows is this: most Jewish leaders are always interested either in getting a story published or getting it suppressed. There is no class of people who read the public press so carefully, with an eye to their own affairs, as do the Jews; and many an editor can vouch for that.

The *Herald* simply adopted the policy from the beginning of this form of harassment that it was not to be permitted to sway the *Herald* from its duty as a public informant. And that this had a reflex advantage for the other newspapers is apparent from the following statement:

If a scandal occurred in Jewish circles, influential Jews would swarm into the editorial offices to arrange for a suppression of the story. But the editors knew that not far away was the *Herald* which would not suppress for anything or anybody. What was the use of one paper suppressing, if another would not? So the editors would say, "We would be very glad to suppress this story, but the *Herald* is going to use it, so we'll have to do the same in self-protection. However, if you can get the *Herald* to suppress it, we will gladly do so, too."

But the *Herald* never succumbed. Neither pressure of influence nor promises of business nor threats of loss availed: it printed the news.

There was a certain Jewish banker who periodically demanded that Bennett discharge the *Herald's* financial editor. This banker was in the business of disposing of Mexican bonds at a time when such bonds were least secure. Once when an unusually large number of bonds were to be unloaded on unsuspecting Americans, the *Herald* published the story of an impending Mexican revolution, which presently ensued. The banker frothed at the mouth and moved every influence he could to change the

Herald's financial staff, but was not able to effect the change even of an office boy.

Once when a shocking scandal involved a member of a prominent family, Bennett refused to suppress it, arguing that if the episode had occurred in a family of any other race it would be published regardless of the prominence of the figures involved. The Jews of Philadelphia secured suppression there, but because of Bennett's unflinching stand there was no suppression in New York.

A newspaper is a business proposition. There are some matters it cannot touch without putting itself in peril of becoming a defunct concern. This is especially true since newspapers no longer receive their support from the public but from the advertisers. The money the reader gives for the paper scarcely suffices to pay for the amount of white paper he receives. In this way, advertisers cannot be disregarded any more than the paper mills can be. And as the most extensive advertisers are the department stores, and as most department stores are owned by Jews, it comes logically that Jews often try to influence the news policies at least, of the papers with whom they deal.

In New York it has always been the burning ambition of the Jews to elect a Jewish mayor. They selected a time when the leading parties were disrupted to push forward their choice. The method which they adopted was characteristic.

They reasoned that the newspapers would not dare refuse the dictum of the combined department store owners, so they drew up a "strictly confidential" letter which they sent to the owners of the New York newspapers, demanding support for the Jewish mayoralty candidate.

The newspaper owners were in a quandary. For several days they debated how to act. All remained silent. The editors of the *Herald* cabled the news to Bennett who was abroad. Then it was that Bennett exhibited that boldness and directness of judgment which characterized him. He cabled back, "*Print the letter.*" It was printed in the *Herald's* editorial columns, the arrogance of the Jewish advertisers was exposed, and non-Jewish New York breathed easier and applauded the action.

215

The *Herald* explained frankly that it could not support a candidate of private interests, because it was devoted to the interests of the public. But the Jewish leaders vowed vengeance against the *Herald* and against the man who dared expose their game. They had not liked Bennett for a long time, anyway. The *Herald* was the real "society newspaper" in New York, but Bennett had a rule that only the names of really prominent families should be printed. The stories of the efforts of newly rich Jews to break into the *Herald's* society columns are some of the best that are told by old newspapermen. But Bennett was obdurate. His policy stood.

Bennett, however, was shrewd enough not to invite open conflict with the Jews. He felt no prejudice against the race; he simply resented their efforts to intimidate him.

The whole matter culminated in a contention which began between Bennett and Nathan Straus, a German Jew whose business house is known under the name of "R. H. Macy & Company," Macy being the Scotchman who built up the business and from whose heirs Straus obtained it. Mr. Straus was something of a philanthropist in the ghetto, but the story goes that Bennett's failure to proclaim him as a philanthropist led to ill feeling between the two. A long newspaper war ensued, the subject of which was the value of the pasteurization of milk—a stupid discussion which no one took seriously, save Bennett and Straus.

The Jews, of course, took Mr. Straus' side. Jewish speakers made the welkin ring with laudation of Nathan Straus and maledictions upon James Gordon Bennett. Bennett was pictured in the most vile business of "persecuting" a noble Jew. It went so far that the Jews were able to put resolutions through the board of aldermen.

Long since, of course, Straus, a very heavy advertiser, had withdrawn every dollar's worth of his business form the *Herald* and the *Evening Telegram*. And now the combined and powerful elements of New York Jewry gathered together to deal a staggering blow at Bennett—as years before they had dealt a blow to another citizen of New York. The Jewish policy of "Dominate or Destroy" was at stake, and Jewry declared war.

As one man, the Jewish advertisers withdrew their advertisements form Mr. Bennett's newspapers. Their assigned reason was that the *Herald* was showing animosity against the Jews. The real purpose of their action was to crush an American newspaper owner who dared be independent of them. The blow they delivered was a staggering one. It meant the loss of $600,000 a year. Any other newspaper in New York would have been put out of business by it. The Jews knew that and sat back, waiting the downfall of the man they chose to consider their enemy.

But Bennett was ever a fighter. Besides, he knew Jewish psychology probably better than any other non-Jew in New York. He turned the tables on his opponents in a startling and unexpected fashion. The coveted positions in his papers had always been used by the Jews. These he immediately turned over to non-Jewish merchants under exclusive contracts. Merchants who had formerly been crowded into the back pages and obscure corners by the more opulent Jewish advertisers, now blossomed forth full page in the most popular spaces. One of the non-Jewish merchants who took advantage of the new situation was John Wanamaker, whose large advertisements from that time forward were conspicuous in the Bennett newspapers.

The Bennett papers came out with undiminished circulation and full advertising pages. The well-planned catastrophe did not occur. Instead, there was a rather comical surprise. Here were the non-Jewish merchants of New York enjoying the choicest service of a valuable advertising medium, while the Jewish merchants were unrepresented. Besides, the "punishment" which the Jews had administered showed no signs of inflicting inconvenience, let alone pain. The "boycott" had been hardest on the boycotters.

Unable to stand the spectacle of trade being diverted to non-Jewish merchants, the Jews dropped their hostile attitude and came back to Bennett, requesting the use of his columns for advertising. Bennett received all who came, displaying no rancor. They wanted back their old positions, but Bennett said,

No. They argued, but Bennett said, No. They offered money, but Bennett said, No. The choice positions had been forfeited.

Then a curious circumstance transpired. A few Jews whose business sense had overcome their racial passions had continued to advertise in the *Herald* all through the "boycott." When they saw their rebellious brethren coming back and taking what positions they could get in the advertising pages, they suspected that Bennett had lured them back by offering a lower rate. So they wrote to Bennett, demanding to know the circumstances, and as usual Bennett published the letter and replied that his rates had not been lowered.

Bennett had triumphed, but it proved a costly victory. The Jews persistently followed the plan which they had inaugurated as early as 1877, for the ruin of another New Yorker who had refused to bow before them. All the time Bennett was fighting them, the Jews were gradually growing more powerful in New York. They were growing more powerful in journalism every year. They were obsessed by the fatuous idea that to control journalism in New York meant to control the thought of the country. They regarded New York as the metropolis of the United States, whereas all balanced minds regard it as a disease.

The number of newspapers gradually diminished through combinations of publications. Adolph S. Ochs, a Philadelphia Jew, acquired the *Times*. He soon made it into a great newspaper, but one whose bias is to serve the Jews. A tabulation of the Jewish publicity that finds its way into the *Times* reveals interesting figures. Of course, it is the quality of the *Times* as a newspaper that makes it so weighty as a Jewish organ. In this paper the Jews are persistently lauded and eulogized and defended. No such tenderness is granted other races. It is quite possible that the staff of the *Times* will not regard this as entirely true. Personally and individually, the majority of them are "not that kind of people." But there is the *Times* itself as evidence.

And then Hearst came into the field—a dangerous agitator because he not only agitates the wrong things, but because he agitates the wrong class of people. He surrounded himself with a coterie of Jews, pandered to them, worked hand in glove with them, even fell out with them, but never told the truth about them—"never gave them away." Naturally, he received large advertising patronage. The trend toward the Jewish-controlled press set in strongly, and has continued that way ever since. The old names, made great by great editors and American policies, slowly dimmed.

A newspaper is founded either on a great editorial mind, in which event it becomes the expression of a powerful personality, or it becomes institutionalized as to policy and becomes a commercial establishment. In the latter event, its chances for a continuing life beyond the lifetime of its founder are much stronger. The *Herald* was Bennett, and with his passing it was inevitable that a certain force and virtue should depart out of it.

Bennett, advancing in age, dreaded lest his newspaper, on his death, should fall into the hands of the Jews. He knew that they regarded it with longing eyes. He knew that they had pulled down, seized, and afterward built up many an agency that had dared speak the truth about them, and boasted about it as a conquest for Jewry, a vindication of the oft misquoted prophecy, "He that curses you I will curse." Bennett loved the *Herald* as a man loves his child. He so arranged his will that the *Herald* should never fall into individual ownership. He devised that its revenues should flow into a fund for the benefit of the men who had worked to make the *Herald* what it was. He died in May, 1918.

The Jewish enemies of the *Herald*, eagerly watchful, more and more withdrew their advertising to force, if possible, the sale of the paper. They knew that if the *Herald* became a losing proposition, the trustees would have no course but to sell, notwithstanding Mr. Bennett's will.

But there were also strong moneyed interests in New York who were beginning to realize the peril of a Jewish press. These interests provided a large sum for the *Herald's* purchase by Frank A. Munsey. Then, to the general astonishment, Mr. Munsey discontinued the gallant old sheet, and bestowed its name as part of the name of the New York *Sun*. But the actual newspaper managed by Bennett is extinct. Even the men who worked upon it are scattered abroad in the newspaper field.

Even though the Jews had not gained possession of the coveted *Herald* they had at least succeeded in driving another non-Jewish newspaper from the field. They set about obtaining control of several evening newspapers, which action is now complete.

But the victory was a financial victory over a dead man. The moral victory, as well as the financial victory, remained with Bennett as long as he lived; the moral victory still remains with the *Herald.* The *Herald* is immortalized as the last bulwark against Jewry in New York. Today the Jews are more completely masters of the journalistic field in New York than they are in any capital in Europe. Indeed, in every capital in Europe there is a newspaper that gives the real news of the Jews. There is none in New York. And thus the situation will remain until Americans shake themselves from their long sleep, and look with steady eyes at the national situation. That look will be enough to show them all, and their very eyes will quail the oriental usurpers.

The moral is: whatever comes out of New York now must be doubly scrutinized, because it comes from the center of that Jewish government which desires to guide and color the thoughts of the people of the United States.

Issue of February 5, 1921.

XL.

Why the Jews Dislike the Morgenthau Report

I T SEEMS a far cry from the Jewish Question in the United States to the same question in Poland, but inasmuch as the Jews of the United States are constantly referring to Poland for propaganda purposes, inasmuch as there are 250,000 Polish Jews arriving in the United States on a schedule made by their brethren here, and inasmuch as the people of Poland have had their own illuminating experience with the World Program, it would seem that Poland has something to teach the United States in this respect.

Especially is this true since it is impossible to pick up an American newspaper without finding traces of Jewish anti-Polish propaganda—a propaganda which is designed to take our eyes away from the thing that is transpiring at the Port of New York. If a reader of these articles should say, "Let us not think about Poland, let us think about the United States," the answer is that he already is thinking about Poland the way the Jews of the United States want him to think, and the fact that he is thinking according to Jewish wishes in this respect incapacitates him up to a certain point to understand the entire Jewish Question in this country.

Three chapters back in this series we presented part of a hearing before a United States Senate committee on the census question as it affected the Jew. The immigration question appeared as part of that inquiry. Then followed an article which showed that Jewish authorities adopt principles exactly opposite to those which had been defended before the United States Senators. A third article followed showing how Jewish leaders resent the influence of the modern State upon Judaism. All these subjects are essential to a well-rounded understanding of the Jewish Question as a whole in its relation to the United States.

Today we go back to the home of that quarter of a million people who are so rapidly being landed on our shores to see what they did there, and to find the basis for Jewish propaganda statements that these people are fleeing from "persecution."

We have five official witnesses whose observations have been printed under the seals of the United States and the British governments. The American document is a "Message from the President of the United States, transmitting pursuant to a Senate Resolution of October 28, 1919, a communication from the Secretary of State submitting a report by the Honorable Henry Morgenthau on the work of The Mission of the United States to Poland." It is Senate Document No. 177.

This document includes also a supplementary report signed by Brigadier-General Edgar Jadwin, United States Army.

There is a certain mystery about this document. Though an edition was printed for public circulation, it soon became extremely rare. It seemed to disappear almost overnight. The copy from which this present examination is made was secured with the utmost difficulty. The head of that American Mission, which remained in Poland from July 13 to September 13, 1919, was Henry Morgenthau, an American Jew, who had been United States Minister to Turkey, a man of excellent public and private reputation.

It is commonly said that the Jews did not like his report, hence its scarcity. This much appears: The Jewish press has never made much of it; it is not cited in Jewish propaganda; it has not had the endorsement of American Jewry. The reason appears to be this—that it told the calm truth about the situation of the Jews in Poland, and made very fair observations.

But it is indirectly that American Jews show the opinion which they hold of the Morgenthau report, and it comes about in this way: When the American Mission left Poland, the British Mission arrived, and remained until December. The chief member of the British Mission was an English Jew, Sir Stuart Samuel, whose brother Herbert is now High Commissioner of Palestine. He was accompanied by a British military officer, Captain P. Wright, who also submitted a supplementary report. The two reports were submitted with an introductory report by Sir H. Rumbold, British representative at Warsaw.

Now, of all five reports, the Morgenthau, Samuel, Jadwin, Wright and Rumbold reports, *the Jews of the United States have circulated only one*—the Samuel report. It has been printed in full in newspapers at advertising rates; it has been circulated broadcast as an American Jewish Congress Bulletin. Any number of Samuel reports may be obtained, but none of the report which a member of the American diplomatic service made and which the President of the United States transmitted as a Message to the Senate.

Why? Because four reports examined the situation all round and reported it without bias, and if they were printed in the United States and spread broadcast before the people, it would throw an entirely different light on the Jewish propaganda in favor of Polish immigration in enormous numbers.

Even when the Jews of the United States published the Samuel report, they did not publish the Captain Wright report which accompanied it. In the American Jewish Congress Bulletin, the Wright report was condensed, mutilated, and shorn of its real meaning; while in the *Maccabaean,* the reports of Rumbold and Wright are treated without courtesy and the Samuel report published in full.

That the reader may form his own conclusions, the testimony of the five official witnesses (or six, if we count Homer H. Johnson, who signed the American report with General Jadwin) will be given on the principal points; the agreements and disagreements will therefore be noticeable.

1. ON THE GENERAL SUBJECT OF PERSECUTION.

SIR STUART SAMUEL says: "Poles generally are of a generous nature, and if the present incitements of the press were repressed by a strong official hand, Jews would be able to live, *as they have done for the past 800 years,* on good terms with their fellow citizens in Poland."

Note how easily Sir Stuart talks about repression of the press. The Polish press has at last obtained freedom of writing. It is exercising a privilege which the Jewish press of Poland has always had. But now that it speaks freely of Jews, repress it with a strong hand, says Sir Stuart. He would not dare suggest that in England where the press also is finding its freedom. As to the Yiddish press in Poland, the reader will find some information in Israel Friedlaender's essay, "The Problem of Polish Jewry." Friedlaender was a Jew and his book is published by a Jewish house in Cincinnati. He says:

"The Yiddish press sprang up and became a powerful civilizing agency among the Jews of Poland. The extent of its influence may be gathered from the fact, which curiously enough is pointed out reproachfully by the Poles, *that the leading Yiddish newspaper of Warsaw commanded but a few years ago a larger circulation than that of all the Polish newspapers combined.*"

HENRY MORGENTHAU says (par. 7)—"The soldiers had been inflamed by the charge that the Jews were Bolsheviks, while at Lemberg it was associated with the idea that the Jews were making common cause with the Ukrainians. *These excesses were, therefore, political* as well as anti-Semitic in character."

And again (par. 8)—"Just as the Jews would resent being condemned as a race for the action of a few of their co-religionists, so it would be correspondingly *unfair to condemn the Polish nation as a whole* for the violence committed by uncontrolled troops or local mobs. These excesses were apparently *not pre-meditated,* for if they had been part of a preconceived plan, the number of victims would have run into *the thousands instead of amounting to about 280.* It is believed that these excesses were the result of a widespread anti-Semitic prejudice aggravated by *the belief that the Jewish inhabitants were politically hostile to the Polish State.*"

SIR H. RUMBOLD says: "It is giving the Jews very little real assistance to single out, as is sometimes done, for reprobation and protest *the country where they have perhaps suffered least.*"

CAPTAIN P. WRIGHT says: "It is an explanation often given of what may be called, according to the point of view, the idiosyncrasies or defects of the Jews, that they have been an oppressed and persecuted people. This is an idea so charitable and humane that I should like to think it, not only of the Jews, but of every other people. It has every merit as a theory, *except that of being true.* When one thinks of what happened to the other 'racial, religious and linguistic minorities' of Europe in modern times. * * * *the Jews appear not as the most persecuted but as the most favored people of Europe.*

BRIGADIER GENERAL JADWIN states clearly that the "persecution" cry may be regarded as propaganda. He says:

"The disorders of November 21 to 23 in Lemberg became, like the excesses in Lithuania, a weapon of *foreign anti-Polish propaganda.* The press bureau of the Central Powers, in whose interest it lay to discredit the Polish Republic before the world, permitted the publication of articles * * * in which an eyewitness estimated the number of victims between 2,500 and 3,000, although the extreme number furnished by the local Jewish committee was 76." (p. 15)

And again: "In common with all free governments of the world, Poland is faced with the danger of the political and *international propaganda* to which the war has given rise. The *coloring,* the *invention,* the *suppression* of news, the *subornation of newspapers* by many different methods, and the *poisoning by secret influences of the instruments affecting public opinion,* in short, all the methods of malevolent propaganda are a menace from which Poland is a notable sufferer." (p. 17).

Of course, all this propaganda has been Jewish. The methods described are typically Jewish.

Speaking about the number killed, Mr. Morgenthau estimates the total at 258; while Sir H. Rumbold says that only 18 were killed "in Poland proper," the others having been killed in the disorders of the war zone. Sir Stuart Samuel estimates the total killed at 348.

2. *ON THE GENERAL CAUSE OF JEWISH TROUBLE BEFORE THE WAR.*

SIR STUART SAMUEL—"The Jews in Poland and Galicia numbered about 3,000,000 * * * Public opinion had been aroused against them by the institution of a virulent boycott. This boycott dates from shortly after the by-election for the Duma, which took place in Warsaw in 1912 * * * Business relations between Poland and Russia were very considerable in the past, and were generally *in the hands of the Jews*, not only in the *handling* of the goods exported, but also in their *manufacture* * * * Initiative in business matters is almost entirely *the prerogative of the Jewish population* * * * Nearly the whole of the *estate agents* who act for the Polish nobility are of the *Jewish race* * * * Attention must be paid to the fact that *Jews form the middle class almost in its entirety.* Above are the aristocracy and below are the peasants. Their relations with the peasants are not unsatisfactory. The young peasants cannot read the newspapers and are therefore but slightly contaminated by anti-Semitism until they enter the army. I was informed that it is not at all unusual for Polish peasants to avail themselves of the arbitrament of the *Jewish rabbi's courts.*"

That shows the Jews to have occupied a very favorable position in Poland and is to be remembered in connection with the previous quotation from Sir Stuart in which he says that if the incitements of the press were repressed by a strong official hand, "the Jews would be able to live, as they have done *for the past 800 years, on good terms* with their fellow citizens in Poland."

Let us take the points made by Sir Stuart, and observe what the other witnesses say about them:

(a) Beginning with the point as to the Jews' monopoly of business in Poland:

SIR H. RUMBOLD—"Sir Stuart Samuel would appear to be mistaken in his appreciation of the part played by the Jews in the pre-war business relations between Poland and Russia and in the *industry* of the former country. Whereas it is true that goods exported from Poland were to a large extent *handled* by the Jews, *only a small percentage of those goods were actually manufactured by them.*"

CAPTAIN P. WRIGHT—"In Poland until the last generation *all business men were Jews:* The Poles were peasants or landowners, and *left commerce to the Jews;* even now certainly much more than half, and perhaps as much as three-quarters, of business men are Jews."

"For both town and country I think it a true generalization to say that the *East Jews are hardly ever producers, but nearly always middlemen.* "

"Economically, the Jews appear at the very outset as *dealers, not as producers,* nor even as artisans, and chiefly *dealers in money:* in course of time the whole business and commerce of Poland became theirs, and they did nothing else."

(b) With regard to the "estate agents" mentioned by Sir Stuart Samuel:

CAPTAIN P. WRIGHT—"Poland is an agricultural country, but the East Jews, unlike the West Jews, play a large part in its country life. Every estate and every village has its Jew, who holds a sort of hereditary position in them; he markets the produce of the peasants and makes their purchases for them in town; every Polish landowner or noble had his own Jew, who did all his business for him, managed the commercial part of his estate, and found him money * * * Besides this, nearly all the population of nearly all the small country towns is Jewish, corn and leather dealers, storekeepers and peddlers, and such like."

(c) Regarding Sir Stuart's assertion that "Jews form the middle class almost to its entirety," with the nobles above them and the peasants beneath them (a typical Jewish position—dividing Gentile society and standing between the parts), this illustration may help to make it clear:

CAPTAIN P. WRIGHT—"It is instructive to try and imagine what England would be like under the same conditions. Arriving in London, a stranger would find every second or third person a Jew, almost all the poorer quarters and slums Jewish, and thousands of synagogues. Arriving at Newbury he would find practically the whole town Jewish, and nearly every printed inscription in Hebrew characters. Penetrating into Berkshire, he would find the only storekeeper in most small villages a Jew, and small market towns mostly composed of Jewish hovels. Going on to Birmingham he would find all the factories owned by Jews, and two shops out of three with Jewish names."

Captain Wright is trying to give the people at home a picture of conditions in order that they may understand how Poland feels. The Jewish press strongly resented this. Sir Stuart Samuel's report is notable for the number of things he mentioned, and the few he explained.

3. *ON THE GENERAL CAUSE OF TROUBLE ARISING DURING THE WAR.*

SIR STUART SAMUEL—'The fact of their language being akin to German often led to their being employed during the German occupation in preference to other Poles. This circumstance caused the Jews to be accused of having had business relations with the Germans * * * The Government publicly declared its disapproval of boycotting, but a certain discrimination seems to have been made in the re-employment of those who served under the German occupation. I find that many Jews who thus served have been relieved of their offices and not reinstated, whereas I can find no evidence of similar procedure in regard to other Poles."

SIR H. RUMBOLD—'The fact of Yiddish being akin to German *may* have been the reason why the Germans employed a large number of Jews during their occupation of Poland, although a great many of the Poles with a good knowledge of German could have been found. *There is this difference, however, that the Poles only served the Germans by compulsion,* as they considered them to be their enemies."

BRIGADIER GENERAL JADWIN—"During the German occupation of Poland, the Germanic character of the Yiddish vernacular and *the readiness of certain Jewish elements to enter into relations with the winning side,* induced the enemy to employ Jews as agents for various purposes and to grant the Jewish population not only exceptional protection, but also *the promise of autonomy.* It is alleged that the Jews were active in *speculation in foodstuffs,* which was encouraged by the armies of occupation with a view to facilitating export to Germany and Austria." That is, the Jews were the means by which Poland was to be drained of its food supply.

CAPTAIN P. WRIGHT—"But the high day and triumph of the Jews was during the German occupation. The Jews in Poland are deeply Germanized, and German carries you over Poland because Jews are everywhere. So the Germans found everywhere people who knew their language and could work for them. *It was with Jews* that the Germans set up their organization to squeeze and drain Poland—Poles and Jews included—of everything it had; *it was in concert with Jews* that German officials and officers toward the end carried on business all over the country. In every department and region they were the instruments of the Germans, *and poor Jews grew rich* and lordly as the servants of the masters. But though Germanized, *the accusation of the Poles that the Jews are devoted to Germany is unfounded* * * * They have no more loyalty to Germany—the home of anti-Semitism— than to Poland. *The East Jews are Jews and only Jews.*

"It has seemed certain that one of two, the German or the Russian Empire, must win, and that *the Jews, who had their money on both,* were safe; but the despised Poland came in first. Even now the Jews can barely believe in its resurrection, and one of them told me it still seemed to him a dream."

Mr. Morgenthau does not touch this matter in his report.

4. *WITH REFERENCE TO THE BOYCOTT, THE METHOD BY WHICH THE POLES SOUGHT TO LIBERATE THEMSELVES FROM THE JEWISH STRANGLEHOLD.*

SIR STUART SAMUEL—'This boycott dates from shortly after the by-election for the Duma, which took place in Warsaw in 1912 * * * During the war, owing to the scarcity of almost everything, the boycott diminished, but with the armistice it revived with much of its original intensity * * * A severe private, social and commercial boycott of Jews, however, exists among the people generally, largely fostered by the Polish press. In Lemburg I found there was a so-called social court presided over by M. Przyluski, a former Austrian vice-president of the Court of Appeals, which goes so far as to summon persons having trade relations with Jews to give an explanation of their conduct. Below will be found a typical cutting from a Polish newspaper giving the name of a Polish countess who sold property to Jews. This was surrounded by a mourning border such as is usual in Poland in making announcements of death.

(translation)

"Countess Anna Jablonowska, resident in Galicia, has sold her two houses, Stryjska street, Nos. 18 and 20, to the Jews, Dogilewski, Hubner and Erbsen. The attorney of the countess was Dr. Dziedzic; her administrator, M. Naszkowski. Will the Polish public forever remain indifferent and passive in such cases?"

This illustration of Sir Stuart brings to mind a practice common in England, It is related on page 123 of "The conquering Jew," by John Fraser, published by Funk & Wagnalls, New York, 1916: "The housing question in the Whitechapel district has reached such a pitch that there are large blocks of buildings where 'No English Need Apply' is a common legend. Whole streets are being bought up by Hebrew syndicates, whose first act is to serve notice on all Gentile tenants."

It is also worth stating in this connection, that some of the feeling which has recently led to race riots in American cities has been engendered by the practice of small Jewish real estate syndicates purchasing a house in the middle of a desirable block, ousting the tenants and installing a Negro family, thereby using race prejudice to depreciate the property in the entire block and render it purchasable by the Jews at a low price. Thereafter the property is lost to Gentile ownership or use.

It may be that in Poland a similar condition exists which makes the sale of property into Jewish hands a kind of disloyalty to the people generally. Apparently the Poles think so. "Racial prejudice" is not a sufficient explanation of such beliefs: there is always something pretty tangible beneath them.

The "boycott" was merely this:—an agreement among Poles to trade with Poles. The Jews were numerous, well-to-do, and in control of all the channels of business. They own practically all the real estate in Warsaw. The Jews claimed that the so-called boycott (the Polish name for it is "the co-operatives") was "persecution."

SIR H. RUMBOLD—"It must be further remembered that under the influence of economic changes and owing to the fact that since 1832 the Poles have not been allowed to hold posts in the government, they were gradually obliged to take to trade, and competition between the Jewish population and the Poles commenced. This competition became stronger when the Russian Government allowed co-operative and agricultural societies to be started in Poland. The co-operative movement is becoming very strong and will undoubtedly form an important factor in the development of economic relations in Poland, so that indirectly it will be bound to affect the position of the small Jewish trader.

"In so far as the Polish Government are able to do so by legislation or proclamations, the boycotting of the Jews should be prohibited. But I would point out that *it is beyond the power of any government to force its subjects to deal with persons with whom they do not wish deal.*"

HENRY MORGENTHAU, however, takes a more reasonable view than his British co-religionist, Sir Stuart Samuel. Mr. Morgenthau says:

"Furthermore, the establishment of co-operative stores is claimed by many Jewish traders to be a form of discrimination. It would seem, however, that *this movement is a legitimate effort* to restrict the activities and therefore the profits of the middleman. Unfortunately, when these stores were introduced into Poland, they were advertised as a means of eliminating the Jewish trader. The Jews have, therefore, been caused to feel that the establishment of co-operatives is an attack upon themselves. While the establishment and the maintenance of co-operatives may have been influenced by anti-Semitic sentiment, *this is a form of economic activity which any community is perfectly entitled to pursue.* "

It is not difficult, therefore, to see through the eyes and minds of these five men the situation that prevailed in Poland. Eight hundred years ago, Poland opened her gates to the persecuted Jews in all Europe. They flocked there and enjoyed complete freedom; they were even allowed to form a "state within a state," governing themselves in all Jewish matters and doing business with the Polish Government only through their own chosen spokesmen and representatives. The Polish people were their friends, evincing neither religious nor racial antipathy to them. Then Europe fell upon Poland, divided her asunder, until in the roster of the nations there was no more Poland, except in the hearts of the Polish people. During this period of Poland's humiliation, the Jews grew to be a mighty power, ruling the Poles, regulating their very lives. The Great War came with its promise of liberation and the restoration of a Polish free government. The Jews were not favorable to that restoration. They were not Poland's friends. The Poles resented this and at the signing of the armistice when they were free to express their resentment, they did so. Many regrettable things occurred, but they were not unintelligible. They had explanatory backgrounds. Even the armistice was not the end. The Bolsheviks from Russia came down upon Poland, and once more, so the Poles strongly declare, the Jews were against the land that had sheltered them for 800 years.

These are a few of the facts. Another article will be required to complete the story. In the meantime enough has been said to show the utter wrong which Jewish propaganda in the United States has done to Poland. But the purpose was not altogether to injure Poland; it was also to blind the American people, and cause them to view with equanimity the great influx of those same Jews into this country.

Issue of October 30, 1920.

XLI.

Jews Use the Peace Conference to Bind Poland

THERE is one difference between the Polish report of Sir Stuart Samuel and those of the others, which illustrates a difference between the Jewish mind and the general mind. The type of mind represented by the other investigators, Captain Wright, Brigadier General Jadwin, Sir H. Rumbold and even Henry Morgenthau is the type of mind which looks behind events for causes.

Here is, for illustration, trouble between the Jews and other people. It is a continuous situation. There is always trouble between the two. We seldom hear of it, however, until the Jew begins to get the worst of it. As long as the Jew remains on top, making the Gentile serve the Jewish plan, there is no publicity whatever. The Gentiles may complain as much as they like, may protest and rebel—no international commissions arrive to investigate the matter.

Trouble between the Jews and other people is designated as trouble only when it begins to grow inconvenient for the Jew. It is then that he sends the cry of "persecution" around the earth, though the plain fact may be that he is only being nipped at his own game. The Poles saw how the Jews clung together in the most admirable teamwork, a minority absolutely controlling the majority because the minority formed a close corporation and the majority did not. So the Poles said: "We will take a leaf out of the Jews' own book. They work co-operatively among themselves; we, therefore, will work co-operatively among ourselves." Which they did, and at once the cry of "persecution" resounded loud and long; propaganda was begun against the good name of the Poles, more resentment followed, regrettable violence ensued, and the dispute still continues.

Jewish reports of these disturbances rarely go beyond the fact that Jews are suffering from certain acts of the Polish populace. Incident after incident is given with full detail, and with a very apparent journalistic appreciation of horror. Names, dates, places, circumstances are all in order.

Very well. It is no part of this article to deny or minimize the suffering of Jews wherever or for whatever cause it may occur. There is nothing whatever to be said in extenuation of injustice inflicted on the humblest human being. The murder of even one person, the terrorizing of even one family, is a very terrible thing to contemplate. It is a great pity that the world has become so accustomed to the piled-up tales of horror that it no longer has any sensibilities left to feel the shame and degradation of these things. From the days of Belgium onward, all races in Europe have suffered, and by sympathy all races in America have suffered with them, though it is a fact that we hear more, far more, about the sufferings of the Jews than of any other people.

There is, however, this reaction of the practical mind: Why do these things occur? Grant that robberies, assaults and murders described in the complaint, have occurred, *why should they occur?*

Are the Polish people naturally given to perpetrating such acts? Have such acts marked the residence of the Jews in Poland for the last 800 years? And if the Polish people are not naturally abusive, if the story of the Jews' residence in Poland has been mostly pleasant, what causes the change now?—that is the way the practical general mind works. It seeks to know the background.

Mr. Morgenthau, apparently, put in too much of this background, though at that he put in very much less than the other investigators, except Mr. Samuel. Therefore, Mr. Morgenthau's report was pigeonholed by American Jewry, because the facts make very poor material for the kind of propaganda which American Jewish leaders had in mind. Apparently they did not dare publicly to criticize or renounce his report; they simply passed it over. Captain Wright, who endeavored to put in all the background he could find to make Polish conditions comprehensible to the British people, has been handled insultingly by the Jewish press. They don't want investigation. They want sympathy for themselves and denunciation for the Poles.

In America, we are inclined to believe that every condition is explainable: it may be reprehensible, but it is intelligible; we believe that the explanation is the first step toward the remedy. Mr. Morgenthau does not speak of "pogroms" at all. In this he sets an example that certain hysterical American Jews ought to follow. The present series of articles in THE DEARBORN INDEPENDENT is a "pogrom" (some Jewish spokesmen speak as if each separate article were a "pogrom") in the hectic but uninstructive oratory of Hebrew lodge meetings. But Mr. Morgenthau exercises more precision in the use of words. He says:

"The mission has purposely avoided the use of the word 'pogrom,' as the word is applied to everything from petty outrages to premeditated and carefully organized massacres * * * "

On one point all the reports agree, namely, that the unjust killing of Jews has been of a scale so much smaller than that alleged by the propagandists that there is no comparison. In that part of Poland where war disorder was less common, 18 persons were unjustly deprived of their lives. For the whole territory during the entire period when it was being overrun by various elements, Sir Stuart Samuel admits, apparently with reluctance, that he can count only 348. Captain Wright says: "I estimate that not more than 200 or 300 have been unjustly killed. One would be too many, but, taking these casualties as a standard with which to measure the excesses committed against them, I am more astonished at their smallness than their greatness." Sir H. Rumbold says: "If the excesses had been encouraged or organized by the civil and military authorities, the number of victims would probably have been much greater."

That the reader may see how the various reports run with reference to specific charges of brutality, the agreements and divergences are set down. Look at the reports concerning what happened at Lemberg.

1. The excesses occurred November 21-23, 1918. The city was taken by Ukrainian troops, formerly in the Austrian service. (Samuel, Morgenthau, Wright, Jadwin)

2. "General Monczyunski raised a Polish army, about 1,500 in number, consisting of men, women, boys, some of them criminals, and, after a severe struggle, succeeded in capturing half the city, the other half of which remained in the occupation of the Ukrainians." (Samuel.) "A few hundred Polish boys, combined with numerous volunteers of doubtful character, recaptured about half the city and held it until the arrival of Polish reinforcements on November 21." (Morgenthau.) "When the German troops revolted all over Poland at the time of the armistice, and the whole edifice of German organization fell to the ground in a day, a few Polish officers raised a small volunteer force in Lemberg, numbering between 1,000 and 2,000, which was composed of boys, roughs and criminals, and even women in uniform. For nearly a fortnight they fought in the streets against the Ukrainians and on the arrival of a similar force * * * drove the Ukrainians out of town. This was really a splendid feat of arms." (Captain Wright.)

3. "The Jewish part of the population of Lemberg declared itself to be neutral." (Samuel.)

"The Jewish population declared themselves neutral, but the fact that the Jewish quarter lay within the section occupied by the Ukrainians, and that the Jews had organized their own militia and, further, the rumor that some of the Jewish population had fired upon the soldiery, stimulated among the Polish volunteers an anti-Semitic bias that readily communicated itself to the relieving troops." (Morgenthau.)

"During the struggle the Jews proclaimed themselves neutral; but, though I do not think they gave any armed assistance to the Ukrainians, their neutrality was highly benevolent to the Ukrainians and probably helpful. They thought the Ukrainians would win." (Captain Wright.)

4. "In the result *none of the military commanders* responsible for these events *has been punished.* (Samuel.) "As early as

December 24, 1918, the Polish Government, through the ministry of justice, began a strict investigation of the events of November 21 and 23 * * * In spite of the crowded dockets of the local courts, where over 7,000 cases are now pending, 164 persons, ten of them Jews, have been tried for complicity in the November disorders, and numerous similar cases await disposal. Forty-four persons are under sentences ranging from 10 days to 18 months. Aside from the civil courts, *the local court-martial has sentenced military persons to confinement for as long as three years* for lawlessness during the period in question." (Morgenthau.) Speaking of the general subject of punishment, Captain Wright says: "The Government has inflicted a good deal, though an insufficient amount of punishment; these punishments it has never published, for fear of Polish public opinion." And Brigadier General Jadwin, of the United States Mission, says: "If complaints as to slowness and uncertainty of military and government punishments and relief were heard, as they were, it seemed nevertheless to indicate that orderly process of government was in operation."

5. *"No compensation has been paid* for the damage done." (Samuel.)

"This mission is advised that on the basis of official investigations the government *has begun the payment of claims* for damages resulting from these events." (Morgenthau.)

"Payments had begun to be made in Wilna, Pinsk and Lemberg before our departure from Poland." (General Jadwin.)

The occurrences in Lemberg were bad enough, to be sure. But Sir Stuart Samuel let it be understood that all the blame rested with the Poles. The other investigators gave reports that explain the matter, although no report could excuse it. And all but Samuel agreed that the Polish Government did what it could to repair what had occurred and to prevent recurrences. This from the American report is worth considering: "General Jadwin was present at the taking of Minsk and a personal witness of the strenuous efforts of the military authorities toward preventing acts of violence." The fact seems to be that as soon as any sort of order could be brought out of the chaos of war, the disorder ceased. And yet we read, even today in our newspapers, of "thousands and tens of thousands of Jews being slaughtered in Poland."

Further, to indicate that these events did not occur without Jewish provocation to a certain extent, there is the case of Pinsk. This was on April 5, 1919.

1. Pinsk had been recaptured from the Bolsheviki a short time before. The population was overwhelmingly Jewish, only 25 per cent being Polish. (General Jadwin, Captain Wright.) The Polish officer had only a very small detachment of men, and the Bolshevist lines were quite close. The Polish officer was treated with coldness by the Jews, and he suspected them of friendly relations with the Bolsheviki; he was very anxious. He had posted notices that any unauthorized meeting would be punishable by death. (Captain Wright.)

2. The Government Organizer of Co-operative societies had given permission for the Jewish co-operatives to meet for discussion of the plan to join other co-operatives. (Samuel, Morgenthau, Wright.)

3. "It seems that *two Polish soldiers* * * * and another soldier * * * informed the military authorities that they had information that the Jews intended to hold a Bolshevik meeting on Saturday in what is known as the People's House, being the headquarters of the Zionists." (Samuel.) "This meeting took place in the offices of the Zionist organization, which is very anti-Polish." (Wright.)

" * * * it is recognized that information of Bolshevist activities in Pinsk had been received by *two Jewish soldiers* * * * " (Morgenthau.)

"The town commander with judgment unbalanced by fear of a Bolshevik uprising of which he had been forewarned by *two Jewish soldier* informers * * * " (General Jadwin.)

"After the meeting had ended and been formally closed, a great many members of the co-operative association remained in the same room talking together; other members of the Zionist organization, including ladies, were in the room at the same time. This collection of people must have presented the appearance of a meeting, and I think the members remaining in one room were numerous enough technically to constitute a meeting. *There was some insolence in this and the previous behavior of the Jews: Sir Stuart Samuel pointed out to the witnesses that their authorized meeting itself had been a breach of the Sabbath,* and therefore a grave religious offense." (Captain Wright.)

All of the investigators agree in denouncing what followed. Captain Wright says the Polish officer would hardly have acted with such promptitude if the prisoners had been others than Jews.

General Jadwin sums it up thus: "The Pinsk outrage * * * was a purely military affair. The town commander with judgment unbalanced by fear of a Bolshevist uprising of which he had been forewarned by *two Jewish soldier informers* sought to terrorize the Jewish population (about 75 per cent of the whole) by the execution of 35 Jewish citizens without investigation of trial, by imprisoning and beating others and by wholesale threats against all Jews. No share in this action can be attributed to any military official higher up, to any of the Polish civil officials, nor to the few Poles resident in that district of White Russia."

Sir Stuart says: "Under the present local administration Pinsk is once more peaceful, and the relations between the Christian and non-Christian inhabitants have become normal."

It is sometimes forgotten here in the United States that for Poland the war is not yet over. Poland is now a free nation—on paper—but her freedom seems to be a day-to-day tenure, dependent on fighting. Bolshevism made serious inroads on her. Wherever the Bolshevik Red armies swept across Poland, the Jews met them with welcomes. This is no longer denied, even in the United States: it is explained by the statement that the Bolsheviki are more friendly to the Jews than are the Poles—a statement which readers of our recent articles on the Jewish character of Sovietism can well understand.

When the Poles beat back the Reds, they commonly found that the Jews had already set up Sovietism, as if they had long awaited it and were well prepared. It is scarcely strange, therefore, that the Poles still retain their suspicions.

The Jews do not want to become Poles. That is the root of the present difficulty between the two peoples. Sir Stuart Samuel barely touches it—"On several occasions the resentment of the soldiery and civil population was aroused by the Zionists' claim to *Jewish nationality as opposed to Polish nationality.*" Mr. Morgenthau goes a step further—"This had led to a conflict with the nationalist declarations of some of the *Jewish organizations which desire to establish cultural autonomy financially supported by the State.*" Mr. Morgenthau, you will observe, gives a wider peep into conditions.

But the best description of the situation is given in the report of Captain Wright: "Their (the Jews') party program in Poland is to have *all Jews on a separate register.* The Jews thus registered are *to elect a representative body of Jews,* with extensive powers of legislation and *taxation*; e. g., it could tax for purposes of emigration. This body to be *handed over by the Polish State a proportionate amount of money* to spend on Jewish charitable and financial institutions. Besides this separate organization, a number of seats proportionate to their numbers to be set aside in every local and in the national legislature. A sixth or seventh of the Polish Diet to be *occupied only by Jews to be elected only by Jews.* Some Jews also demand separate law courts, or at least the right to use Yiddish as well as Polish in legal proceedings. This is the practical program, but the ambition of the advanced section is *national personal autonomy* granted in the Ukraine by one of the ephemeral governments of the Ukraine, the Ukrainian Central Rada, on January 9, 1918, and called the Statute of National Personal Autonomy, of which I have a copy. It organizes the Jews as a nation with full sovereign powers; the Ukrainian *bank notes were printed in Yiddish* as well as in Ukrainian."

People sometimes ask, where is the proof of the program of the Protocols? It is everywhere the Jewish leaders have attained power, and everywhere they are striving for power. The Protocols can be written out of Jewish rabbinical writings; they can be written out of Jewish tendencies in the United States; they can be written out of Jewish demands in the Balkans; they can be written out of Jewish achievements in Russia. They represent the Jewish program, ideal and real, at every stage of modern history.

Do you ever hear of this Jewish program in Poland when you are invited to sympathize with the 250,000 Jews who are being brought from Poland to the United States? Will these people leave their ideas outside New York harbor?

Incidentally, Captain Wright's full investigation of the Jewish program may throw some light on the refusal of the American Jews to circulate his report, although it was attached to the report of Sir Stuart Samuel which is being to widely circulated.

However, that his government at home might fully understand the situation, Captain Wright draws an illustrative parallel:

"If the Jews in England—after multiplying their numbers by twenty or thirty—demanded that the Jewish Board of Guardians should have extensive powers, including the right to tax for purposes of emigration, and that a separate number of seats should be set aside in the London County Council, the Manchester Town Council, the House of Commons, and the House of Lords, to be occupied only by Jews chosen by Jews; that the president of the board of education should hand over yearly to the Jews sums proportionate to their numbers; if some were to demand the right to have separate Jewish law courts, or at least to be allowed to use Yiddish as well as English in the King's Bench and Chancery Division; if the most advanced even looked forward to a time when Bank of England notes were to be printed in Yiddish as well as in English, then they might well find public opinion, even in England, less well disposed to them * * *"

In view of this state of affairs, it cannot be regarded as a fact of minor significance that the Jewish investigators who must have known all this virtually concealed it, and that the other investigators brought it forth to general knowledge. Neither is it of minor significance that the Jewish press has absolutely suppressed these facts even while pretending to give the results of the British

Missions' investigations. Insulting references have been made to Captain Wright's report in a Jewish publication of the better class, because he made references to certain practices which are common among the Jews in Poland. It may be said, however, that the references made by Captain Wright are in great restraint compared with the number given in the recent book by Arthur Goodhart. ·Whether Mr. Goodhart is a Jew or not, the present writer cannot now say. He is a Fellow of Corpus Christi College, Cambridge. He is "lately Captain, United States Army." He was transferred from the army at the suggestion of Mr. Morgenthau, to act as counsel for the Mission. And he says on page 161, "After dinner Mr. Morgenthau attended a meeting of the B'nai B'rith Lodge, the only chapter of this Jewish organization in Poland. No branches had been permitted in Russia before the war, as it was a secret society and therefore illegal in the Czar's Empire. Major Otto and I, not being members, walked round the town." Mr. Goodhart, as counsel of the American mission, makes an excellent witness as to the kind of people who are coming in such large numbers to this country. But their sense of their own political importance and power is the principal point for Americans to consider.

The Peace Conference did not tend to bring unity in Poland; it rather established the disunity for as long a period as the treaty of Versailles remains to rule the world. The reader has just seen Captain Wright's description of what the Jews demanded. Let the reader now understand what the Peace Conference decreed.

Poland is prohibited from having an election on Saturday. Poland is prohibited from having a registration on Saturday. The Jewish Sabbath is established by law, and government and courts must govern themselves accordingly. Do what you like on Sunday—order elections on Sunday, as the Poles sometimes do—but not Saturday; it is the Jews' Sabbath!

"Article 11—Jews shall not be compelled to perform *any act which constitutes a violation of their Sabbath,* nor shall they be placed under any disability by reason of their refusal to attend courts of law or to perform any legal business on their Sabbath* * * Poland declares her intention to refrain from ordering or permitting elections, whether general or local, to be held on a *Saturday,* nor will registration for electoral or other purposes be compelled to be performed on a *Saturday*."

What the Bolsheviki did in Russia, the Peace Conference did in Poland—established the Jewish Sabbath.

The people who saw this strange setting up of Jewish customs as a part of the law of the land, one of the authorities for such action being the President of the United States, are now flocking to the United States in large numbers. Is it unreasonable for them to believe that if the President of the United States could bind Poland to Jewish custom, it is all right to bind the United States too?

Moreover, the Jewish separate schools were established by law in Poland. Poland's great trouble has resulted from her lack of schools in which *all* the population could imbibe Polish ideals expressed in the Polish language. The Peace Conference authorizes the continuance of that source of trouble.

In Article 11, "the Jews" were mentioned. In Article 9, the term used is "Polish nationals." The reader will save himself a great deal of misunderstanding in the perusal of European news if he will translate the clause "racial, religious and linguistic minorities" to mean simply Jews. They are the "minority" that is at the bottom of most of the difficulty, and they are the minority that is most heard of. It was this minority that dominated the Peace Conference.

"Article 9—Poland will provide in the educational system in towns and districts in which a considerable proportion of Polish nationals of other than Polish speech are residents, adequate facilities for insuring that in the primary schools instruction shall be given to the children of such Polish nationals through the medium of their own language. * * *

"In towns and districts where there is a considerable proportion of Polish nationals belonging to racial, linguistic or religious minorities, *these minorities shall be assured an equitable share in the enjoyment and application of the sums which may be provided out of public funds* under the state, municipal or other budgets for education, religious or charitable purposes."

But even that is not all. The Polish State is to hand over the money, but the Jews will distribute it:

"Educational committees appointed locally by the *Jewish* communities of Poland will, subject to the general control of the state, provide for the distribution of the proportional share of the public funds allocated to *Jewish* schools in accordance with Article 9 * * *"

It is most amazing how "racial minorities" are dropped the moment money comes into view, and the definite term "Jew" is substituted.

More than all this, "the United States of America, the British Empire, France, Italy, and Japan, the principal allied and associated powers, on the one hand; and Poland, on the other hand," (so the text of the treaty begins) together make of all these special privileges, not a national agreement on the part of hard-pressed Poland, but an international demand on the part of the League of Nations. Article 12 stipulates that all the agreements affecting "racial, linguistic and religious minorities," which is mere diplomatic camouflage for "Jews," shall be placed under the guaranty of the League of Nations. This lifts the Jews in Poland completely out of Polish obligation. All they will have to do is to complain to the League of Nations—and International Jewry will do the rest.

The United States was a party toward the writing of these stipulations into the treaty. The American people are not yet a party to their enforcement.

There are a quarter of a million of these Jews coming to the United States from Poland. You have read their demands in Poland. You have read their achievements in the Peace Conference.

Do you say, as an American citizen, that you are ready to take for the United States the dose of Jewish medicine, which the Peace Conference gave to Poland?

Do you say, in view of what has been said about the whole situation, that the Jews are showing anything besides a wicked and gloating spirit of revenge in the way they have propagandized against Poland after humiliating her in the Peace Conference?

Issue of November 6, 1920

XLII.

The Present Status of the
Jewish Question

THE Jewish Question in the United States has existed for years, but until now in silence and suspicion. Every one knew that there was such a Question; the Jew himself knew best of all; but very few possessed the courage to open the Question to the sanitary influences of sunlight and speech. The mention of courage in this connection is needful to explain the silence. A few men of insight have attempted publicly to define the Question in the United States, and they have been so effectually dealt with by an invisible power of which the public could have no knowledge, that Free Speech on the Jewish Question naturally became unpopular. The fact, it is true, reflects more seriously on non-Jews than on Jews. But it is a fact nevertheless. He who undertakes to speak truth on this question must expect far more opposition that he could ever withstand were he not speaking the truth.

One fact that militated against Free Speech on the Jewish Question was the condition into which our American people have been trained, of expecting applause and approval to follow every act and word. There was a time in American history, and it was the most glorious period of our past, when opposition was considered an often desirable attitude. A man's weight was accounted equal, whether computed by the number of his enemies or his friends. But a softening change has come over us. We have grown to like applause. Hisses used to stir our fathers; hisses cow their sons. Public speech has thus become neutral; we have grown pudgy and futile in our programs of "helping the weak," so pudgy and futile that we no longer have gristle to attack the strong who have brought weakness on the others.

As a people, we have passed the "bunk" around so habitually; we have enervated our judgment and moral convictions so seriously by our fake "philosophy of Boost," we have become so accustomed to measure the effectiveness of work by the applause it immediately provokes, that we have lost all stomach for courses that call for contest, unless it be those spurious contests of the political arena which are all managed from the same Great Headquarters, or those verbal assaults against "Big Business" which bring no reaction. We have lost all taste for tangible foes who have a ready retaliation.

Nevertheless it is true that, whereas a year ago it was not possible to speak the word "Jew" in the United States, it is now possible. The name appears on the front page of every newspaper nearly every day. It is the subject of discussion everywhere. For the time at least, speech has been liberated, although our friends of the B'nai B'rith in every state are doing their best to throttle it.

This freedom is of benefit both to Jew and non-Jew. The Jew need no longer look askance at the name of his race on the lips of a non-Jew. It only means that suppression and deceit are past, that is all; the Jew is a Jew, is recognized as a Jew, is spoken of as a Jew; and thus an honest relation between the mind and the fact is established in both the Jew and the non-Jew. The air is cleared. Concealment on the one hand is done away; on the other hand a missing fact, whose absence meant confusion, is supplied. The Jew may now say, "I am a Jew," as casually as any other man might claim his race. We may even see some noted Americans who all their lives have tried to conceal their race, come forward now and say, "We are Jews." It is freedom to the Jew; it is interpretation to the non-Jew. *Half the confusion which men meet in their efforts to account for the world is due to their ignorance of just where the Jew is.* He is always a key. But if the key be disguised as something else, how can it be used?

About eight months ago THE DEARBORN INDEPENDENT began a series of studies on the Jewish Question. It was an attempt to state the facts on which the Question is based. It was not at its beginning, nor has it since developed into, an attack on Jews as Jews. Its purpose was enlightenment, and if it secretly indulged a hope, it was this—that the leaders of American Jewry might be wise to see that this is the country and this is the time in which the causes of distress and distrust and disrepute might be removed from Jewry and a genuine modus operandi, not of toleration, but of reconciliation, arrived at.

The proof that these articles have contained facts and only facts is found in the failure of the Jewish spokesmen to show any one of them to be false. The record stands that way—not one disproof. The reason for the record is this: when only facts are sought, and are subjected to the tests, only facts are found. If, however, one embarks on a "campaign" whose purpose is to besmirch an opponent or create a prejudice, one's partisan zeal may induce him to accept as facts what is merely probability. These articles, however, do not constitute a campaign. They are the lighting of lamps here and there about the country, in this industry and that, in corners heretofore kept dark by those who should serve more faithfully on the watchtower of the Press.

What THE DEARBORN INDEPENDENT has said could have had no weight at all, had not the people been able to see the same facts all about them. It is not information, but illumination, that has given these articles the importance they have found among hundreds of thousands of readers.

The Jewish response to these articles has in one way been gratifying, and in another way quite disappointing.

The Jewish response has been gratifying in that it has furnished substantial proof of all the statements made in THE DEARBORN INDEPENDENT. This journal has no doubt of the truth of its statements, and is possessed of a very substantial reserve of evidence, but none the less the corroborative evidence produced by the Jewish leaders themselves in endeavoring to meet the issue is appreciated. There is no reason to believe that this was an intentional contribution on the part of Jewish leaders; it was simply impossible for them to move without revealing further evidence.

It is quite well known what is the position of Jewish leaders today: it is one of fear. For once they themselves are possessed with the fear of the unknown. Knowing how much of truth exists behind the statements made in this series, they are in fear of what may yet come forth. They do not even make any more pretense of considering it a joke; in their own conclaves they do not rave and roar like the rabbinical editors, they behave themselves like sober frightened men, who sometimes have a desire to own up to some of the things that have been charged, but who are halted by a doubt as to how far the owning-up process would lead them if once begun. They are in fear of the truth, but mostly of the whole truth.

Needless to say a responsibility rests also on those who hold the whole truth. The purpose determines everything. If the purpose is to breed hatred of the Jews, that involves one course of action. If the purpose is to excite the public mind with startling facts, that involves another course of action. If the purpose is to lay a basis for an intelligent, straightforward understanding and possible solution of the question, then such information as defines the question and presents all essential material, is all that is necessary. It is within these limits that this series has endeavored to keep. If there are facts which are unfavorable to the Jews, that is a matter for the Jews. If the Jews do despite to a certain class of facts, it may be necessary to produce still another class of facts. If the leaders of the Jews have been fair, just argumentatively, oppositionally fair, they would not now be in fear of what may yet be produced.

Jews, for illustration, have proved the statement that they are the best organized people in the United States. They have proved that they are more closely grouped together in their own national interest than are the citizens of the United States whose whole nationality is defined by their citizenship. The government of the United States itself is not so well organized as American Jewry—and that fact is not due to anything American; it is the same in every country. Telegraphic speed and instantaneous mass action have marked every move organized Jewry has made in this country in the last six months.

It is not for nothing that they control the avenues of communication in this country. It is not for nothing that the wireless of the world is under ironclad Jewish control. They are not loosely organized in social lodges for occasional fellowship; they are organized as states of the Jewish people, with officials who do nothing whatever but attend to the advancement of Jewish power in this and other countries. They have proved by the mass play of their synagogues, their newspapers, their alleged "social" organizations, their conservative clubs and their Bolshevik-Socialist groups—all of them working together, under orders—that they are a separate people within the American people, a people that do not agree with the genius of the American people, and a people that constantly make distinctions between Jewish and American rights.

In every state, in every city, there is a Jewish organization with a definite policy, and the first policy is to suffocate, destroy, put the "fear of the Jew" upon any man, newspaper, or institution that gives the least indication of independent thought on the Jewish Question. These organizations have special committees to do certain work. One of these works is to start "a whispering drive" against the person or institution aimed at. This "whispering drive" is a most hideous oriental device; it can be sustained only by groups of minds which bear a certain racial twist.

Without giving a full description of the devices used, it can be seen that the fact of their being centrally controlled and working simultaneously in all parts of the country, creates a considerable force. No other institution now operating in the United States can accomplish that so quickly and unitedly.

Jewish solidarity would be above criticism were it used for the benefit of the whole communal life, but it is not; it is not only Jewish, but its operations show it to be largely anti-American. This does not mean anti-American in the sense of being pro-German or pro-Mexican, but in this sense, that it opposes many things that have been conceded to constitute the American tradition. The Jew assumes that the United States is still an unformed entity which is fair prey to any who can seize it and mold it. That is his attitude today. He refuses to assume that

America is here; he adopts the belief that part of his duty is to bring America into being, on Jewish lines, of course.

Now, in a sense, the United States is private property. It is the property of those who share the ideals of the founders of the government. And those ideals were ideals held by a white race of Europeans. They were fundamentally Christian ideals. And with most of these the Jews not only disagree, but hold them in contempt. Indeed, a Jewish leader recently said in New York that the United States was not a Christian land, and the context of his statement shows that he clearly intended that it should never be. He was condemning the Christian Sunday, though he is an officer of a society whose purpose is the establishment of the Mosaic Sabbath.

The Jews have also proved the charge that they exercise disproportionate influence in governmental affairs. This charge has only been stated in this series. The mass of proof has not yet been brought to bear. But it exists, fixed beyond all change. However, another important bit of evidence has been transpiring before the country's eyes. When the immigration bill was first put up to Congress, the vote was overwhelmingly in favor of restricting entry into the country. Congress voted upon the facts and its patriotic convictions. Taking the question just as it was, no other verdict could have been given.

Hardly had the vote been taken, however, than the wires were hot and the trains crowded and Jewish protests and Jewish agents began flocking to Washington. The magic name Jew was uttered. Legislators fled to cover. Learned speeches were made. Compromises were suggested. Modifications of the original law were framed. Under the magic of Jew the whole proposal simply melted like an icicle before a fire.

The only protest made against the Congressional vote was made by Jews. Their wonderful teamwork in all parts of the country gave their protest the air of national importance. *BUT* there was one point the Jews were not able this year to deny, and that is that *the majority of the immigrants are Jews.* That fact, fortunately, was established beforehand. The hand of the Congress of the United States was stayed by the Jews in a matter of serious importance to national protection, just as a few years ago the hand of the Congress of the United States was forced to break the treaty with Russia when President Taft held it would be wrong to break it.

This proof of political power, based on nothing but sheer force and sheer determination to have what they want regardless of what the United States wants, has appeared broadcast as a matter of public knowledge.

And let the reader mark this: it will be found that this present immigration move is as much a part of the Jewish World Program as was the breaking of the treaty with Russia. Readers of the article of January 15 will recall how at the behest of the Jews, the United States' trade with Russia was thrown into the hands of German Jews who were using it to further their plans for the destruction of the Russian Empire, which later came to pass. The Jews "used" the United States to put across an essential part of that plan.

Well, what are they using the United States for now? We may well believe that the Jews are not without several reasons for what they are doing. The Jew excels as a chess player because he plays a game wherever he may be. The immigration matter amounts to this: Jews are streaming out of Poland as speedily as they can. It is not "pogroms" that are driving them out. "Pogroms" have been proved to be immigration propaganda for consumption outside Poland.

The Jews are leaving Poland because they know something is going to happen.

And if they are leaving Poland it is a sign it is going to happen to Poland.

And if the Jews have advance news of it, it is a sign that what will occur will be inflicted by Jews.

Plainly it is this: Jewish Bolshevism in Russia has made a secret decree against Poland. The Jews are getting out of the way. American Jewish agents are constantly passing into Poland. Rich American Jews are sending agents to bring back groups of "relatives." There is an *exodus* from Poland and there is a reason for it which spells trouble for Poland. The United

States is being used as the chief means by which the Jews are to clear out. France protests against them and will not have them. England most decidedly refuses to have them. The Jews of the United States are powerful enough to compel this country to take them. We are utilized to effect the entrance of Bolshevism into Russia; it went from our East Side thither. We are now being utilized to assist at the destruction of Poland. It is possible, however, that by the time the Jewish program reaches that point, something may have intervened.

The Jews of the United States have also given a splendid illustration of what THE DEARBORN INDEPENDENT said of their control of American newspapers. Of course, the local newspaper editor is not dominated by any Jewish authority seated at Washington, New York or Chicago, of course not; but he is very amenable to the twenty richest Jews in his community who advertise in his paper, and it is they who take orders from Washington, New York and Chicago. So the editor gets his orders from Jewish headquarters just the same, though he may not realize it.

This, however, is one instance where publicity does not count, because it represents a business favor oftener than it does an *editorial conviction.* The knowledge of the Jewish Question which newspaper men possess is quite complete, and a confidential council of the best informed editors of the United States would include all that the government or the people would need to know for a complete handling of the Jewish Question. The publicity demanded and received by the organized Jews has proved a roorback; it has served the cause of truth more than the cause they desired, which was suppression.

Gratifying as these proofs are to the producers of the facts, there is a very decided element of disappointment in the Jewish answers. Either Jewry is feinting, or is defenseless; certainly the present status of the defense must be humiliating to those who have any conception of the importance of the matter.

The answer signed by the Jews themselves—a list of signatures which showed as in panorama the close-locked corporational solidarity of the Jewish race in this country—was devoid of a single fact which threw light. In this, the Jewish answer was almost a confession of "no defense."

But aside from its ineptitude was its utter lack of frankness. It refuses to face the question. It will not meet a single statement, either in the substance of the Protocols or in the substance of this series. It veers off whenever it approaches a concrete theme, and loses itself in a vapor of denials. If a statement is wrong, it is provably wrong, especially a statement which deals with matters now actual in daily life.

The official Jewish answer, signed by a few, not all, of the Jewish leaders, is at least decent in its language, and that is more than can be said for most of the other Jewish answers. But it is indecent in its attempt to create the impression that anti-Semitism is abroad in the country.

Mark this: All the anti-Semitism that exists in the United States today is the deliberate creation of the Jewish leaders and is a recent creation.

The Jewish leaders want anti-Semitism here. Unable to create it among non-Jews, they are seeking the effects of it among the Jews by telling them that it exists.

The Jewish leaders of the United States have done everything possible to keep THE DEARBORN INDEPENDENT away from the Jews, to prevent their reading it and learning the fact that *NO ATTACK IS BEING MADE ON THE JEWS AS JEWS.*

From the first, after wrestling for weeks to discover a way of meeting these articles without having to confess too much, these leaders threw up their hands and took refuge in the lie of anti-Semitism.

What they ought to fear now is not the force of an anti-Semitic feeling among the non-Jews, but the force of a righteous indignation among American Jews when they discover the deceit and incompetence of their leaders.

"Anti-Semitism" has always been the last resort of scoundrelly Jewish leaders when cornered by the truth, and they have been known deliberately to incite it among the Gentile rabble in order through it to maintain their hold on their own people.

Recently there was printed in the newspapers "A Protest Against Anti-Semitism," signed by various non-Jews. The "protest" was printed twice, in fact, because it did not "go big" the first time. The newspapers were evidently growing a little weary of printing daily communiques from Jewish Great Headquarters. So, to give it more vim for a thorough circulation, the signature of Woodrow Wilson was obtained. And of course that put it on the telegraph wires again.

It was quite proper for President Wilson to sign a protest against anti-Semitism. It was quite proper for all the other signers to do so, provided that was what they meant to do.

If the protest had been sent to THE DEARBORN INDEPENDENT, its responsible officials would have signed also. THE DEARBORN INDEPENDENT *is against anti-Semitism* and protests against leading Jews using its name to foment that spirit.

The "protest," however innocent the signers may have been of this fact, *was against any public discussion of the Jewish Question,* and especially against this one.

The dispatches are careful to state that the Jews had nothing to do with that protest. A supposedly non-Jewish organization has been in the service of a coterie of New York Jews for a long time. The assertion that the "protest" was written by "a single citizen, a non-Jew, acting upon his own initiative and responsibility, and without consultation with anybody," is mildly amusing.

There was just enough "consultation" to make the whole "non-Jewish protest" nothing more nor less than a previously approved document, and the citizen who did the job has known for a long time where it pays to please.

As to Mr. John Spargo, whose name is beginning to appear prominently as a Gentile defender of the Jews, this much is known: he did not undertake the Jewish defense without several secret consultations with a group of New York Jews, who had to overcome several of Spargo's scruples before they could make much headway with him. Spargo's attitude was something like this: "Gentlemen, they've got it on you. It is not a matter that can be whitewashed." Spargo told a lot of truth in that New York room. The Jewish conferees knew it was truth. If Spargo should speak one-twentieth as much truth on the platform, his lecture engagements would dwindle in number.

All of the literature of the Anti-Defamation Society, all of the speech of the retained defenders, is very welcome. Open the Question up! If the Jews engage enough Gentile defenders, the time will come when Gentile logical faculties will bring about a real discussion of the Question. The Jewish spokesmen must, on pain of losing their position, limit themselves to denials, abuse and threats; but the Gentile defenders are constitutionally unable to dwell in that state of mind for long; they will probe through to the truth; in which event real discussion may be expected.

There is not a single Jewish publication, however vituperative and truthless, that we would forbid the mails or exclude from a public library. There is not a single Jewish spokesman whom we would heckle or hinder on the public platform. There is not a single Jewish enterprise that we would recommend for boycott. We believe in Free Speech and unfettered conviction. By means of these the people may yet hope to clean up the United States.

The Jews do *not* believe in Free Speech. They do *not* believe in a Free Press.

In every state in the Union the B'nai B'rith is introducing into the local legislatures a bill that will prevent any publication from saying anything derogatory of the Jews.

That is the Jews' *answer* to the facts produced in this publication.

In scores and hundreds of public libraries, the Jews are using the members of their race who happen to be on library boards, or are using committees of their race to influence library boards to clear the libraries of all books, pamphlets and papers that deal with the Jewish Question in a manner to leave any doubt that the Jews are paragons of virtue and The Chosen People.

This is occurring in the United States. It is occurring in some of those eastern American states that stood most valiantly for the cause of Free Speech and a Free Press in other days.

Let it go on! Multiply the instances! Add madness to madness! Each act of this nature simply gives a local proof, visible and intelligible to each community where it transpires, that what is written about the Jews is true.

The present status of the Jewish Question in the United States is this:

A beginning has been made on the too-long accumulating facts.

Jewish recognition of the truth has been expressed in soberness among the leaders.

Jewish action in response has been, for themselves, denial; for others, *SUPPRESSION.*

The result to date is:—abject failure to meet the case.

Issue of January 29, 1921.